THE INCREDIBLE HERCULES

SECRET INVASION

Writers: **GREG PAK** & **FRED VAN LENTE**
Penciler: **RAFA SANDOVAL**
Inker: **ROGER BONET** with **GREG ADAMS** (Issue #120)
Colorist: **MARTEGOD GRACIA**
with **DENNIS CALERO** and **RAUL TREVIÑO** (Issue #120)
Letterer: **VIRTUAL CALLIGRAPHY'S JOE CARAMAGNA**
Cover Artists: **JOHN ROMITA JR., KLAUS JANSON** & **DEAN WHITE**

Assistant Editor: **NATHAN COSBY**
Editor: **MARK PANICCIA**

Collection Editor: **CORY LEVINE**
Editorial Assistant: **ALEX STARBUCK**
Assistant Editor: **JOHN DENNING**
Editors, Special Projects: **JENNIFER GRÜNWALD** & **MARK D. BEAZLEY**
Senior Editor, Special Projects: **JEFF YOUNGQUIST**
Senior Vice President of Sales: **DAVID GABRIEL**
Production: **JERRON QUALITY COLOR**

Editor in Chief: **JOE QUESADA**
Publisher: **DAN BUCKLEY**

INCREDIBLE HERCULES: SECRET INVASION. Contains material originally published in magazine form as INCREDIBLE HERCULES #116-120. First printing 2008. ISBN# 978-0-7851-3333-9. Published by MARVEL PUBLISHING, INC., a subsidiary of MARVEL ENTERTAINMENT, INC. OFFICE OF PUBLICATION: 417 5th Avenue, New York, NY 10016. Copyright © 2008 Marvel Characters, Inc. All rights reserved. $19.99 per copy in the U.S. and $21.00 in Canada (GST #R127032852); Canadian Agreement #40668537. All characters featured in this issue and the distinctive names and likenesses thereof, and all related indicia are trademarks of Marvel Characters, Inc. No similarity between any of the names, characters, persons, and/or institutions in this magazine with those of any living or dead person or institution is intended, and any such similarity which may exist is purely coincidental. **Printed in the U.S.A.** ALAN FINE, CEO Marvel Toys & Publishing Divisions and CMO Marvel Characters, Inc.; DAVID GABRIEL, SVP of Publishing Sales & Circulation; DAVID BOGART, SVP of Business Affairs & Talent Management; MICHAEL PASCIULLO, VP of Merchandising & Communications; JIM O'KEEFE, VP of Operations & Logistics; DAN CARR, Executive Director of Publishing Technology; JUSTIN F. GABRIE, Director of Editorial Operations; SUSAN CRESPI, Editorial Operations Manager; OMAR OTIEKU, Production Manager; STAN LEE, Chairman Emeritus. For information regarding advertising in Marvel Comics or on Marvel.com, please contact Mitch Dane, Advertising Director, at mdane@marvel.com. For Marvel subscription inquiries, please call 800-217-9158.

10 9 8 7 6 5 4 3 2 1

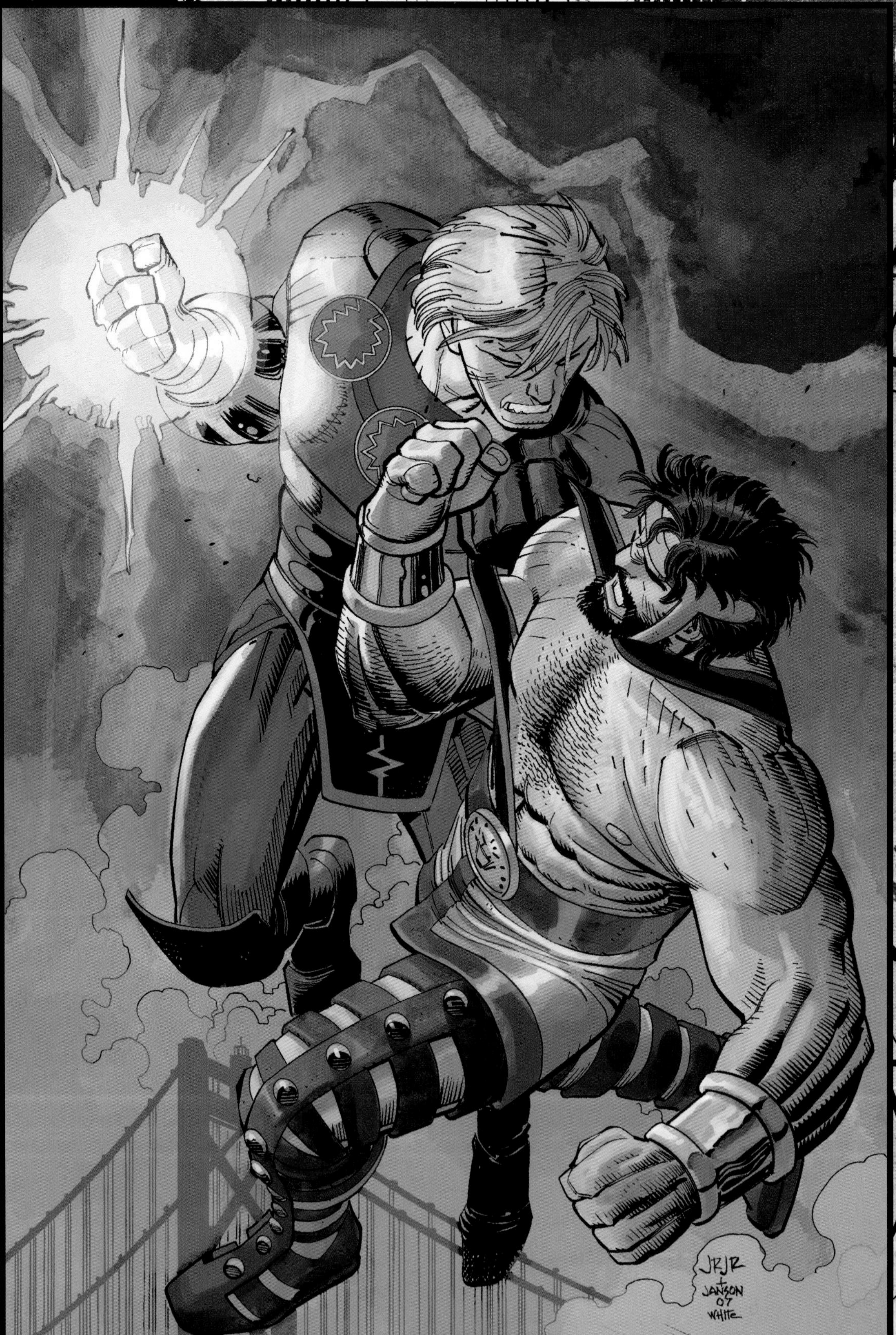
JRJR
+
JANSON
07
WHITE

INCREDIBLE HERCULES #116

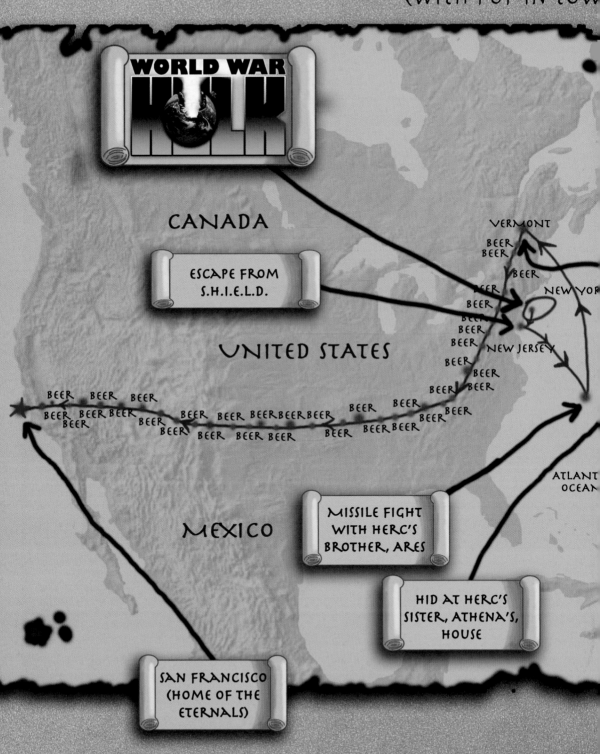

THE JOURNEYS OF
HERCULES & AMADEUS CHO
(WITH PUP IN TOW

WORLD WAR HULK

CANADA

ESCAPE FROM S.H.I.E.L.D.

UNITED STATES

VERMONT
BEER
BEER
BEER
BEER
BEER
BEER
BEER
BEER
BEER
BEER
BEER
BEER

NEW YOR

NEW JERSEY

BEER BEER BEER
BEER BEER BEER
BEER
BEER
BEER BEER BEERBEERBEER BEER BEER
BEER BEER BEER BEER BEERBEER
BEER BEER

ATLANT
OCEAN

MEXICO

MISSILE FIGHT WITH HERC'S BROTHER, ARES

HID AT HERC'S SISTER, ATHENA'S, HOUSE

SAN FRANCISCO (HOME OF THE ETERNALS)

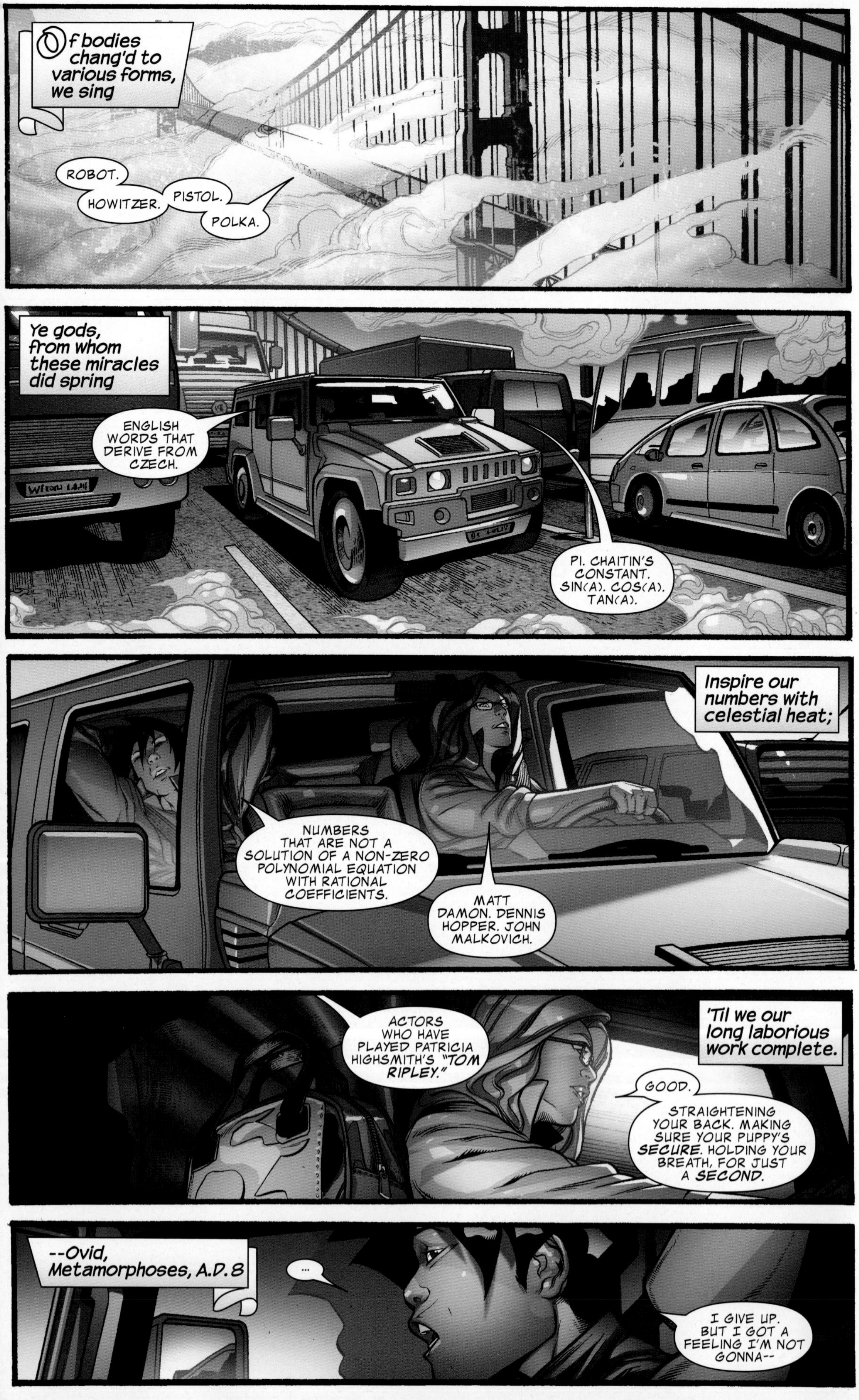
Of bodies chang'd to various forms, we sing
ROBOT.
HOWITZER.
PISTOL.
POLKA.
Ye gods, from whom these miracles did spring
ENGLISH WORDS THAT DERIVE FROM CZECH.
PI. CHAITIN'S CONSTANT. SIN(A). COS(A). TAN(A).
Inspire our numbers with celestial heat;
NUMBERS THAT ARE NOT A SOLUTION OF A NON-ZERO POLYNOMIAL EQUATION WITH RATIONAL COEFFICIENTS.
MATT DAMON. DENNIS HOPPER. JOHN MALKOVICH.
ACTORS WHO HAVE PLAYED PATRICIA HIGHSMITH'S "TOM RIPLEY."
'Til we our long laborious work complete.
GOOD.
STRAIGHTENING YOUR BACK. MAKING SURE YOUR PUPPY'S SECURE. HOLDING YOUR BREATH, FOR JUST A SECOND.
--Ovid, Metamorphoses, A.D. 8
...
I GIVE UP. BUT I GOT A FEELING I'M NOT GONNA--

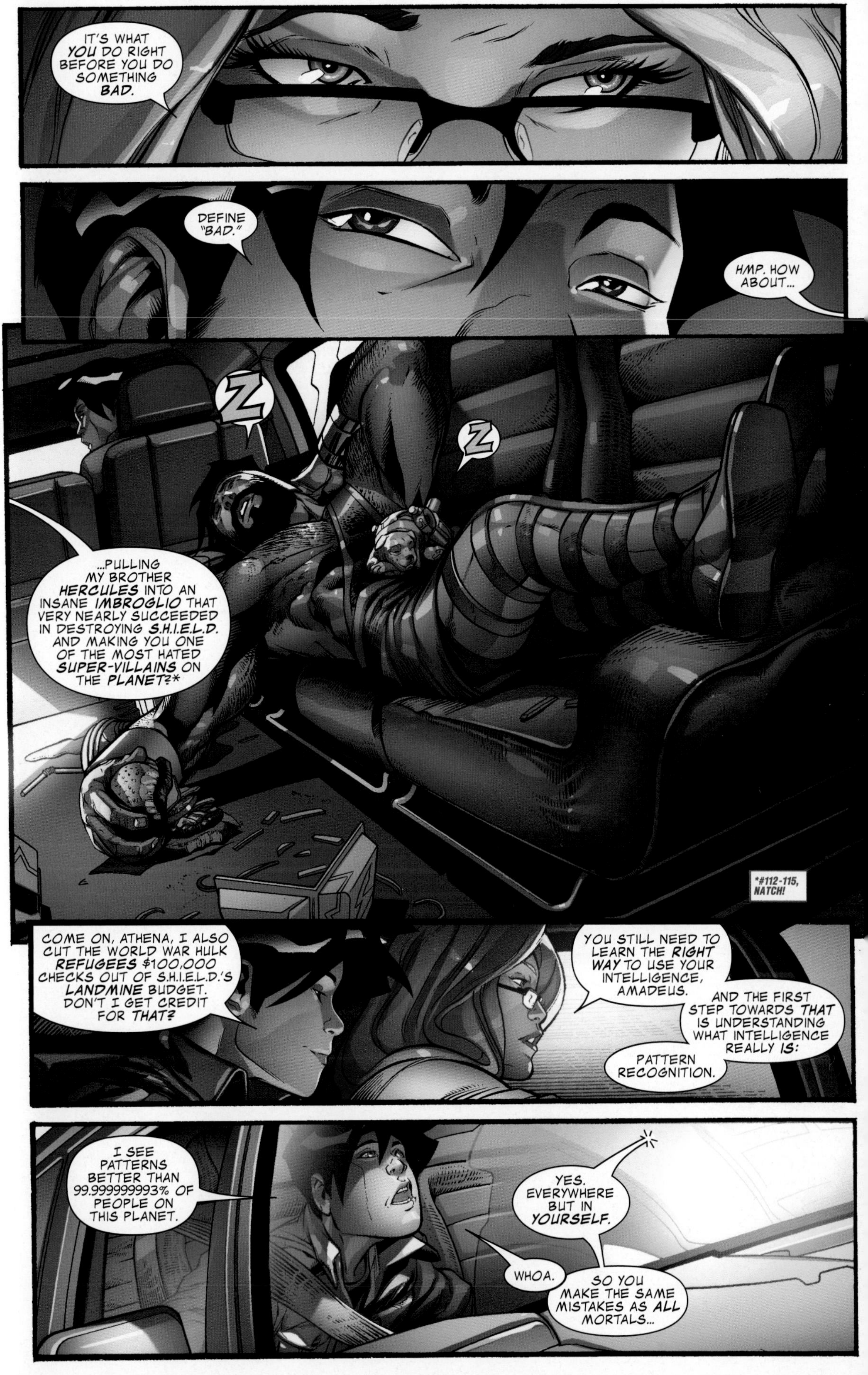
IT'S WHAT YOU DO RIGHT BEFORE YOU DO SOMETHING BAD.
DEFINE "BAD."
HMP. HOW ABOUT...
Z
Z
...PULLING MY BROTHER HERCULES INTO AN INSANE IMBROGLIO THAT VERY NEARLY SUCCEEDED IN DESTROYING S.H.I.E.L.D. AND MAKING YOU ONE OF THE MOST HATED SUPER-VILLAINS ON THE PLANET?*
*#112-115, NATCH!
COME ON, ATHENA, I ALSO CUT THE WORLD WAR HULK REFUGEES $100,000 CHECKS OUT OF S.H.I.E.L.D.'S LANDMINE BUDGET. DON'T I GET CREDIT FOR THAT?
YOU STILL NEED TO LEARN THE RIGHT WAY TO USE YOUR INTELLIGENCE, AMADEUS.
AND THE FIRST STEP TOWARDS THAT IS UNDERSTANDING WHAT INTELLIGENCE REALLY IS:
PATTERN RECOGNITION.
I SEE PATTERNS BETTER THAN 99.99999993% OF PEOPLE ON THIS PLANET.
YES. EVERYWHERE BUT IN YOURSELF.
WHOA.
SO YOU MAKE THE SAME MISTAKES AS ALL MORTALS...

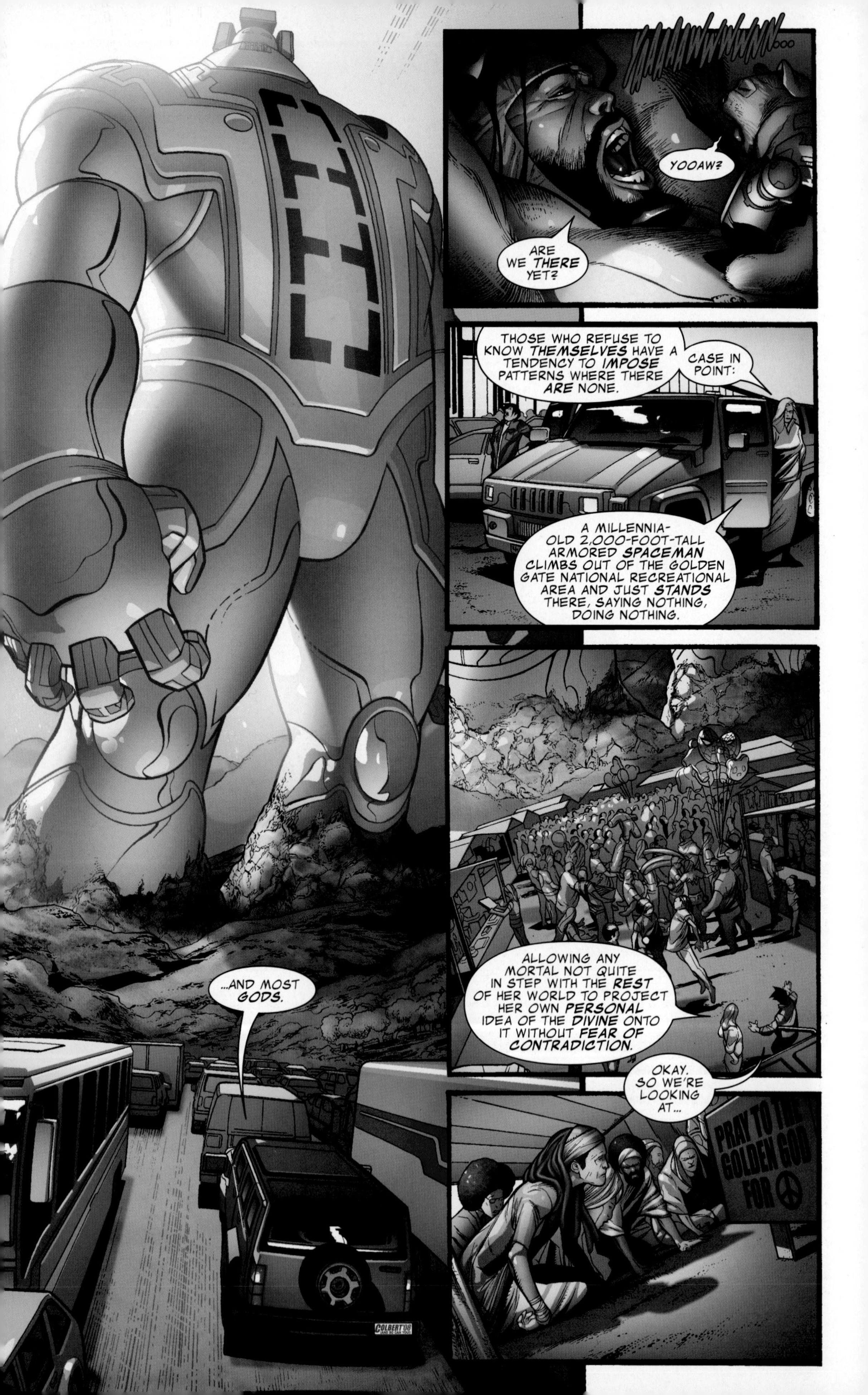
YAAAAWWWWWN...
YOOAW?
ARE WE THERE YET?
THOSE WHO REFUSE TO KNOW THEMSELVES HAVE A TENDENCY TO IMPOSE PATTERNS WHERE THERE ARE NONE.
CASE IN POINT:
A MILLENNIA-OLD 2,000-FOOT-TALL ARMORED SPACEMAN CLIMBS OUT OF THE GOLDEN GATE NATIONAL RECREATIONAL AREA AND JUST STANDS THERE, SAYING NOTHING, DOING NOTHING.
ALLOWING ANY MORTAL NOT QUITE IN STEP WITH THE REST OF HER WORLD TO PROJECT HER OWN PERSONAL IDEA OF THE DIVINE ONTO IT WITHOUT FEAR OF CONTRADICTION.
OKAY. SO WE'RE LOOKING AT...
...AND MOST GODS.
PRAY TO THE GOLDEN GOD FOR ☮
COLBERT '08

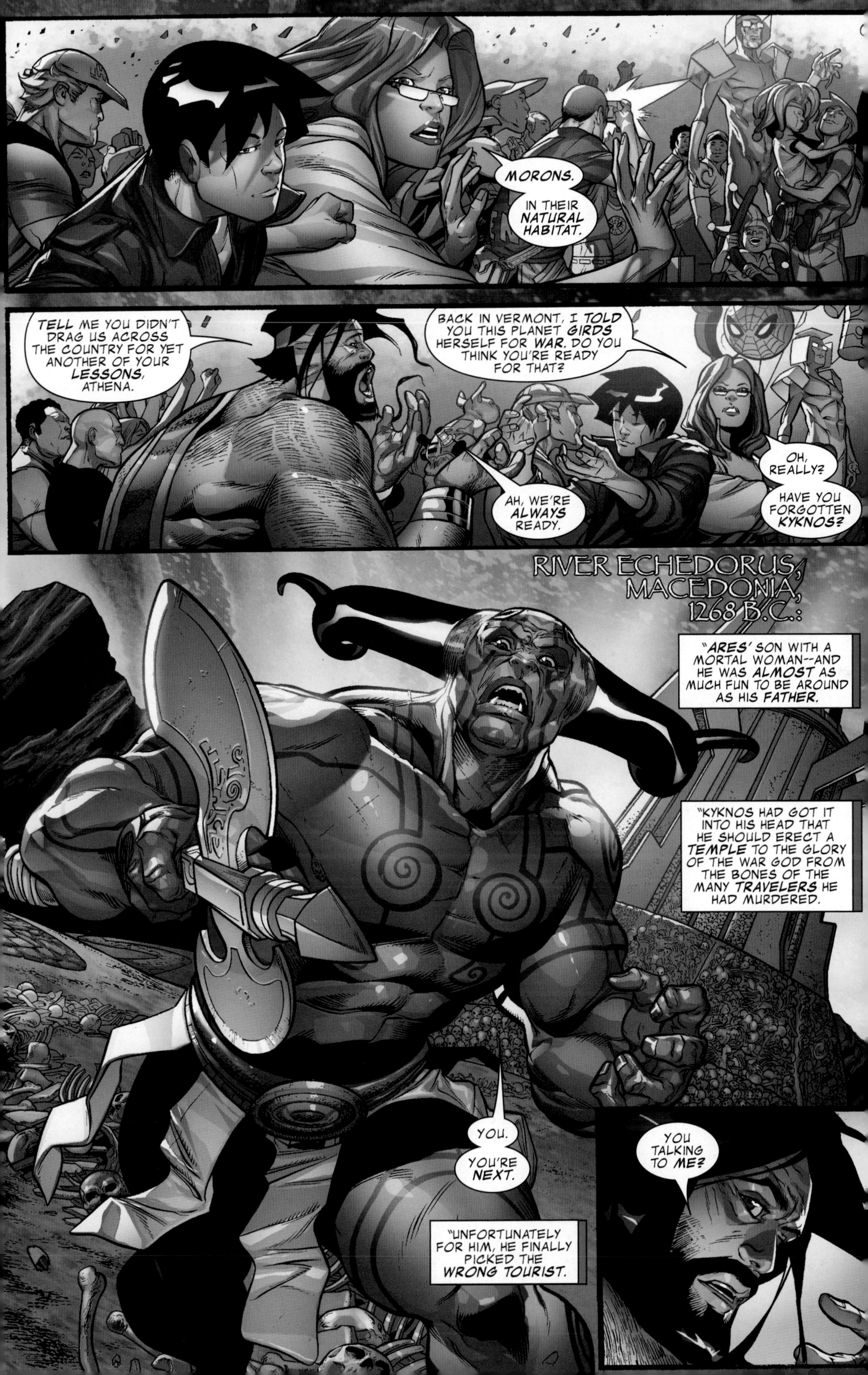
MORONS.
IN THEIR NATURAL HABITAT.
TELL ME YOU DIDN'T DRAG US ACROSS THE COUNTRY FOR YET ANOTHER OF YOUR LESSONS, ATHENA.
BACK IN VERMONT, I TOLD YOU THIS PLANET GIRDS HERSELF FOR WAR. DO YOU THINK YOU'RE READY FOR THAT?
AH, WE'RE ALWAYS READY.
OH, REALLY?
HAVE YOU FORGOTTEN KYKNOS?
RIVER ECHEDORUS, MACEDONIA, 1268 B.C.:
"ARES' SON WITH A MORTAL WOMAN--AND HE WAS ALMOST AS MUCH FUN TO BE AROUND AS HIS FATHER.
"KYKNOS HAD GOT IT INTO HIS HEAD THAT HE SHOULD ERECT A TEMPLE TO THE GLORY OF THE WAR GOD FROM THE BONES OF THE MANY TRAVELERS HE HAD MURDERED.
YOU.
YOU'RE NEXT.
YOU TALKING TO ME?
"UNFORTUNATELY FOR HIM, HE FINALLY PICKED THE WRONG TOURIST.

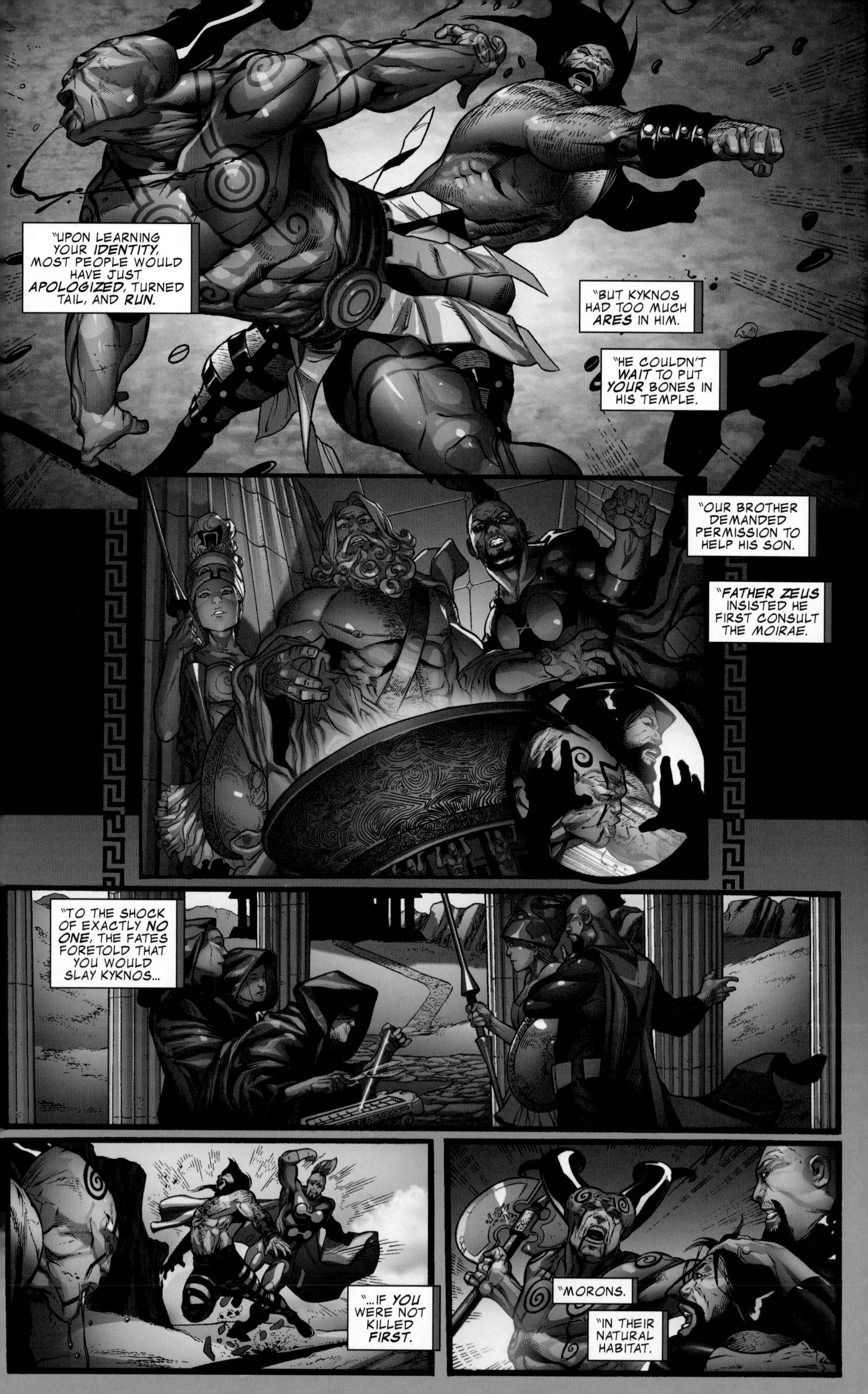
"UPON LEARNING YOUR IDENTITY, MOST PEOPLE WOULD HAVE JUST APOLOGIZED, TURNED TAIL, AND RUN.
"BUT KYKNOS HAD TOO MUCH ARES IN HIM.
"HE COULDN'T WAIT TO PUT YOUR BONES IN HIS TEMPLE.
"OUR BROTHER DEMANDED PERMISSION TO HELP HIS SON.
"FATHER ZEUS INSISTED HE FIRST CONSULT THE MOIRAE.
"TO THE SHOCK OF EXACTLY NO ONE, THE FATES FORETOLD THAT YOU WOULD SLAY KYKNOS...
"...IF YOU WERE NOT KILLED FIRST.
"MORONS.
"IN THEIR NATURAL HABITAT.

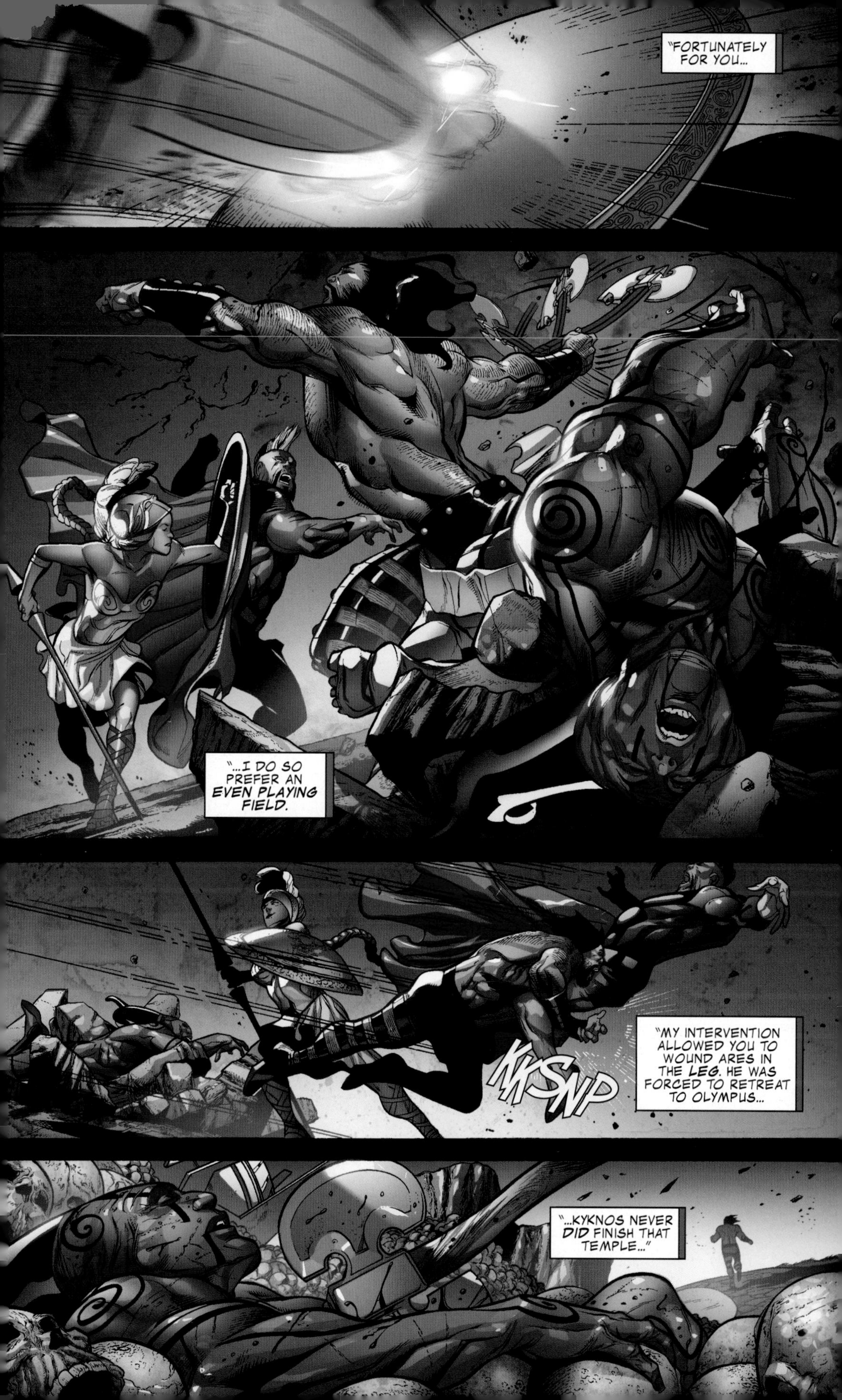
"FORTUNATELY FOR YOU...
"...I DO SO PREFER AN EVEN PLAYING FIELD.
"MY INTERVENTION ALLOWED YOU TO WOUND ARES IN THE LEG. HE WAS FORCED TO RETREAT TO OLYMPUS...
KKSNP
"...KYKNOS NEVER DID FINISH THAT TEMPLE..."

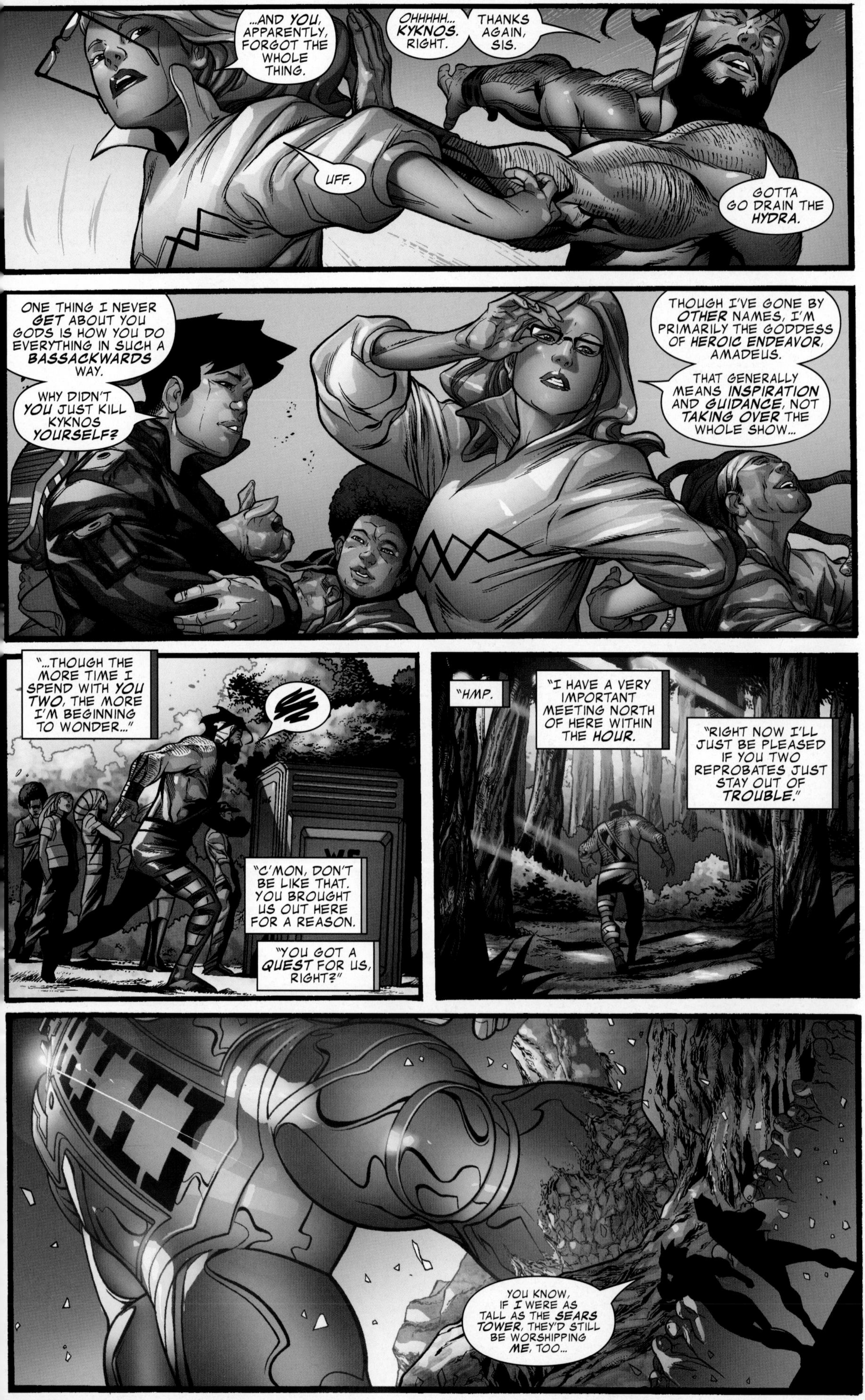
...AND YOU, APPARENTLY, FORGOT THE WHOLE THING.
OHHHHH... KYKNOS. RIGHT.
THANKS AGAIN, SIS.
UFF.
GOTTA GO DRAIN THE HYDRA.
ONE THING I NEVER GET ABOUT YOU GODS IS HOW YOU DO EVERYTHING IN SUCH A BASSACKWARDS WAY.
WHY DIDN'T YOU JUST KILL KYKNOS YOURSELF?
THOUGH I'VE GONE BY OTHER NAMES, I'M PRIMARILY THE GODDESS OF HEROIC ENDEAVOR, AMADEUS.
THAT GENERALLY MEANS INSPIRATION AND GUIDANCE, NOT TAKING OVER THE WHOLE SHOW...
"...THOUGH THE MORE TIME I SPEND WITH YOU TWO, THE MORE I'M BEGINNING TO WONDER..."
"C'MON, DON'T BE LIKE THAT. YOU BROUGHT US OUT HERE FOR A REASON.
"YOU GOT A QUEST FOR US, RIGHT?"
"HMP.
"I HAVE A VERY IMPORTANT MEETING NORTH OF HERE WITHIN THE HOUR.
"RIGHT NOW I'LL JUST BE PLEASED IF YOU TWO REPROBATES JUST STAY OUT OF TROUBLE."
YOU KNOW, IF I WERE AS TALL AS THE SEARS TOWER, THEY'D STILL BE WORSHIPPING ME, TOO...

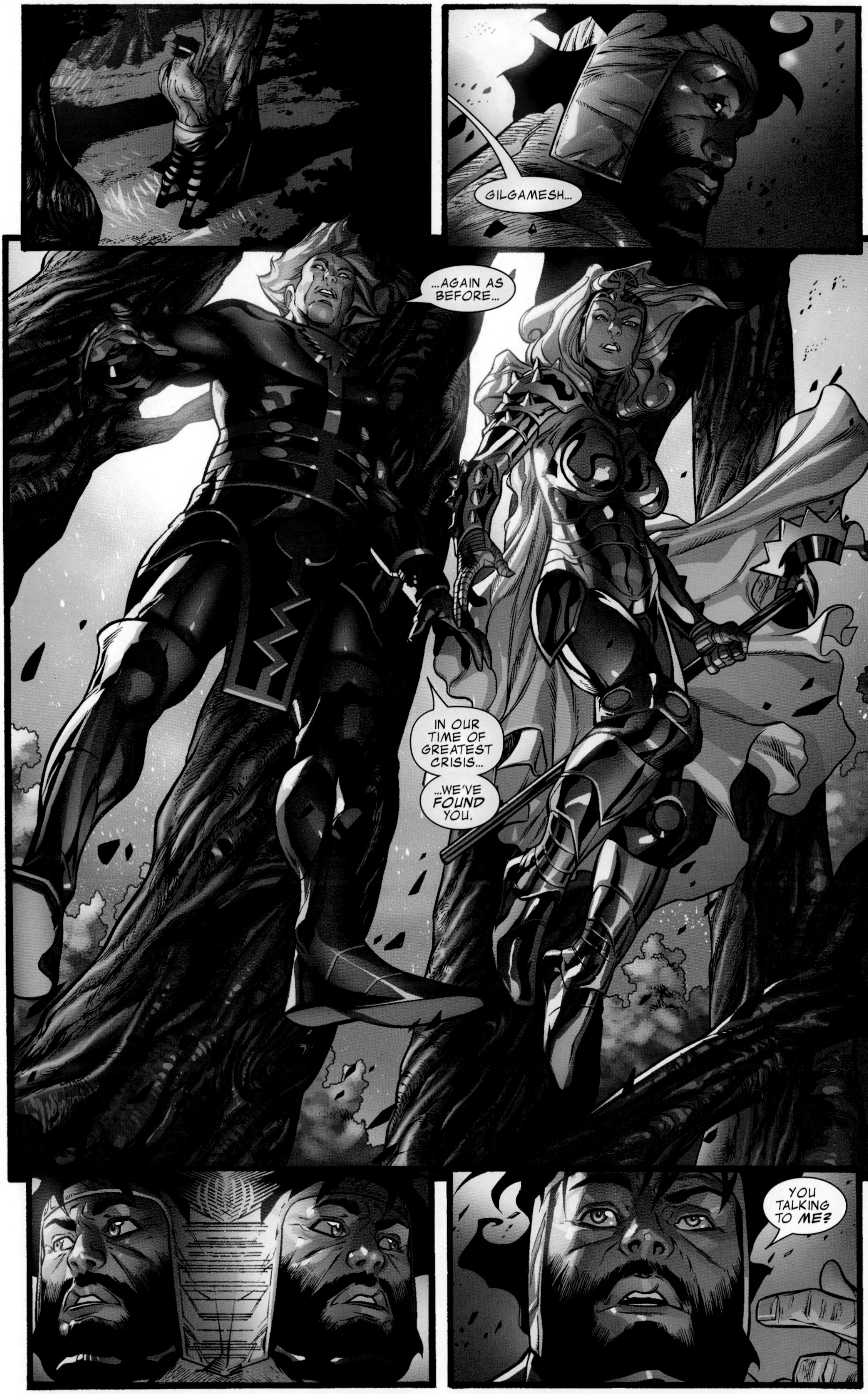
GILGAMESH...
...AGAIN AS BEFORE...
IN OUR TIME OF GREATEST CRISIS...
...WE'VE FOUND YOU.
YOU TALKING TO ME?

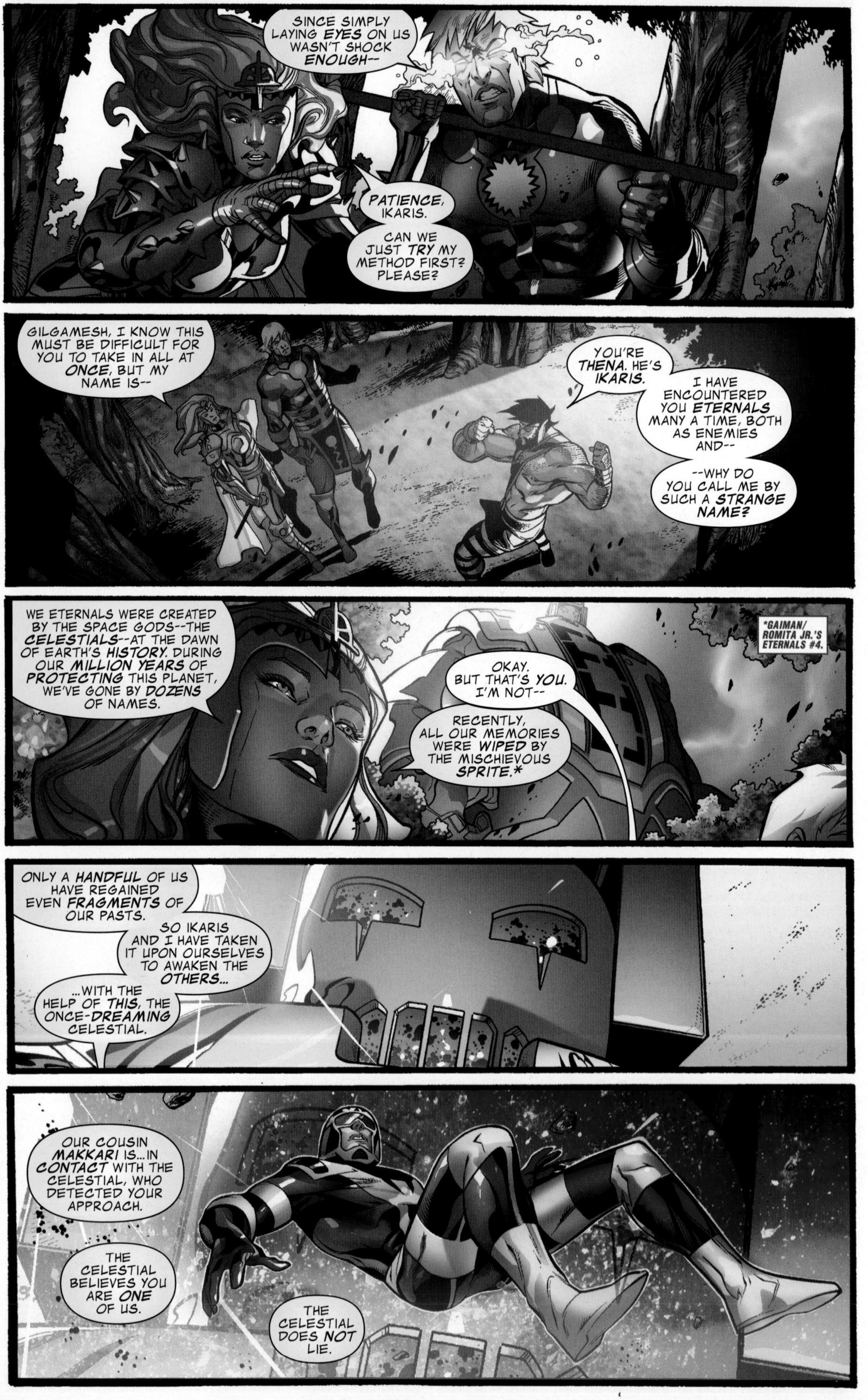
SINCE SIMPLY LAYING EYES ON US WASN'T SHOCK ENOUGH--
PATIENCE, IKARIS.
CAN WE JUST TRY MY METHOD FIRST? PLEASE?
GILGAMESH, I KNOW THIS MUST BE DIFFICULT FOR YOU TO TAKE IN ALL AT ONCE, BUT MY NAME IS--
YOU'RE THENA. HE'S IKARIS.
I HAVE ENCOUNTERED YOU ETERNALS MANY A TIME, BOTH AS ENEMIES AND--
--WHY DO YOU CALL ME BY SUCH A STRANGE NAME?
WE ETERNALS WERE CREATED BY THE SPACE GODS--THE CELESTIALS--AT THE DAWN OF EARTH'S HISTORY. DURING OUR MILLION YEARS OF PROTECTING THIS PLANET, WE'VE GONE BY DOZENS OF NAMES.
*GAIMAN/ ROMITA JR.'S ETERNALS #4.
OKAY. BUT THAT'S YOU. I'M NOT--
RECENTLY, ALL OUR MEMORIES WERE WIPED BY THE MISCHIEVOUS SPRITE.*
ONLY A HANDFUL OF US HAVE REGAINED EVEN FRAGMENTS OF OUR PASTS.
SO IKARIS AND I HAVE TAKEN IT UPON OURSELVES TO AWAKEN THE OTHERS...
...WITH THE HELP OF THIS, THE ONCE-DREAMING CELESTIAL.
OUR COUSIN MAKKARI IS...IN CONTACT WITH THE CELESTIAL, WHO DETECTED YOUR APPROACH.
THE CELESTIAL BELIEVES YOU ARE ONE OF US.
THE CELESTIAL DOES NOT LIE.

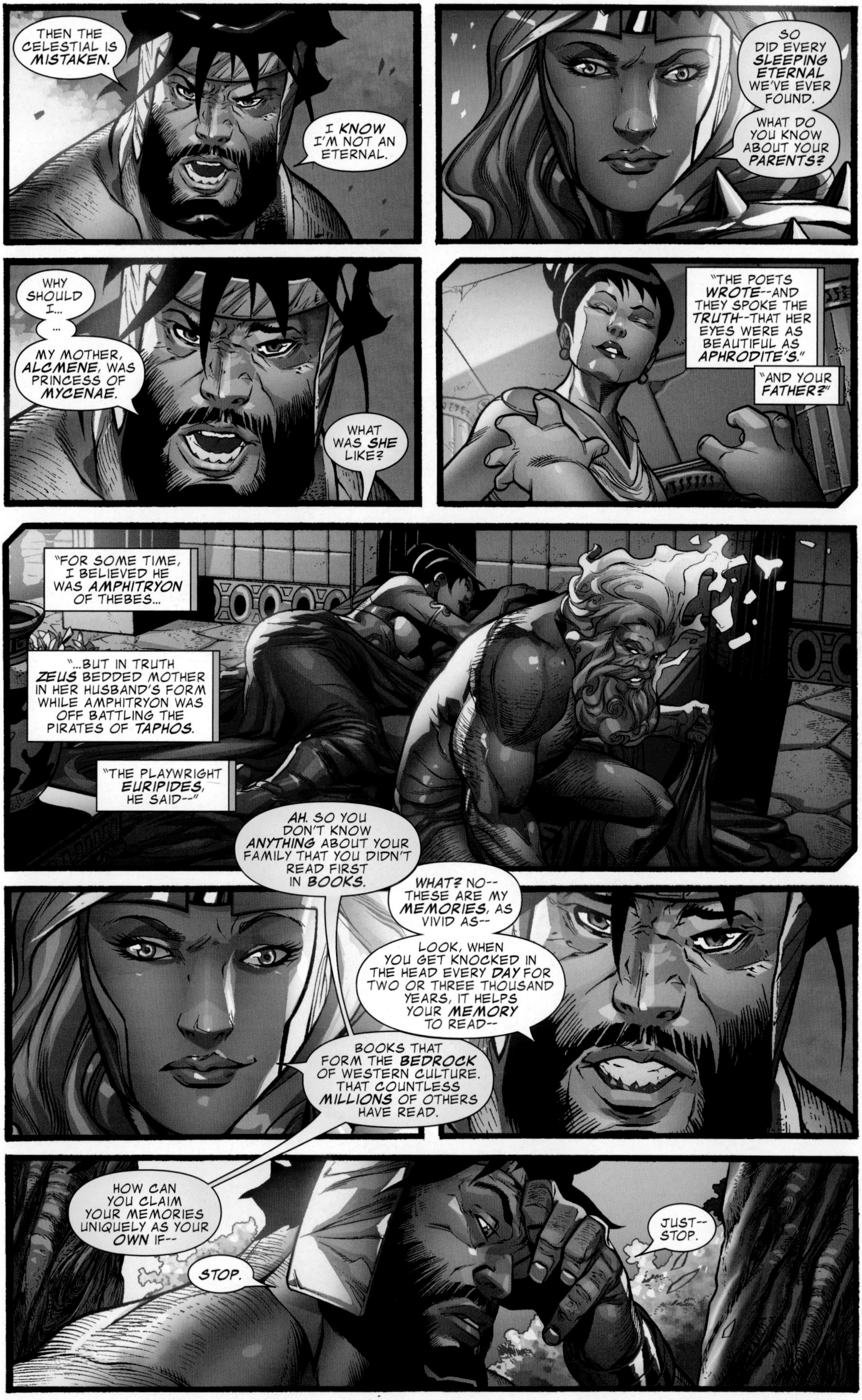
THEN THE CELESTIAL IS MISTAKEN.
I KNOW I'M NOT AN ETERNAL.
SO DID EVERY SLEEPING ETERNAL WE'VE EVER FOUND.
WHAT DO YOU KNOW ABOUT YOUR PARENTS?
WHY SHOULD I...
...
MY MOTHER, ALCMENE, WAS PRINCESS OF MYCENAE.
WHAT WAS SHE LIKE?
"THE POETS WROTE--AND THEY SPOKE THE TRUTH--THAT HER EYES WERE AS BEAUTIFUL AS APHRODITE'S."
"AND YOUR FATHER?"
"FOR SOME TIME, I BELIEVED HE WAS AMPHITRYON OF THEBES...
"...BUT IN TRUTH ZEUS BEDDED MOTHER IN HER HUSBAND'S FORM WHILE AMPHITRYON WAS OFF BATTLING THE PIRATES OF TAPHOS.
"THE PLAYWRIGHT EURIPIDES, HE SAID--"
AH. SO YOU DON'T KNOW ANYTHING ABOUT YOUR FAMILY THAT YOU DIDN'T READ FIRST IN BOOKS.
WHAT? NO--THESE ARE MY MEMORIES, AS VIVID AS--
LOOK, WHEN YOU GET KNOCKED IN THE HEAD EVERY DAY FOR TWO OR THREE THOUSAND YEARS, IT HELPS YOUR MEMORY TO READ--
BOOKS THAT FORM THE BEDROCK OF WESTERN CULTURE. THAT COUNTLESS MILLIONS OF OTHERS HAVE READ.
HOW CAN YOU CLAIM YOUR MEMORIES UNIQUELY AS YOUR OWN IF--
STOP.
JUST--STOP.

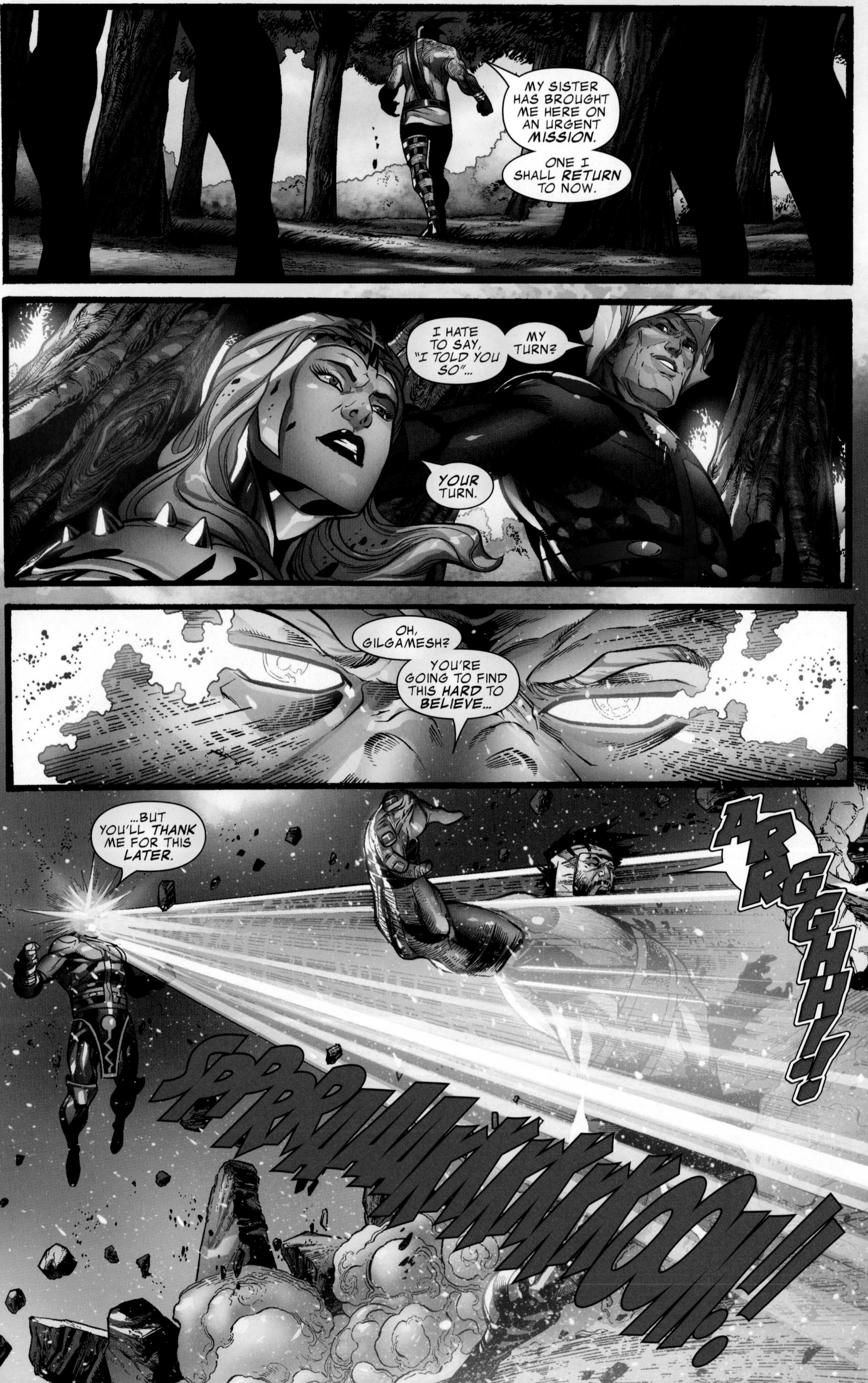
MY SISTER HAS BROUGHT ME HERE ON AN URGENT MISSION.
ONE I SHALL RETURN TO NOW.
I HATE TO SAY, "I TOLD YOU SO"...
MY TURN?
YOUR TURN.
OH, GILGAMESH?
YOU'RE GOING TO FIND THIS HARD TO BELIEVE...
...BUT YOU'LL THANK ME FOR THIS LATER.
ARRGGHH!!
SPRRAAMMMMOOM!!

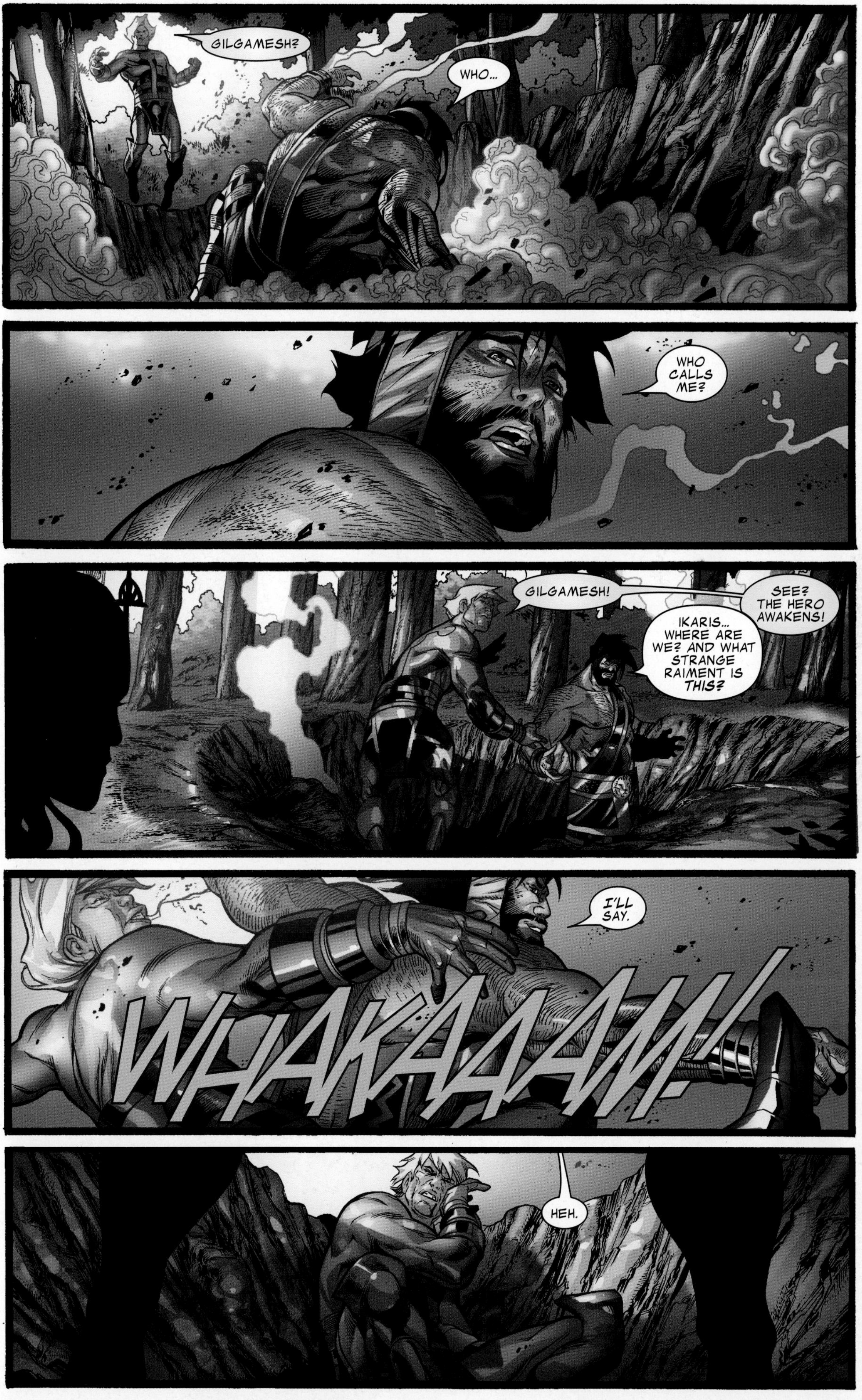
GILGAMESH?
WHO...
WHO CALLS ME?
GILGAMESH!
SEE? THE HERO AWAKENS!
IKARIS... WHERE ARE WE? AND WHAT STRANGE RAIMENT IS THIS?
I'LL SAY.
WHAKAAAM!
HEH.

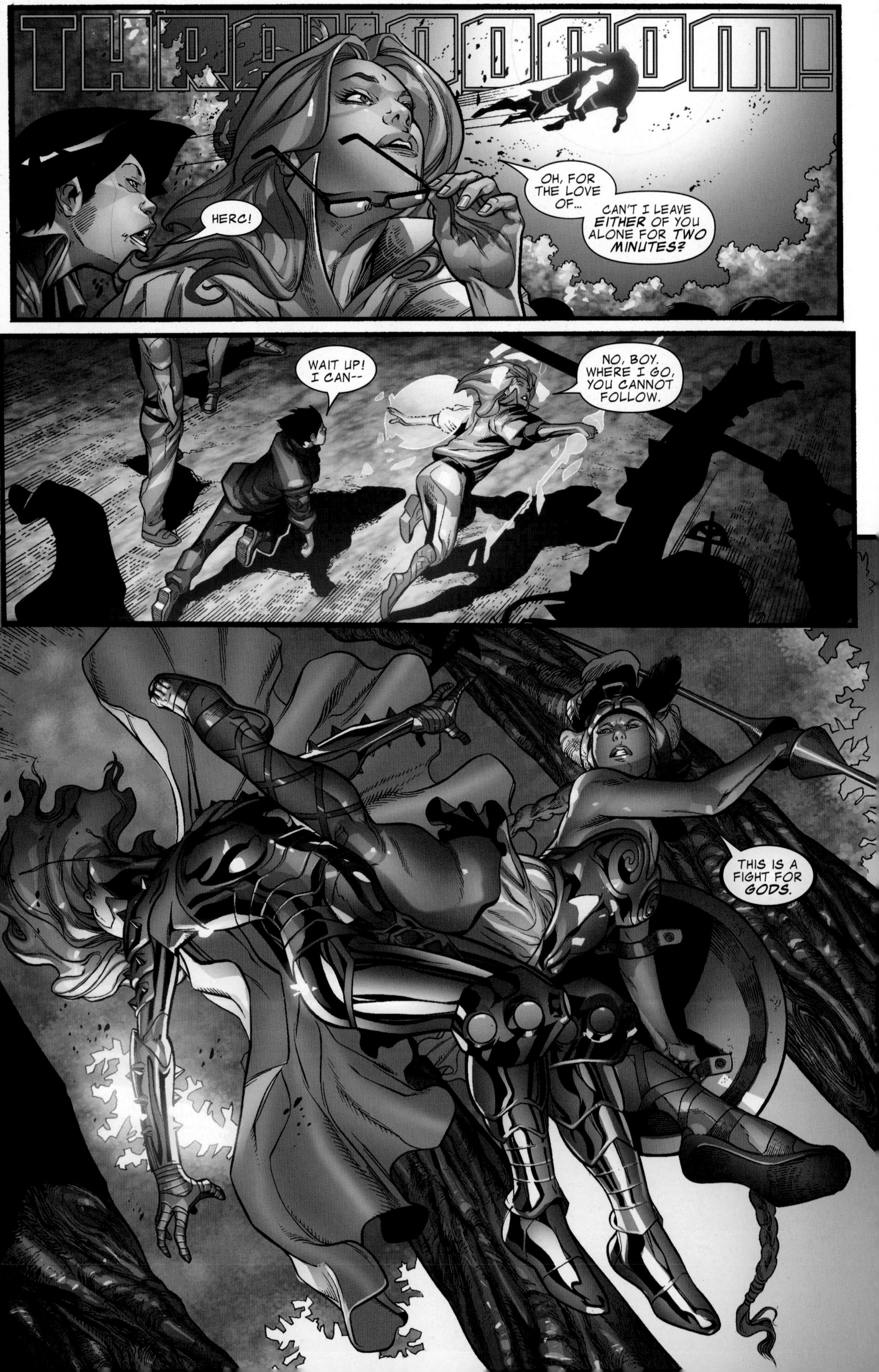
THRAKOOOOM!
HERC!
OH, FOR THE LOVE OF...
CAN'T I LEAVE EITHER OF YOU ALONE FOR TWO MINUTES?
WAIT UP! I CAN--
NO, BOY. WHERE I GO, YOU CANNOT FOLLOW.
THIS IS A FIGHT FOR GODS.

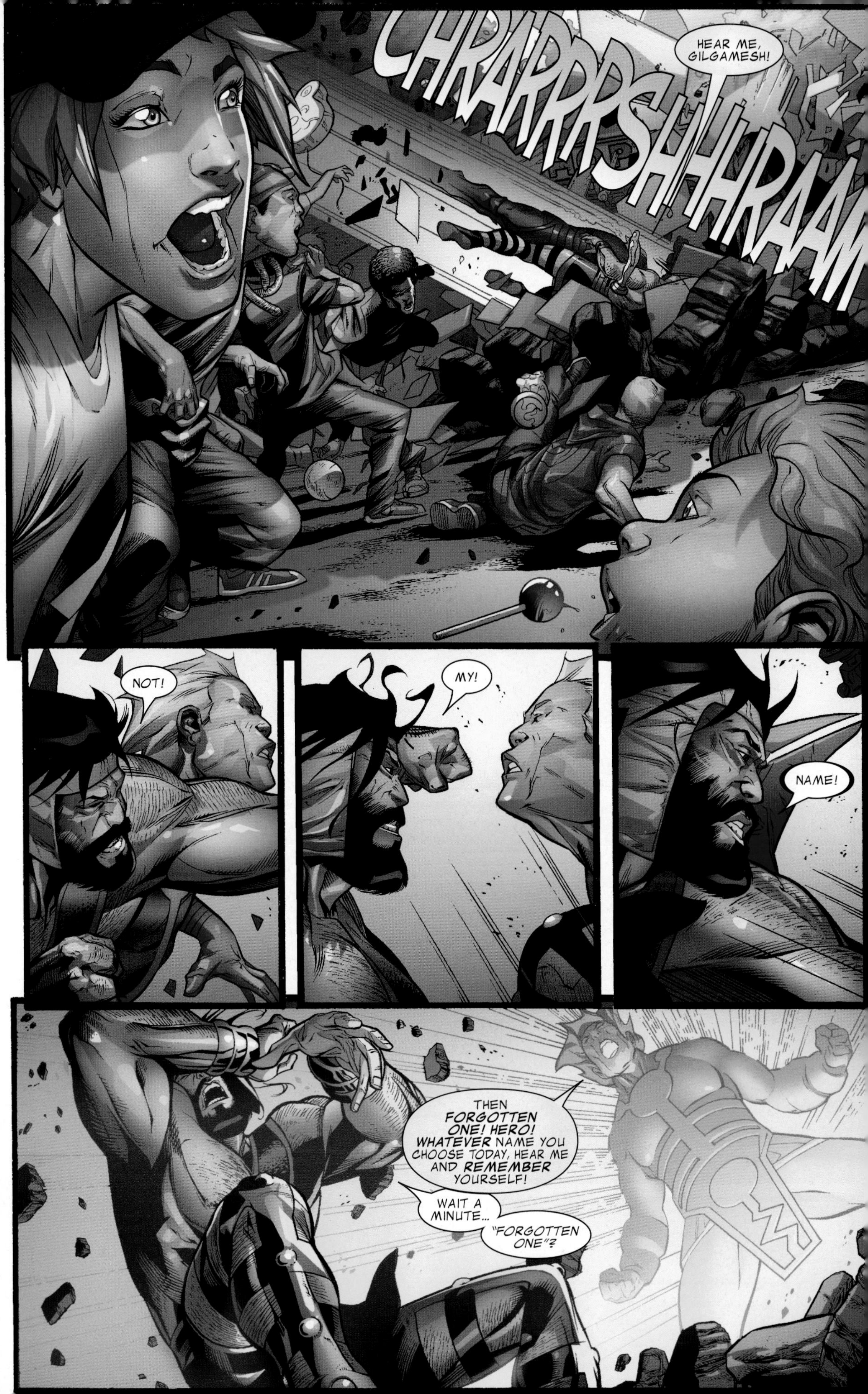
CHRARRRSHHHRAAM
HEAR ME, GILGAMESH!
NOT!
MY!
NAME!
THEN FORGOTTEN ONE! HERO! WHATEVER NAME YOU CHOOSE TODAY, HEAR ME AND REMEMBER YOURSELF!
WAIT A MINUTE...
"FORGOTTEN ONE"?

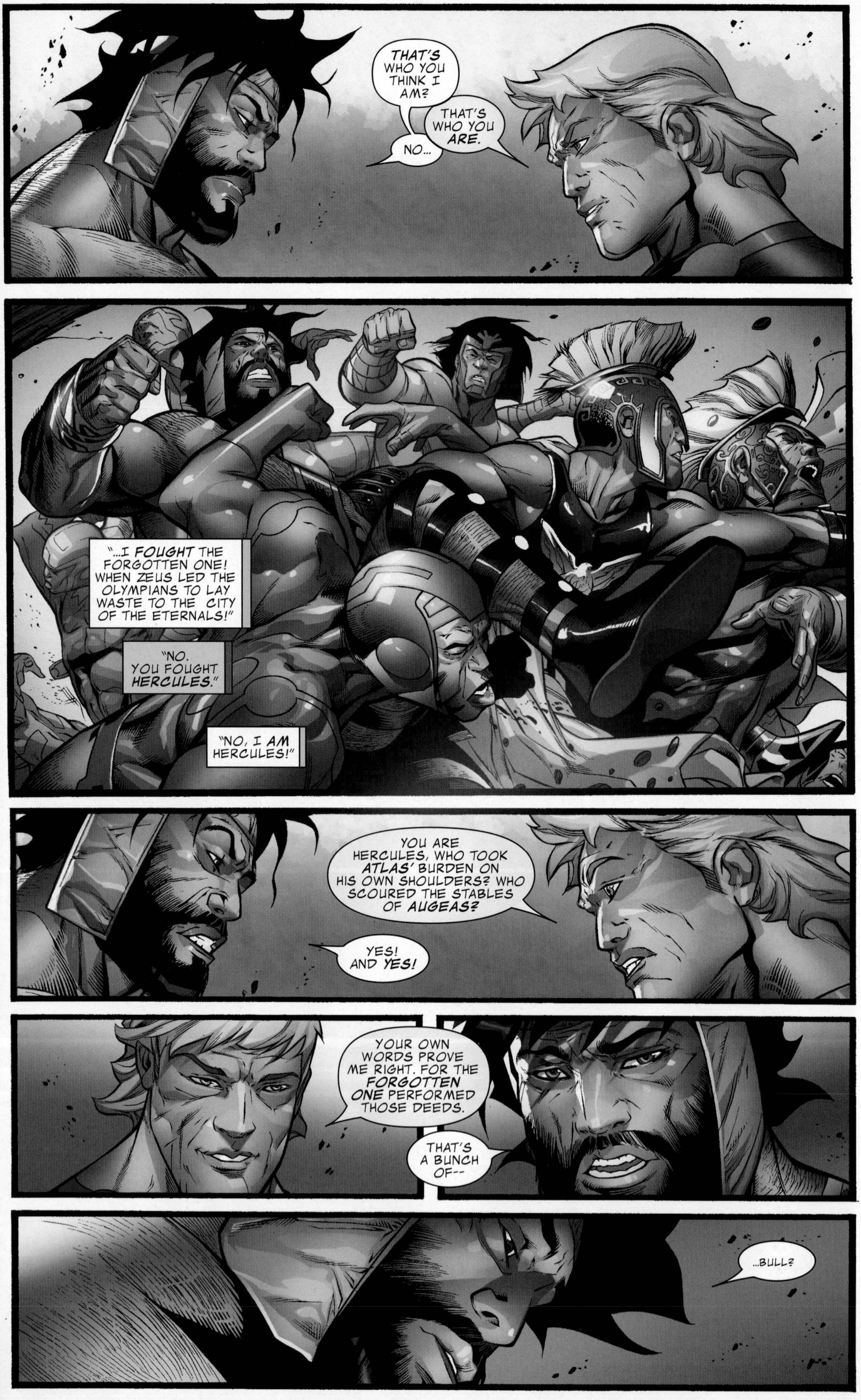
THAT'S WHO YOU THINK I AM?
NO...
THAT'S WHO YOU ARE.
"...I FOUGHT THE FORGOTTEN ONE! WHEN ZEUS LED THE OLYMPIANS TO LAY WASTE TO THE CITY OF THE ETERNALS!"
"NO. YOU FOUGHT HERCULES."
"NO, I AM HERCULES!"
YOU ARE HERCULES, WHO TOOK ATLAS' BURDEN ON HIS OWN SHOULDERS? WHO SCOURED THE STABLES OF AUGEAS?
YES! AND YES!
YOUR OWN WORDS PROVE ME RIGHT. FOR THE FORGOTTEN ONE PERFORMED THOSE DEEDS.
THAT'S A BUNCH OF--
...BULL?

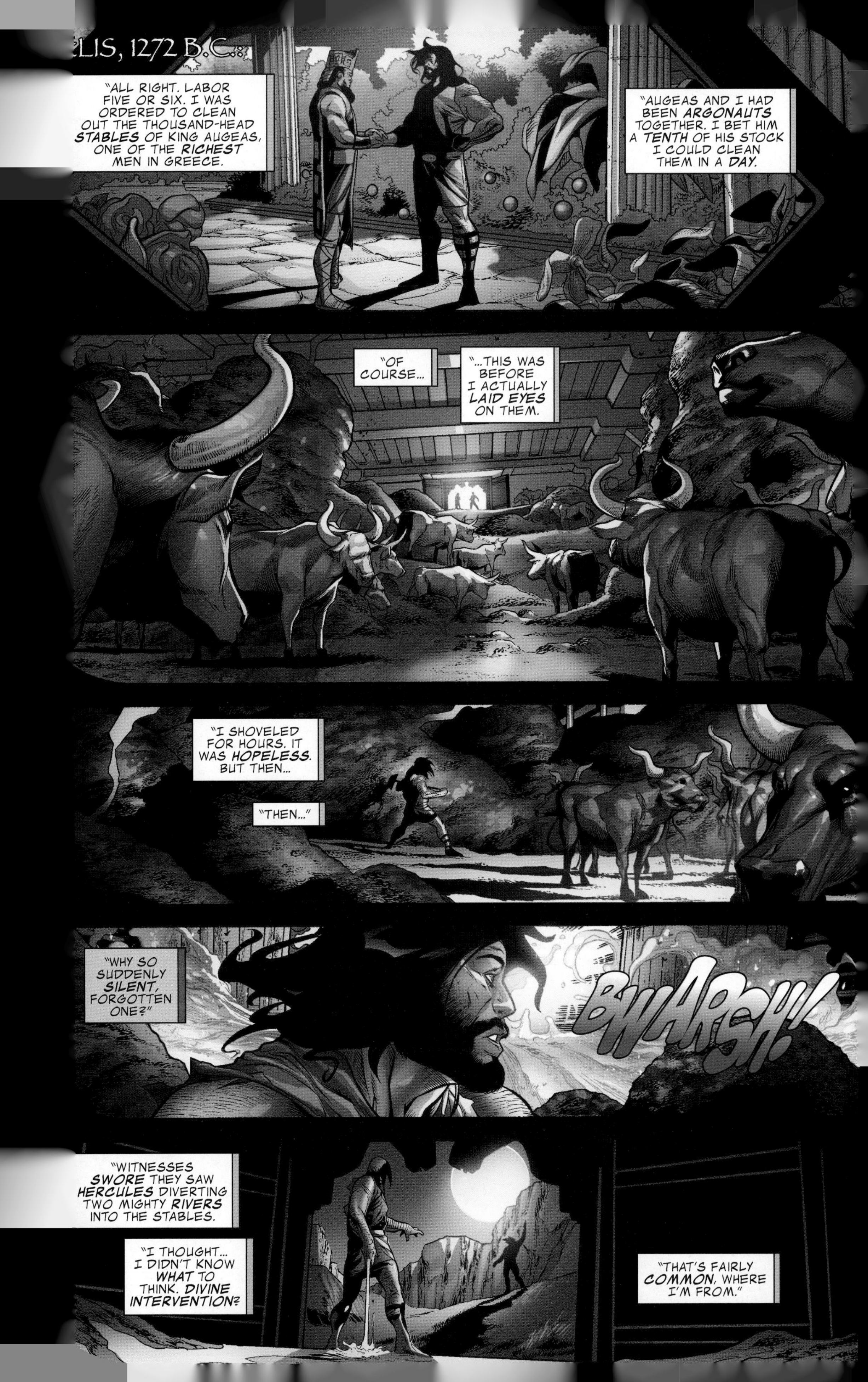

ELIS, 1272 B.C.:
"ALL RIGHT. LABOR FIVE OR SIX. I WAS ORDERED TO CLEAN OUT THE THOUSAND-HEAD STABLES OF KING AUGEAS, ONE OF THE RICHEST MEN IN GREECE.
"AUGEAS AND I HAD BEEN ARGONAUTS TOGETHER. I BET HIM A TENTH OF HIS STOCK I COULD CLEAN THEM IN A DAY.
"OF COURSE...
"...THIS WAS BEFORE I ACTUALLY LAID EYES ON THEM.
"I SHOVELED FOR HOURS. IT WAS HOPELESS. BUT THEN...
"THEN..."
"WHY SO SUDDENLY SILENT, FORGOTTEN ONE?"
BWARSH!
"WITNESSES SWORE THEY SAW HERCULES DIVERTING TWO MIGHTY RIVERS INTO THE STABLES.
"I THOUGHT... I DIDN'T KNOW WHAT TO THINK. DIVINE INTERVENTION?
"THAT'S FAIRLY COMMON, WHERE I'M FROM."

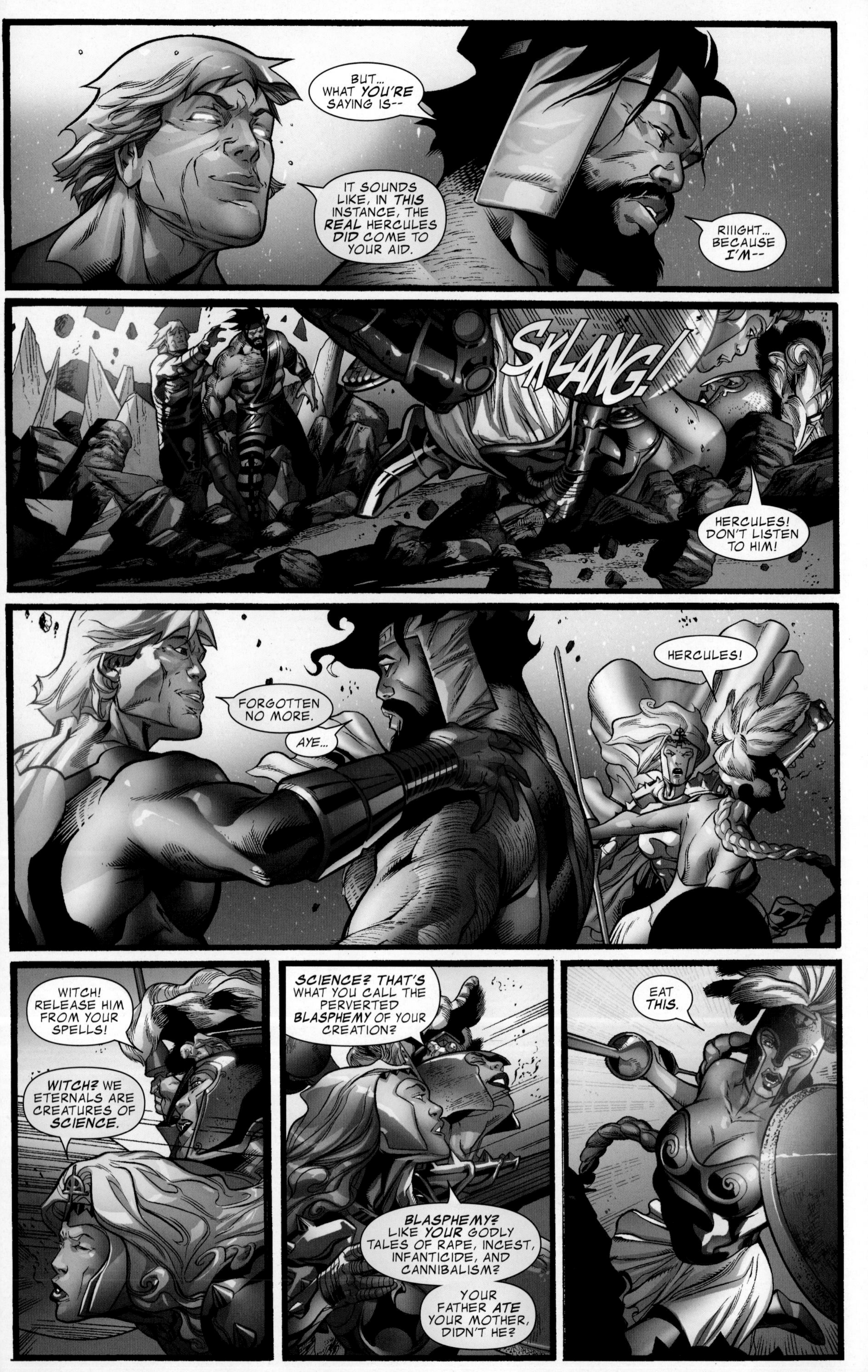
BUT... WHAT YOU'RE SAYING IS--
IT SOUNDS LIKE, IN THIS INSTANCE, THE REAL HERCULES DID COME TO YOUR AID.
RIIIGHT... BECAUSE I'M--
SKLANG!
HERCULES! DON'T LISTEN TO HIM!
FORGOTTEN NO MORE.
AYE...
HERCULES!
WITCH! RELEASE HIM FROM YOUR SPELLS!
WITCH? WE ETERNALS ARE CREATURES OF SCIENCE.
SCIENCE? THAT'S WHAT YOU CALL THE PERVERTED BLASPHEMY OF YOUR CREATION?
BLASPHEMY? LIKE YOUR GODLY TALES OF RAPE, INCEST, INFANTICIDE, AND CANNIBALISM?
YOUR FATHER ATE YOUR MOTHER, DIDN'T HE?
EAT THIS.

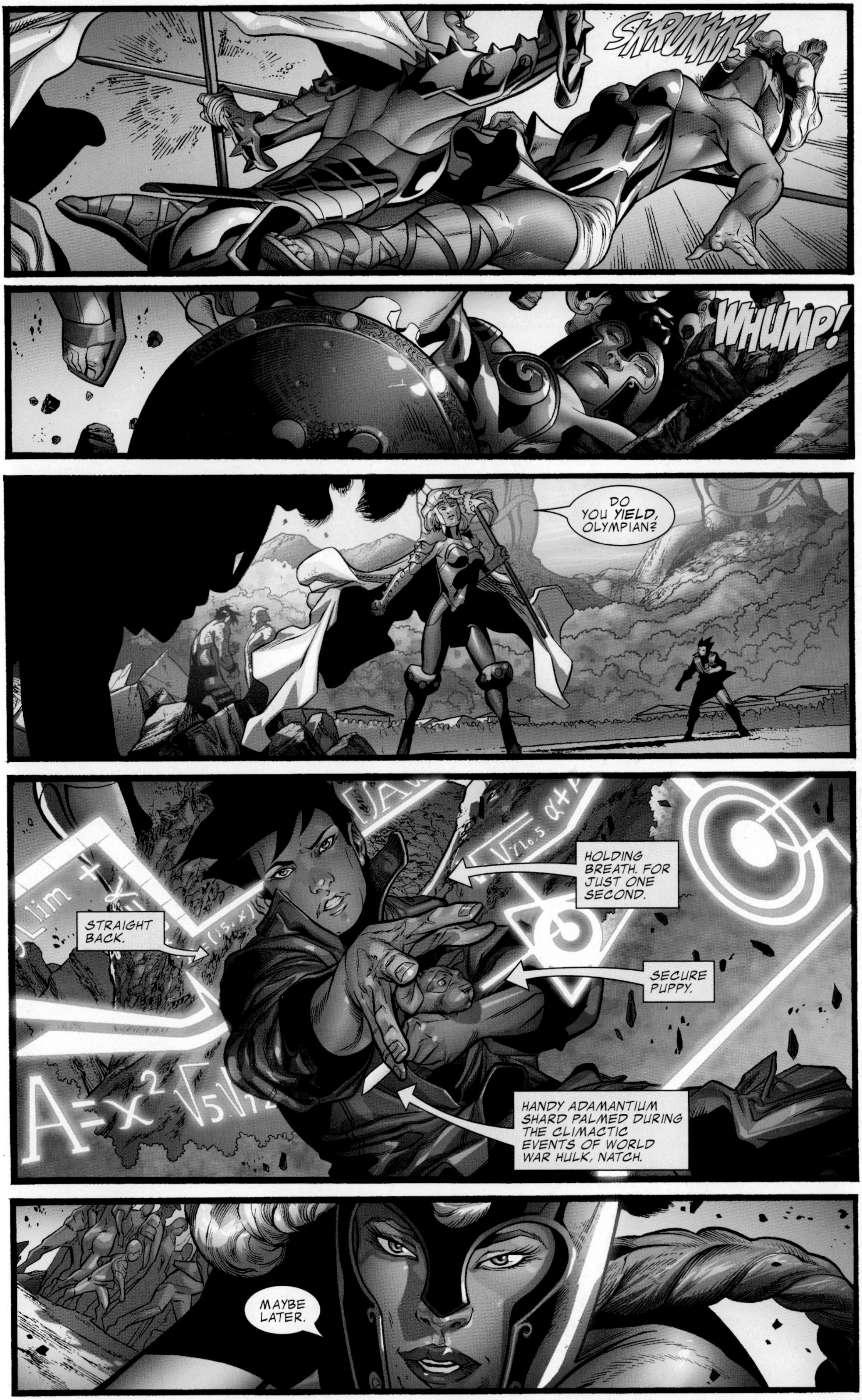
SKRUNKK!
WHUMP!
DO YOU YIELD, OLYMPIAN?
HOLDING BREATH. FOR JUST ONE SECOND.
STRAIGHT BACK.
SECURE PUPPY.
HANDY ADAMANTIUM SHARD PALMED DURING THE CLIMACTIC EVENTS OF WORLD WAR HULK, NATCH.
MAYBE LATER.

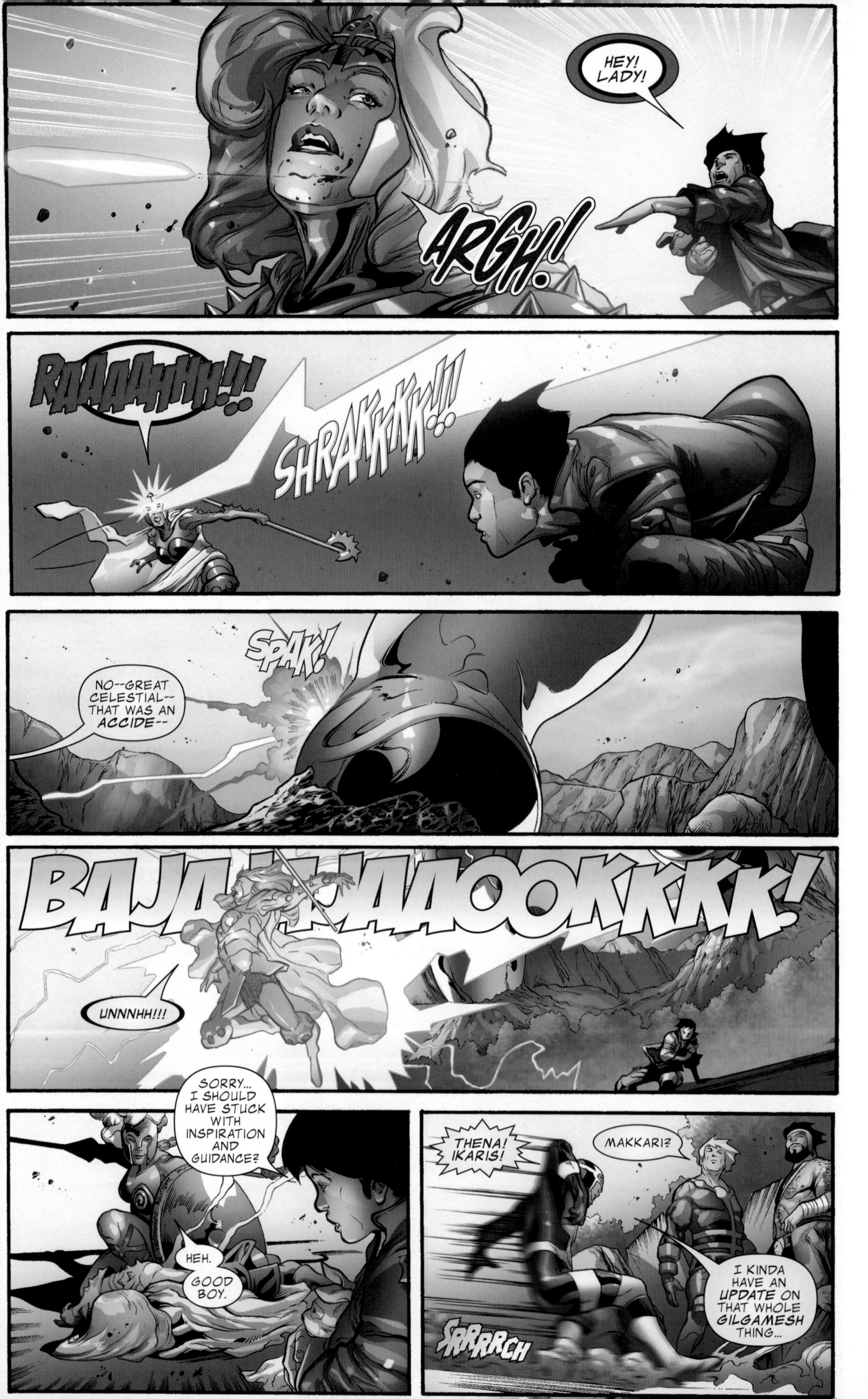
HEY! LADY!
ARGH!
RAAAAHHH!!!
SHRAKKKK!!!
SPAK!
NO--GREAT CELESTIAL--THAT WAS AN ACCIDE--
BAJAAAAAOOKKKK!
UNNNHH!!!
SORRY... I SHOULD HAVE STUCK WITH INSPIRATION AND GUIDANCE?
HEH. GOOD BOY.
THENA! IKARIS!
MAKKARI?
I KINDA HAVE AN UPDATE ON THAT WHOLE GILGAMESH THING...
SRRRRCH

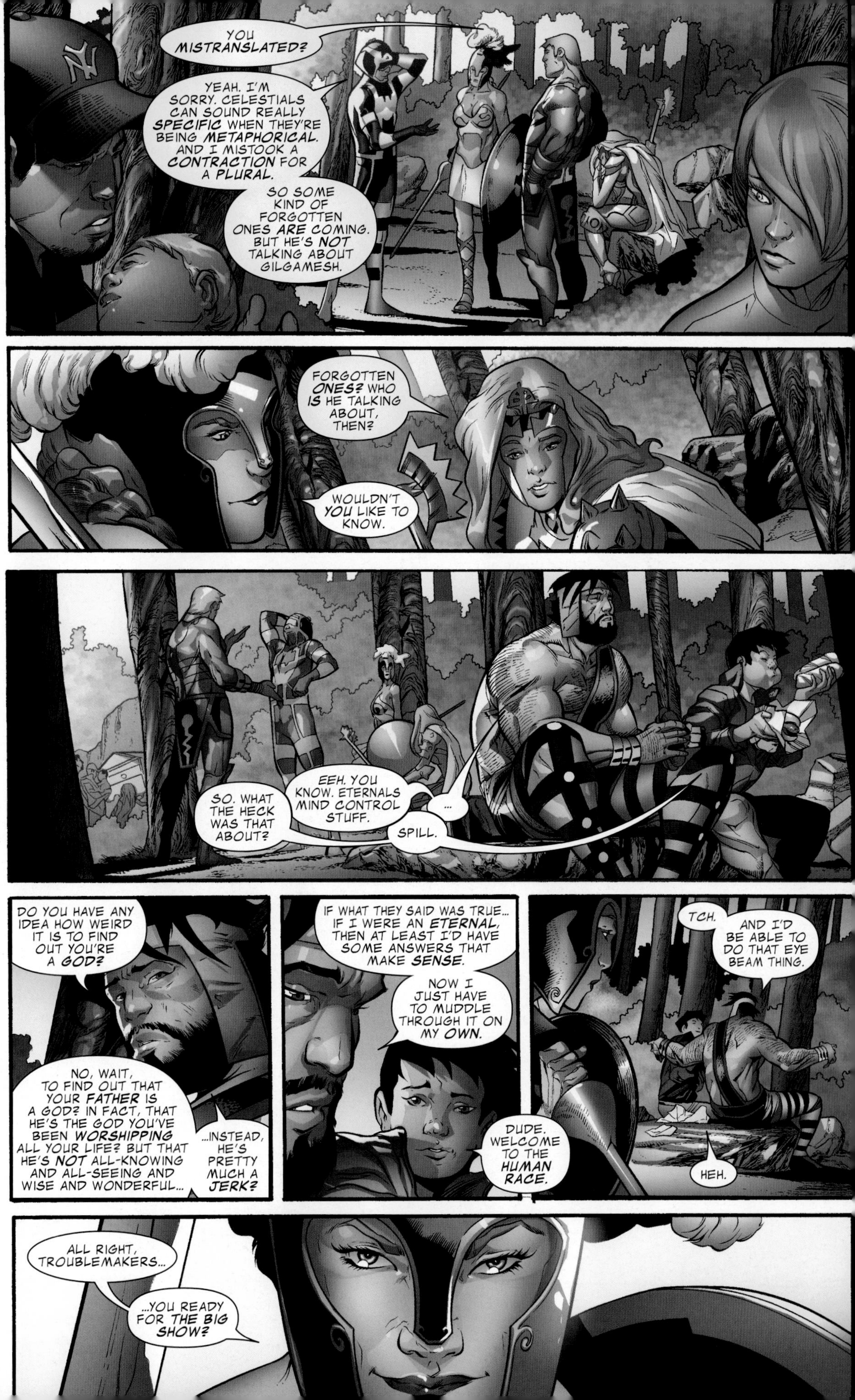
YOU MISTRANSLATED?
YEAH. I'M SORRY. CELESTIALS CAN SOUND REALLY SPECIFIC WHEN THEY'RE BEING METAPHORICAL. AND I MISTOOK A CONTRACTION FOR A PLURAL.
SO SOME KIND OF FORGOTTEN ONES ARE COMING. BUT HE'S NOT TALKING ABOUT GILGAMESH.
FORGOTTEN ONES? WHO IS HE TALKING ABOUT, THEN?
WOULDN'T YOU LIKE TO KNOW.
SO. WHAT THE HECK WAS THAT ABOUT?
EEH. YOU KNOW. ETERNALS MIND CONTROL STUFF.
...
SPILL.
DO YOU HAVE ANY IDEA HOW WEIRD IT IS TO FIND OUT YOU'RE A GOD?
NO, WAIT, TO FIND OUT THAT YOUR FATHER IS A GOD? IN FACT, THAT HE'S THE GOD YOU'VE BEEN WORSHIPPING ALL YOUR LIFE? BUT THAT HE'S NOT ALL-KNOWING AND ALL-SEEING AND WISE AND WONDERFUL...
...INSTEAD, HE'S PRETTY MUCH A JERK?
IF WHAT THEY SAID WAS TRUE... IF I WERE AN ETERNAL, THEN AT LEAST I'D HAVE SOME ANSWERS THAT MAKE SENSE.
NOW I JUST HAVE TO MUDDLE THROUGH IT ON MY OWN.
DUDE. WELCOME TO THE HUMAN RACE.
TCH.
AND I'D BE ABLE TO DO THAT EYE BEAM THING.
HEH.
ALL RIGHT, TROUBLEMAKERS...
...YOU READY FOR THE BIG SHOW?

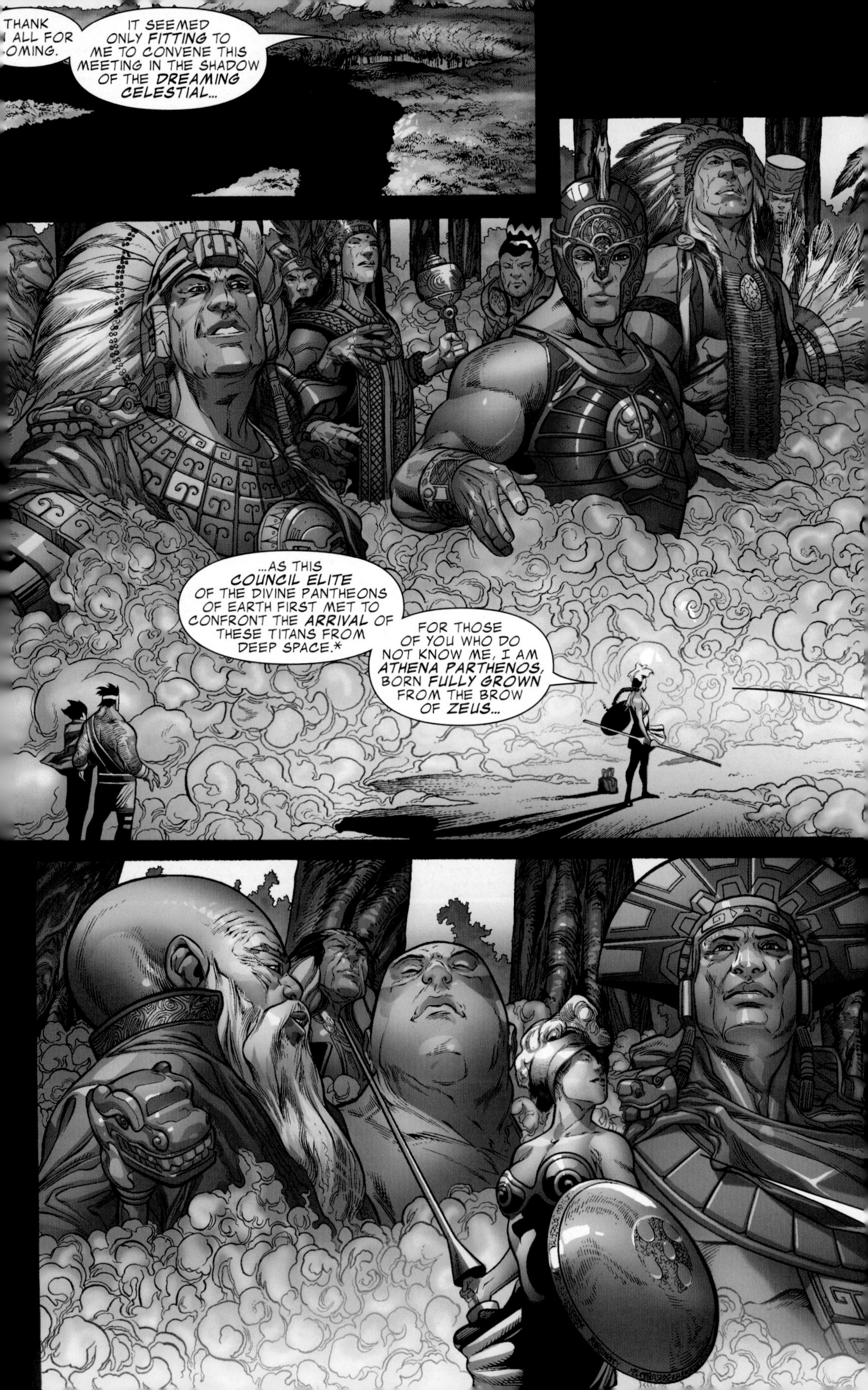
THANK
ALL FOR
OMING.
IT SEEMED ONLY FITTING TO ME TO CONVENE THIS MEETING IN THE SHADOW OF THE DREAMING CELESTIAL...
...AS THIS COUNCIL ELITE OF THE DIVINE PANTHEONS OF EARTH FIRST MET TO CONFRONT THE ARRIVAL OF THESE TITANS FROM DEEP SPACE.*
FOR THOSE OF YOU WHO DO NOT KNOW ME, I AM ATHENA PARTHENOS, BORN FULLY GROWN FROM THE BROW OF ZEUS...

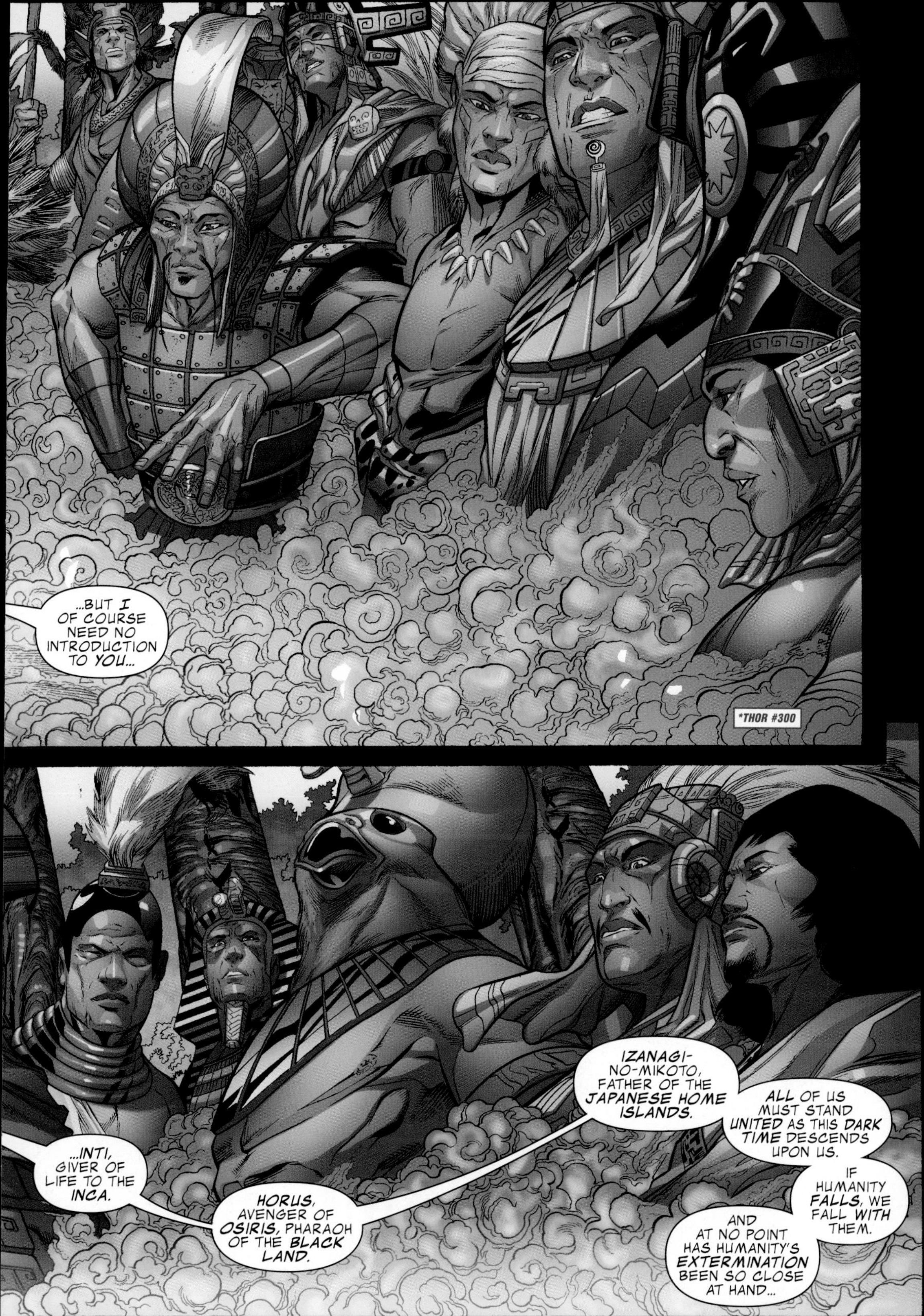
...BUT I OF COURSE NEED NO INTRODUCTION TO YOU...
*THOR #300
...INTI, GIVER OF LIFE TO THE INCA.
HORUS, AVENGER OF OSIRIS, PHARAOH OF THE BLACK LAND.
IZANAGI-NO-MIKOTO, FATHER OF THE JAPANESE HOME ISLANDS.
ALL OF US MUST STAND UNITED AS THIS DARK TIME DESCENDS UPON US.
IF HUMANITY FALLS, WE FALL WITH THEM.
AND AT NO POINT HAS HUMANITY'S EXTERMINATION BEEN SO CLOSE AT HAND...

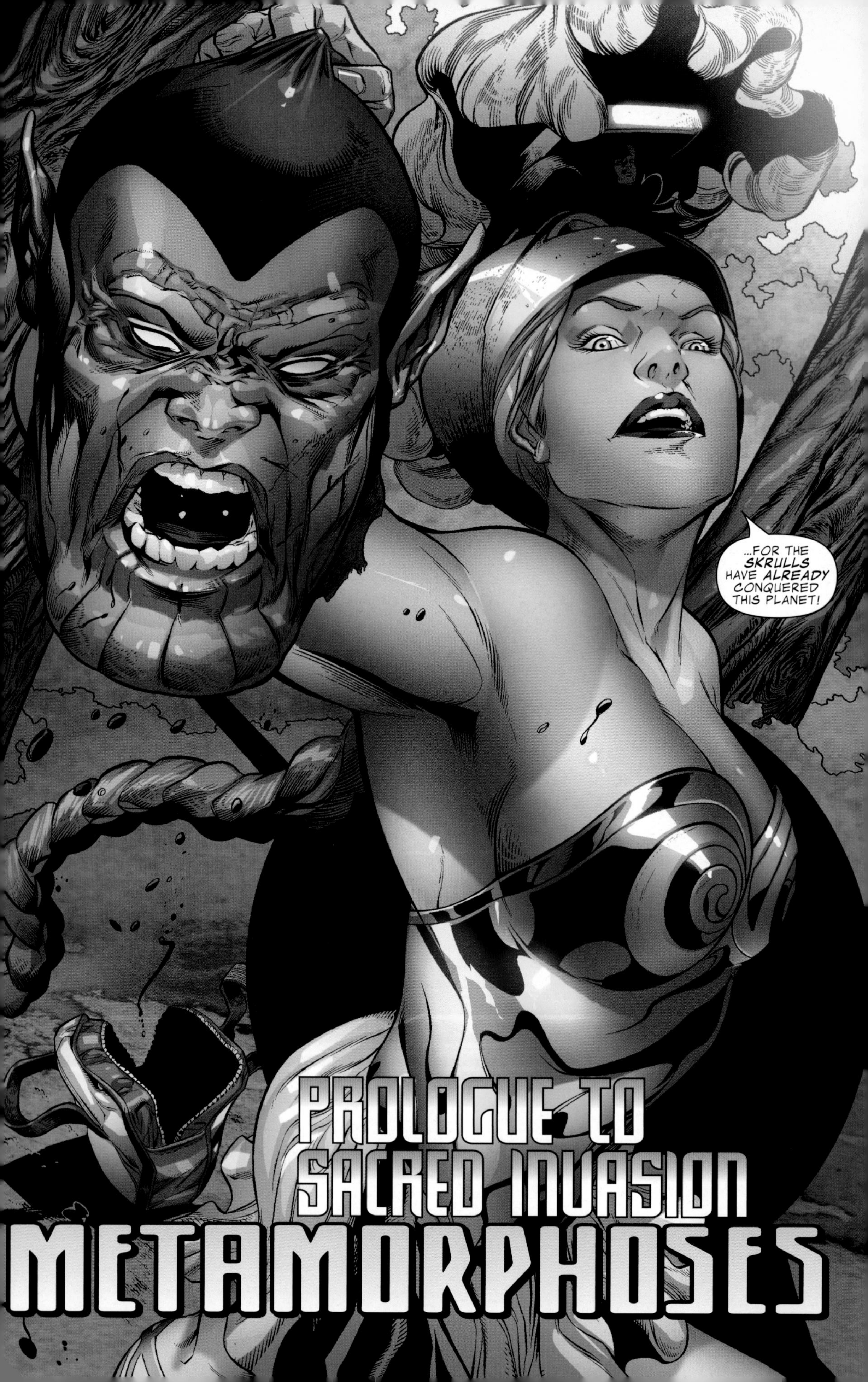
...FOR THE SKRULLS HAVE ALREADY CONQUERED THIS PLANET!
PROLOGUE TO SACRED INVASION
METAMORPHOSES

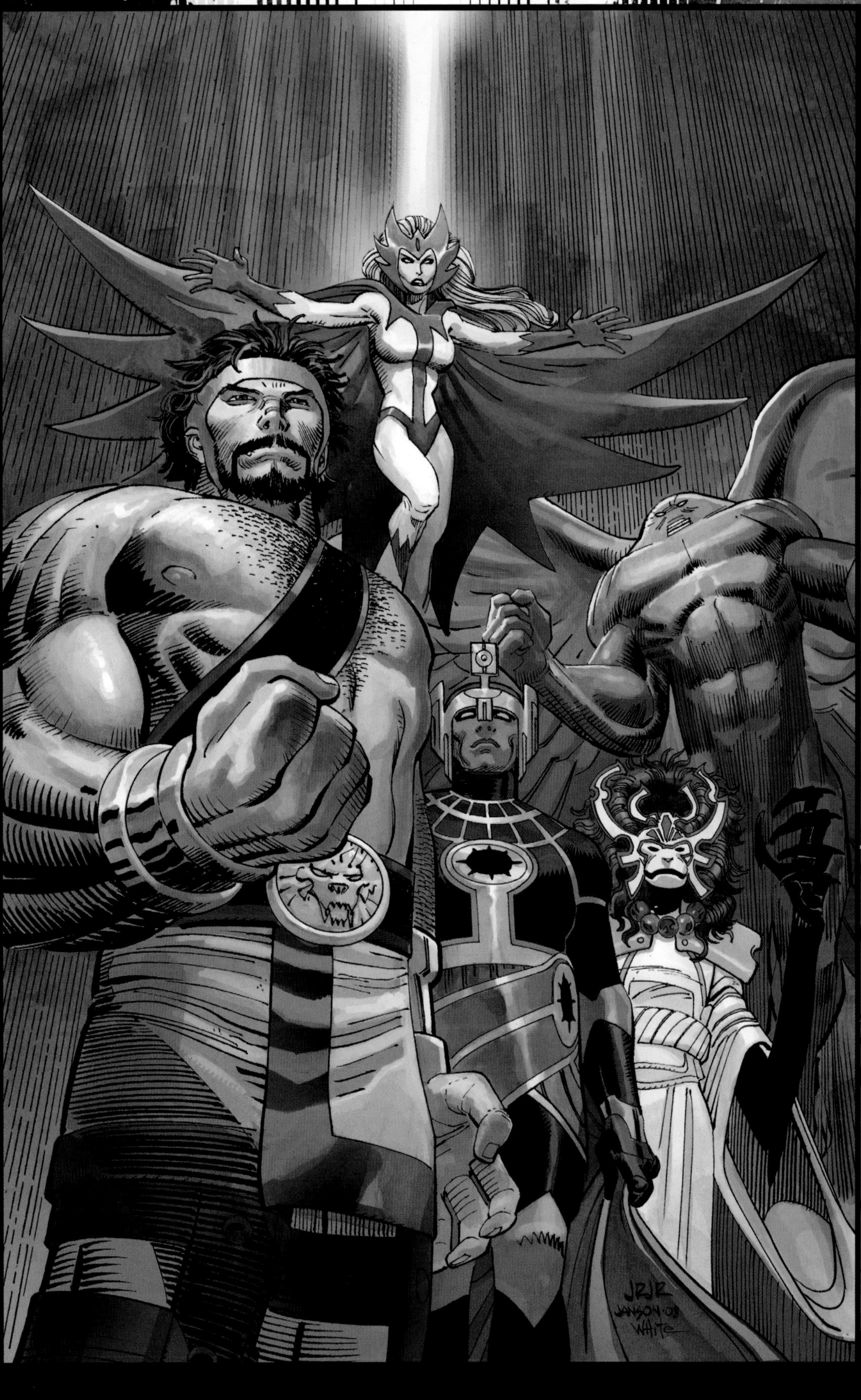
JRJR
JANSON·08
WHITE

INCREDIBLE HERCULES #117

A MINISTERING ANGEL SHALL MY SISTER BE.
~ WILLIAM SHAKESPEARE

BIG SISTERS ARE THE CRAB GRASS IN THE LAWN OF LIFE.
~CHARLES M. SCHULZ

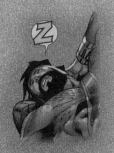

THE MIGHTY **HERCULES**.

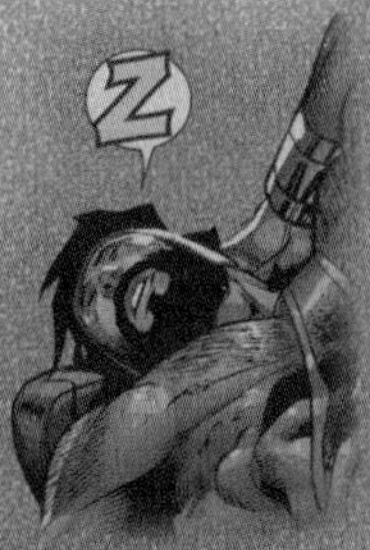
Z

A GOD AMONGST MEN.
A WARRIOR SUPERB.

HIS SISTER

ATHENA

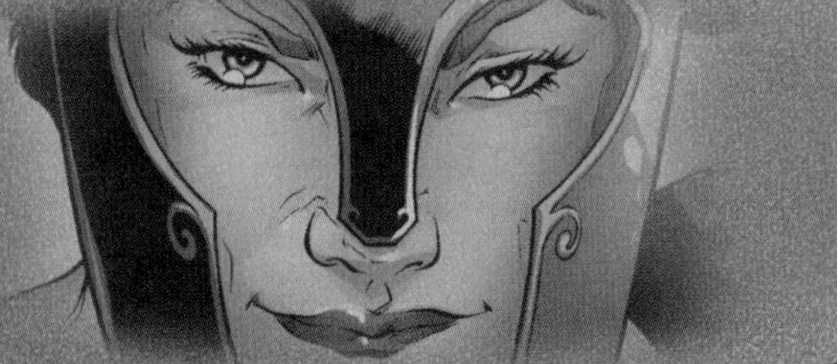

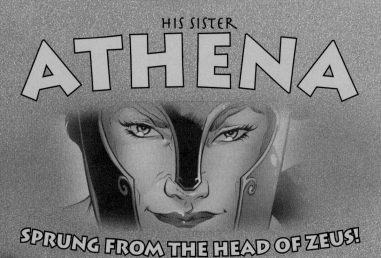

SPRUNG FROM THE HEAD OF ZEUS!

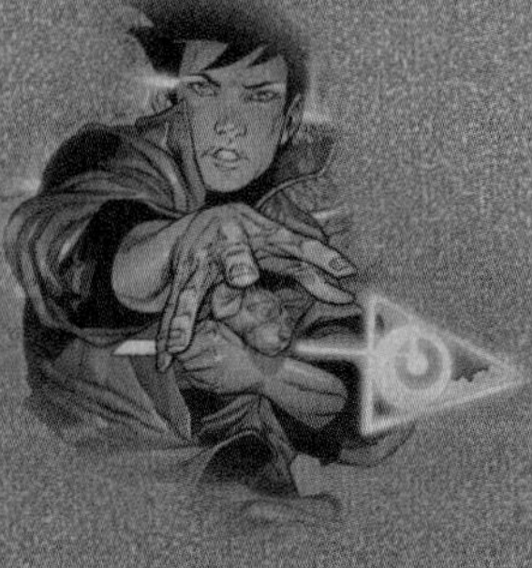

HATH LED HE AND **AMADEUS CHO** (WITH PUP IN TOW) TO A **COUNCIL OF GODS**, FOR MYSTERIOUS SKRULL-RELATED REASONS.

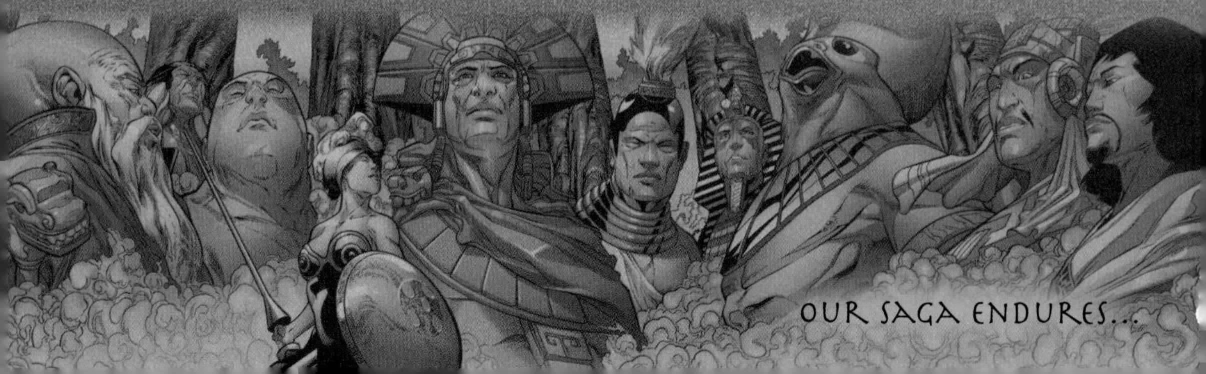

OUR SAGA ENDURES...

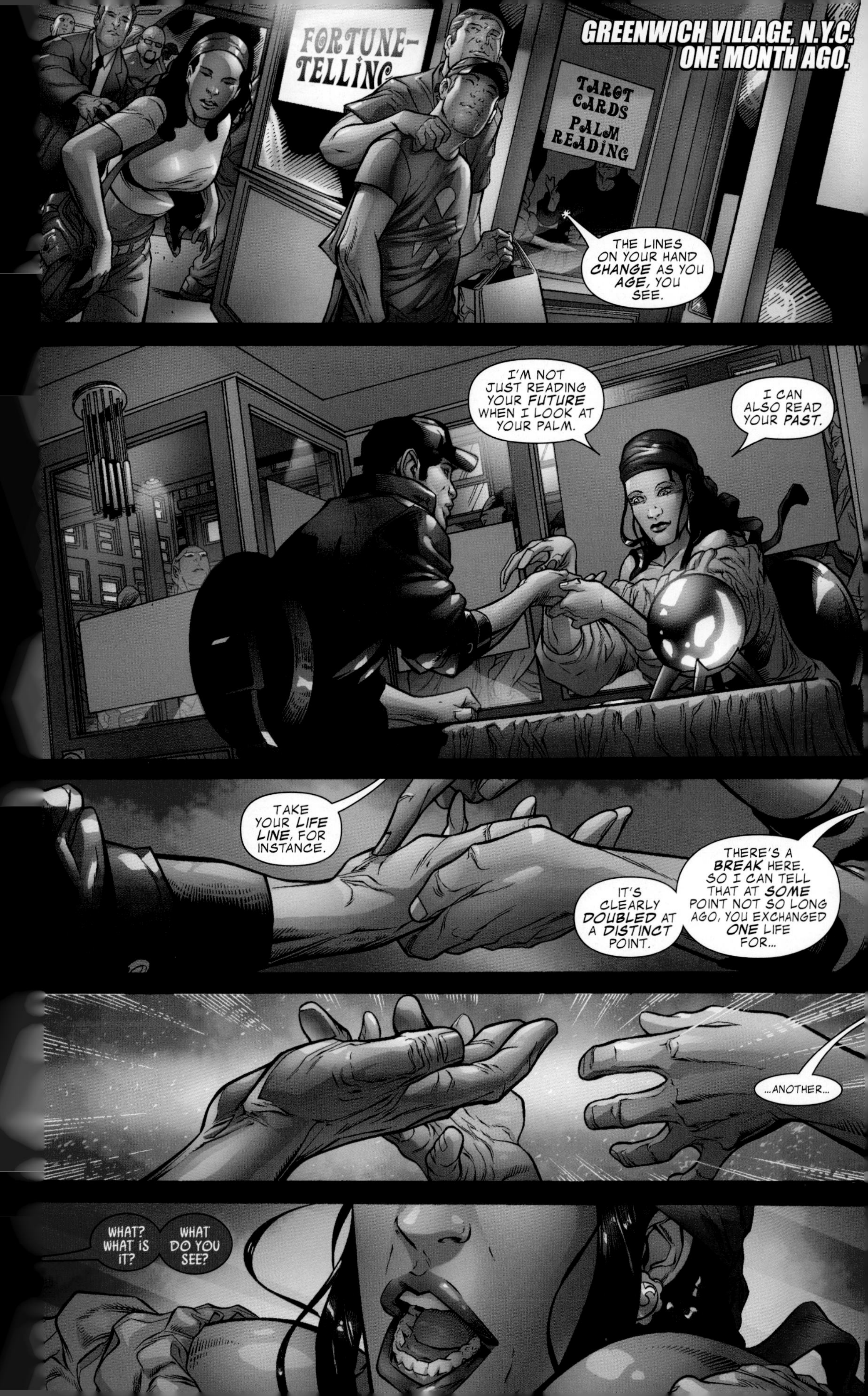

GREENWICH VILLAGE, N.Y.C. ONE MONTH AGO.
FORTUNE-TELLING
TAROT CARDS PALM READING
THE LINES ON YOUR HAND CHANGE AS YOU AGE, YOU SEE.
I'M NOT JUST READING YOUR FUTURE WHEN I LOOK AT YOUR PALM.
I CAN ALSO READ YOUR PAST.
TAKE YOUR LIFE LINE, FOR INSTANCE.
IT'S CLEARLY DOUBLED AT A DISTINCT POINT.
THERE'S A BREAK HERE. SO I CAN TELL THAT AT SOME POINT NOT SO LONG AGO, YOU EXCHANGED ONE LIFE FOR...
...ANOTHER...
WHAT? WHAT IS IT?
WHAT DO YOU SEE?

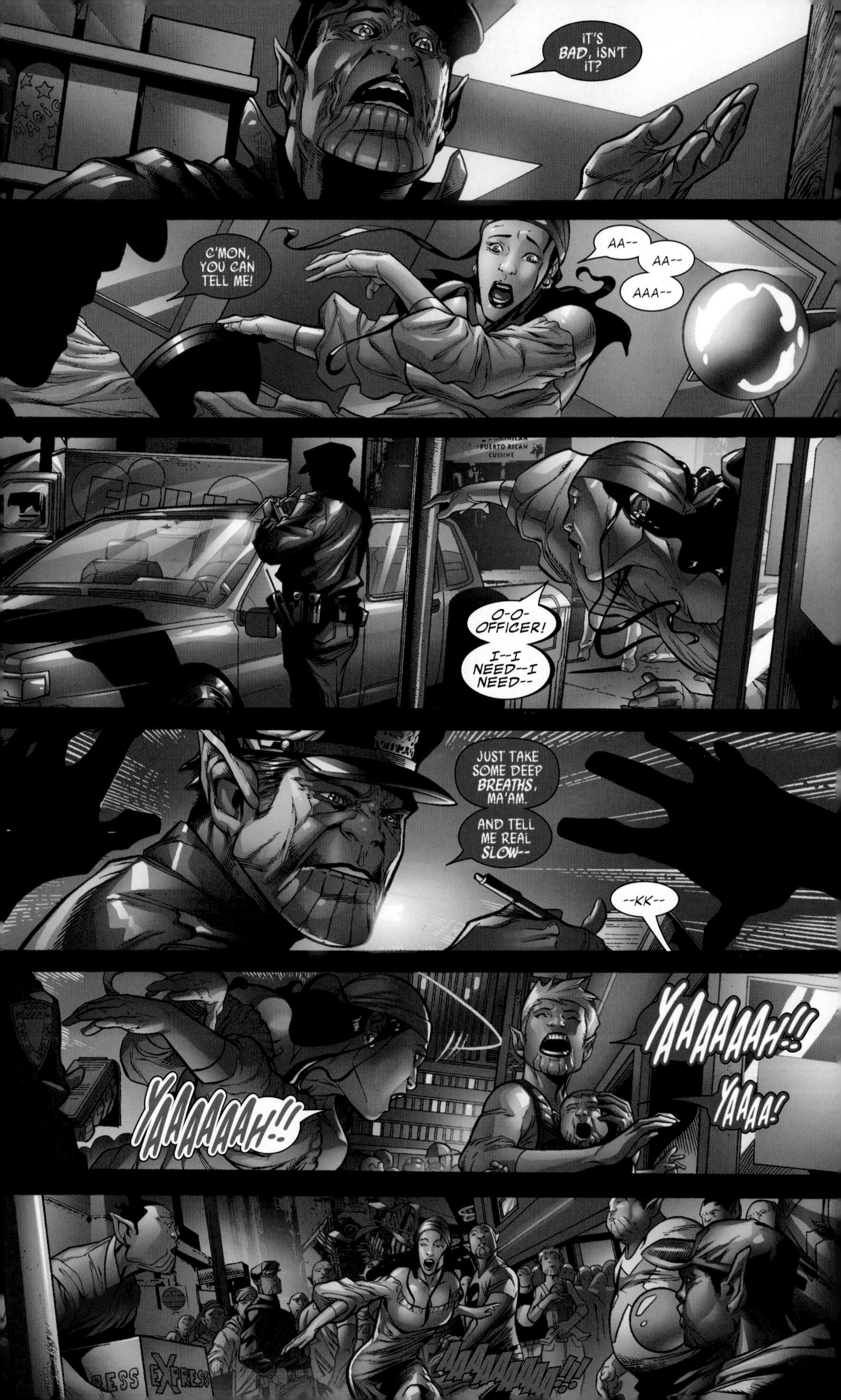
IT'S BAD, ISN'T IT?
C'MON, YOU CAN TELL ME!
AA--
AA--
AAA--
DOMINICAN PUERTO RICAN CUISINE
O-O-OFFICER!
I--I NEED--I NEED--
JUST TAKE SOME DEEP BREATHS, MA'AM.
AND TELL ME REAL SLOW--
--KK--
YAAAAAAH!!
YAAAAAAH!!
YAAAA!
RESS
EXPRESS

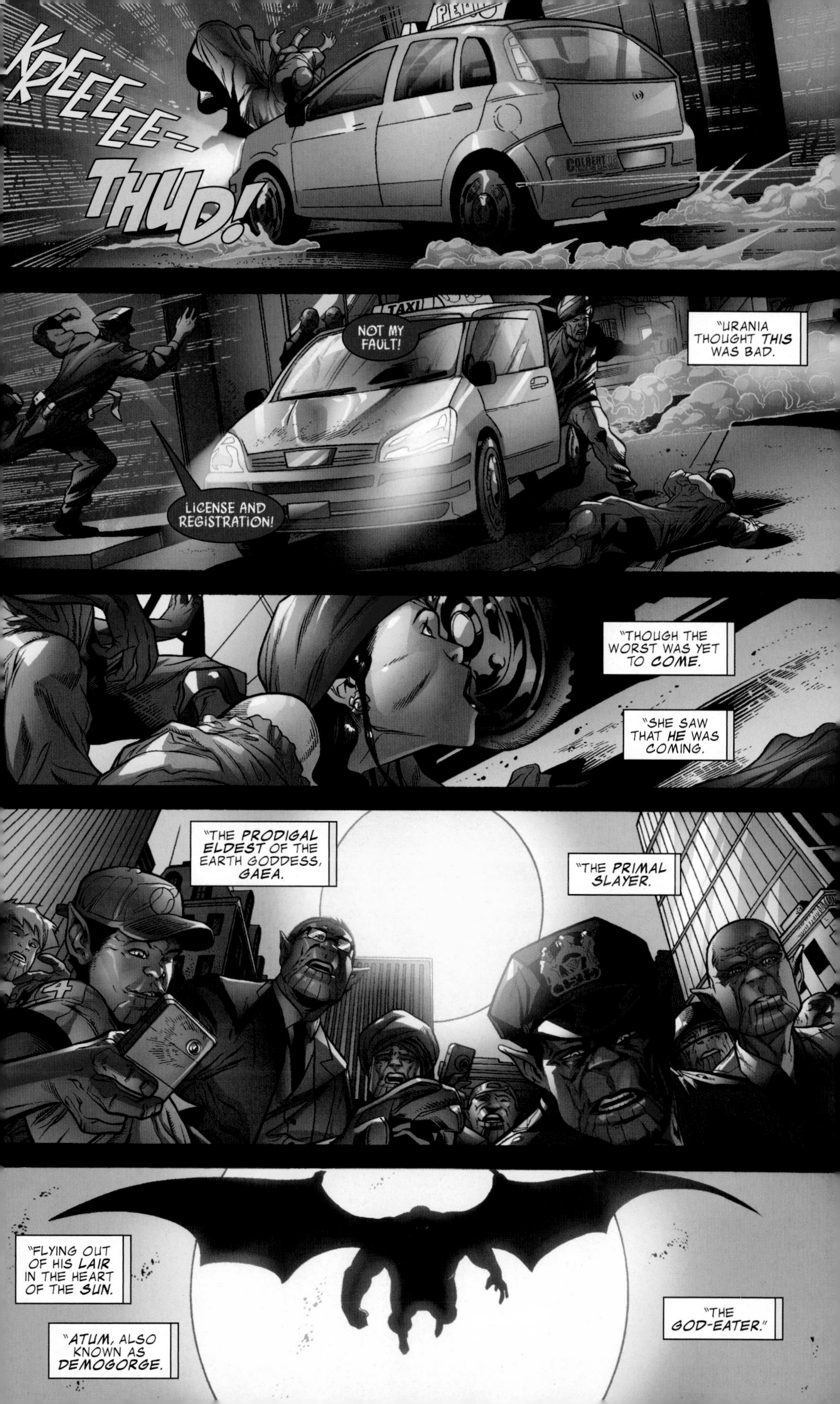
KREEEEEE--
THUD!
NOT MY FAULT!
"URANIA THOUGHT THIS WAS BAD.
LICENSE AND REGISTRATION!
"THOUGH THE WORST WAS YET TO COME.
"SHE SAW THAT HE WAS COMING.
"THE PRODIGAL ELDEST OF THE EARTH GODDESS, GAEA.
"THE PRIMAL SLAYER.
"FLYING OUT OF HIS LAIR IN THE HEART OF THE SUN.
"ATUM, ALSO KNOWN AS DEMOGORGE.
"THE GOD-EATER."

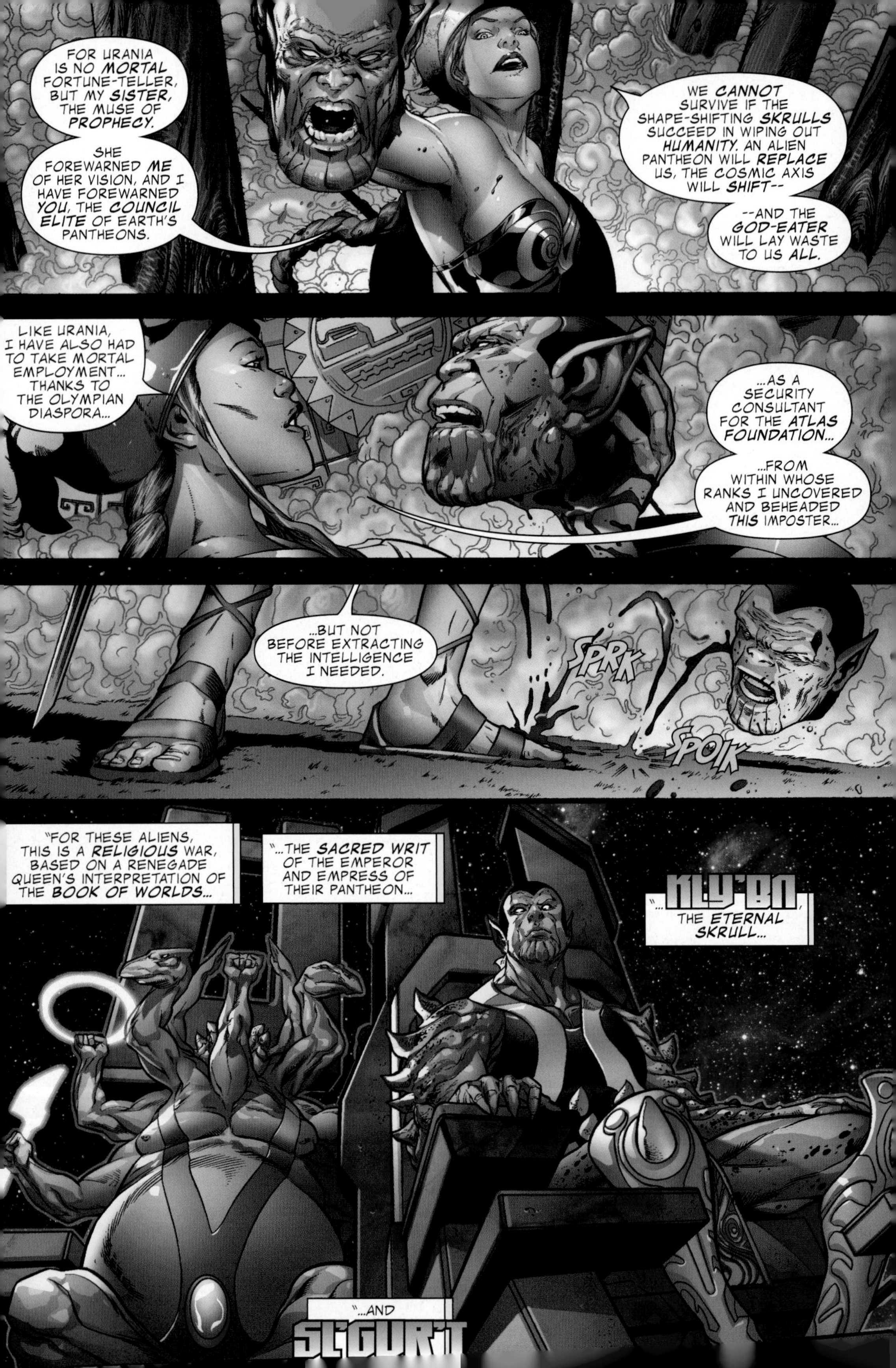

FOR URANIA IS NO MORTAL FORTUNE-TELLER, BUT MY SISTER, THE MUSE OF PROPHECY.
SHE FOREWARNED ME OF HER VISION, AND I HAVE FOREWARNED YOU, THE COUNCIL ELITE OF EARTH'S PANTHEONS.
WE CANNOT SURVIVE IF THE SHAPE-SHIFTING SKRULLS SUCCEED IN WIPING OUT HUMANITY. AN ALIEN PANTHEON WILL REPLACE US, THE COSMIC AXIS WILL SHIFT--
--AND THE GOD-EATER WILL LAY WASTE TO US ALL.
LIKE URANIA, I HAVE ALSO HAD TO TAKE MORTAL EMPLOYMENT... THANKS TO THE OLYMPIAN DIASPORA...
...AS A SECURITY CONSULTANT FOR THE ATLAS FOUNDATION...
...FROM WITHIN WHOSE RANKS I UNCOVERED AND BEHEADED THIS IMPOSTER...
...BUT NOT BEFORE EXTRACTING THE INTELLIGENCE I NEEDED.
SPRK
SPOIK
"FOR THESE ALIENS, THIS IS A RELIGIOUS WAR, BASED ON A RENEGADE QUEEN'S INTERPRETATION OF THE BOOK OF WORLDS...
"...THE SACRED WRIT OF THE EMPEROR AND EMPRESS OF THEIR PANTHEON...
"...KLY'BN, THE ETERNAL SKRULL...
"...AND SL'GUR'T

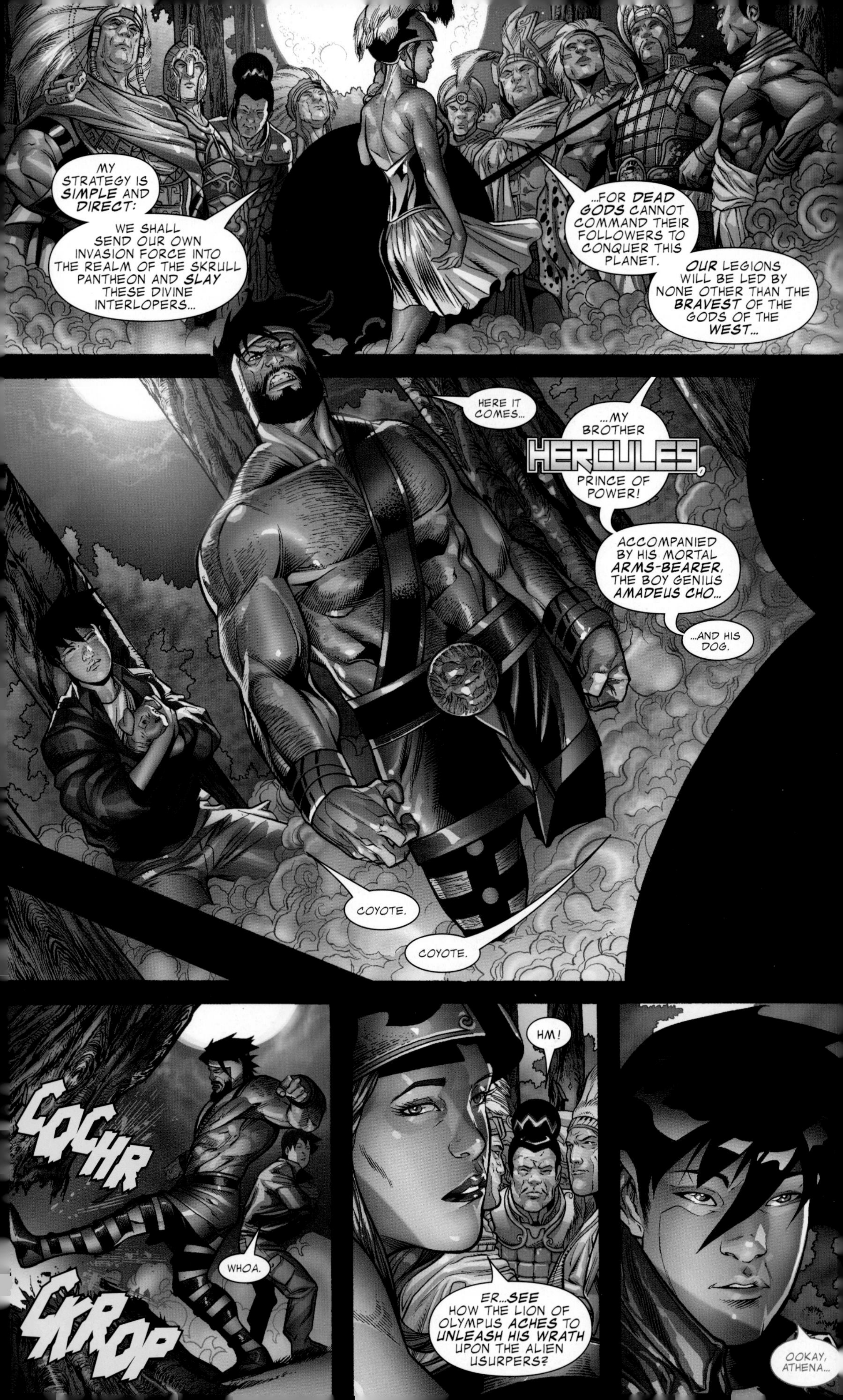

MY STRATEGY IS **SIMPLE** AND **DIRECT:**
WE SHALL SEND OUR OWN INVASION FORCE INTO THE REALM OF THE SKRULL PANTHEON AND **SLAY** THESE DIVINE INTERLOPERS...
...FOR **DEAD GODS** CANNOT COMMAND THEIR FOLLOWERS TO CONQUER THIS PLANET.
OUR LEGIONS WILL BE LED BY NONE OTHER THAN THE **BRAVEST** OF THE GODS OF THE **WEST...**
HERE IT COMES...
...MY BROTHER
HERCULES,
PRINCE OF POWER!
ACCOMPANIED BY HIS MORTAL **ARMS-BEARER,** THE BOY GENIUS **AMADEUS CHO...**
...AND HIS DOG.
COYOTE.
COYOTE.
COCHR
CKROP
WHOA.
HM!
ER...**SEE** HOW THE LION OF OLYMPUS **ACHES** TO **UNLEASH HIS WRATH** UPON THE ALIEN USURPERS?
OOKAY, ATHENA...

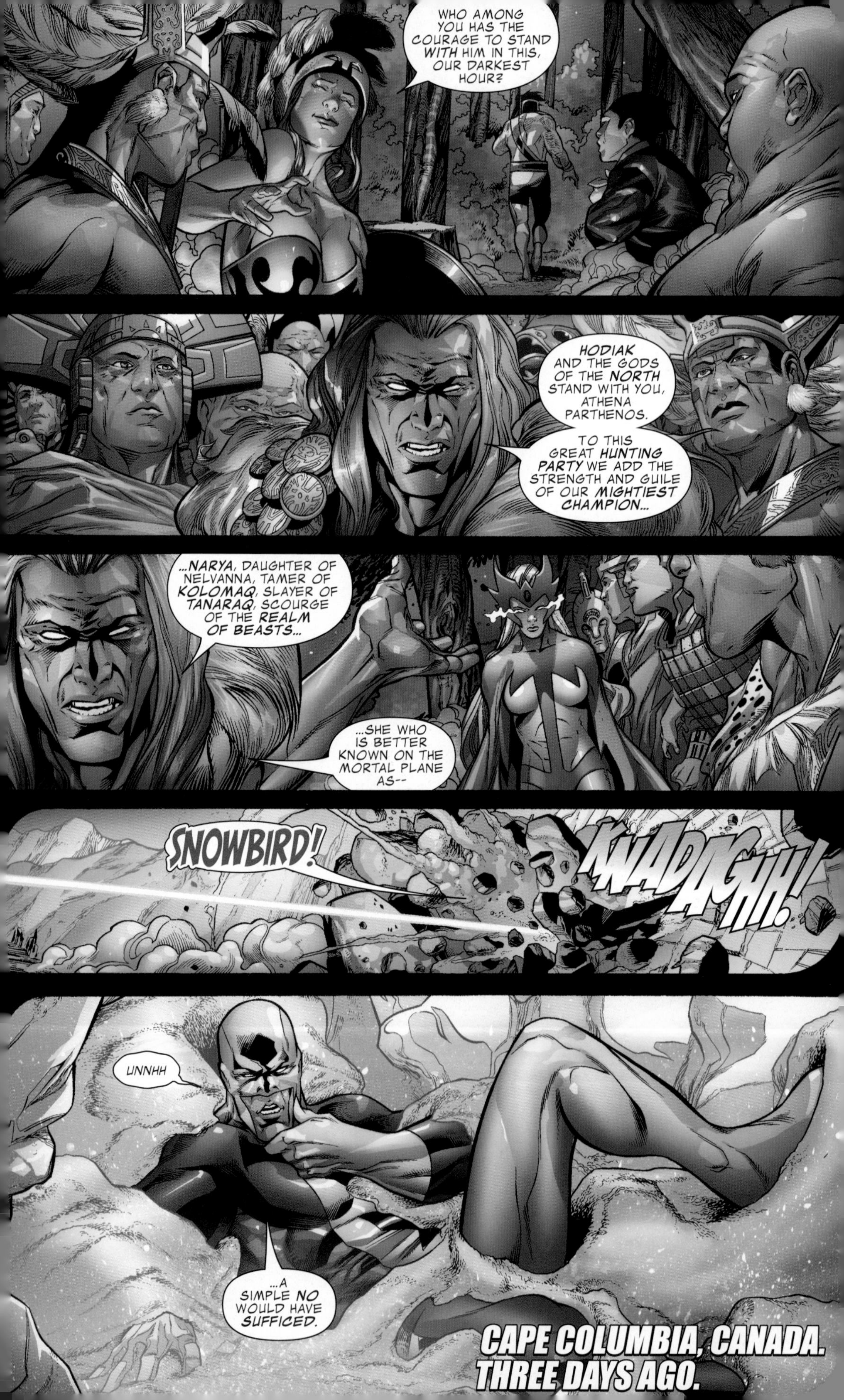
WHO AMONG YOU HAS THE COURAGE TO STAND WITH HIM IN THIS, OUR DARKEST HOUR?
HODIAK AND THE GODS OF THE NORTH STAND WITH YOU, ATHENA PARTHENOS.
TO THIS GREAT HUNTING PARTY WE ADD THE STRENGTH AND GUILE OF OUR MIGHTIEST CHAMPION...
...NARYA, DAUGHTER OF NELVANNA, TAMER OF KOLOMAQ, SLAYER OF TANARAQ, SCOURGE OF THE REALM OF BEASTS...
...SHE WHO IS BETTER KNOWN ON THE MORTAL PLANE AS--
SNOWBIRD!
KWADAGHH!
UNNHH
...A SIMPLE NO WOULD HAVE SUFFICED.
CAPE COLUMBIA, CANADA. THREE DAYS AGO.

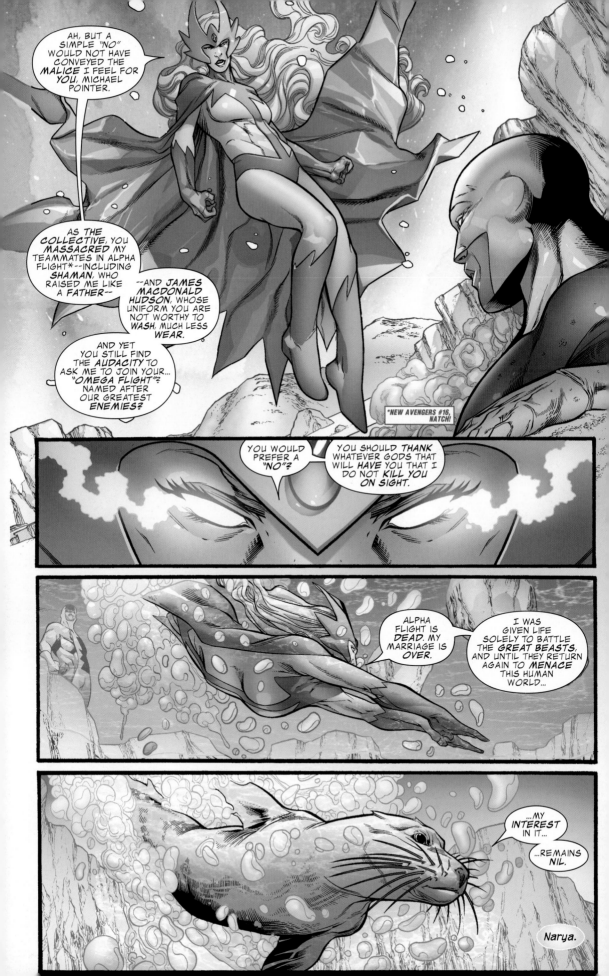

AH, BUT A SIMPLE "NO" WOULD NOT HAVE CONVEYED THE MALICE I FEEL FOR YOU, MICHAEL POINTER.

AS *THE COLLECTIVE*, YOU *MASSACRED* MY TEAMMATES IN ALPHA FLIGHT*--INCLUDING *SHAMAN*, WHO RAISED ME LIKE A *FATHER*--

--AND *JAMES MACDONALD HUDSON*, WHOSE UNIFORM YOU ARE NOT WORTHY TO WASH, MUCH LESS WEAR.

AND YET YOU STILL FIND THE *AUDACITY* TO ASK ME TO JOIN YOUR... "*OMEGA FLIGHT*"? NAMED AFTER OUR GREATEST *ENEMIES*?

*NEW AVENGERS #16, NATCH!

YOU WOULD PREFER A "NO"?

YOU SHOULD *THANK* WHATEVER GODS THAT WILL *HAVE* YOU THAT I DO NOT *KILL YOU ON SIGHT.*

ALPHA FLIGHT IS *DEAD.* MY MARRIAGE IS *OVER.*

I WAS GIVEN LIFE SOLELY TO BATTLE THE *GREAT BEASTS,* AND UNTIL THEY RETURN AGAIN TO *MENACE* THIS HUMAN WORLD...

...MY INTEREST IN IT...

...REMAINS NIL.

Narya.

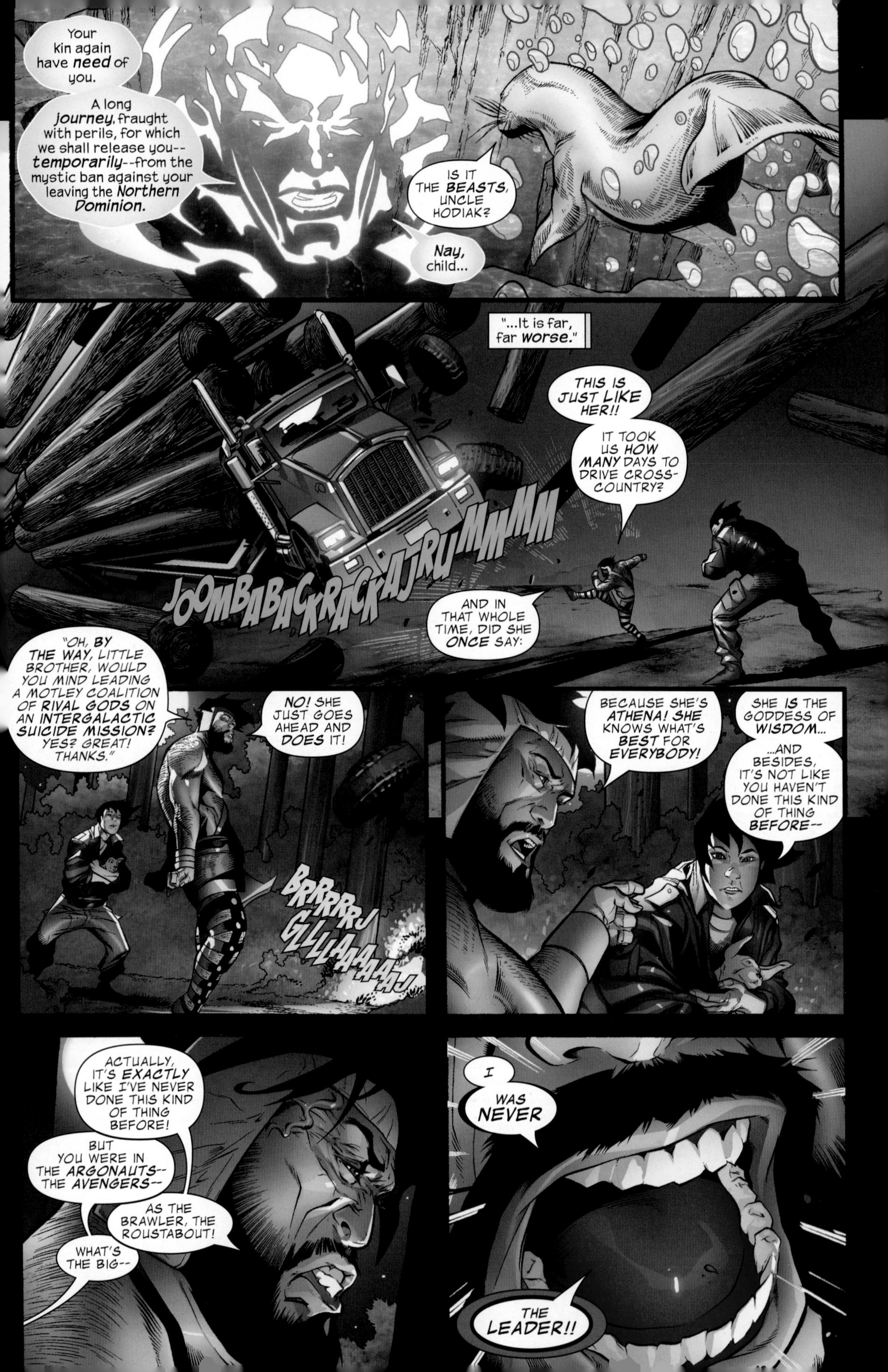
Your kin again have need of you.
A long journey, fraught with perils, for which we shall release you--temporarily--from the mystic ban against your leaving the Northern Dominion.
IS IT THE BEASTS, UNCLE HODIAK?
Nay, child...
"...It is far, far worse."
THIS IS JUST LIKE HER!!
IT TOOK US HOW MANY DAYS TO DRIVE CROSS-COUNTRY?
JOOMBABACKRACKAJRUMMMMM
AND IN THAT WHOLE TIME, DID SHE ONCE SAY:
"OH, BY THE WAY, LITTLE BROTHER, WOULD YOU MIND LEADING A MOTLEY COALITION OF RIVAL GODS ON AN INTERGALACTIC SUICIDE MISSION? YES? GREAT! THANKS."
NO! SHE JUST GOES AHEAD AND DOES IT!
BRRRRRJ GLLLAAAAAJ
BECAUSE SHE'S ATHENA! SHE KNOWS WHAT'S BEST FOR EVERYBODY!
SHE IS THE GODDESS OF WISDOM...
...AND BESIDES, IT'S NOT LIKE YOU HAVEN'T DONE THIS KIND OF THING BEFORE--
ACTUALLY, IT'S EXACTLY LIKE I'VE NEVER DONE THIS KIND OF THING BEFORE!
BUT YOU WERE IN THE ARGONAUTS--THE AVENGERS--
AS THE BRAWLER, THE ROUSTABOUT!
WHAT'S THE BIG--
I
WAS NEVER
THE LEADER!!

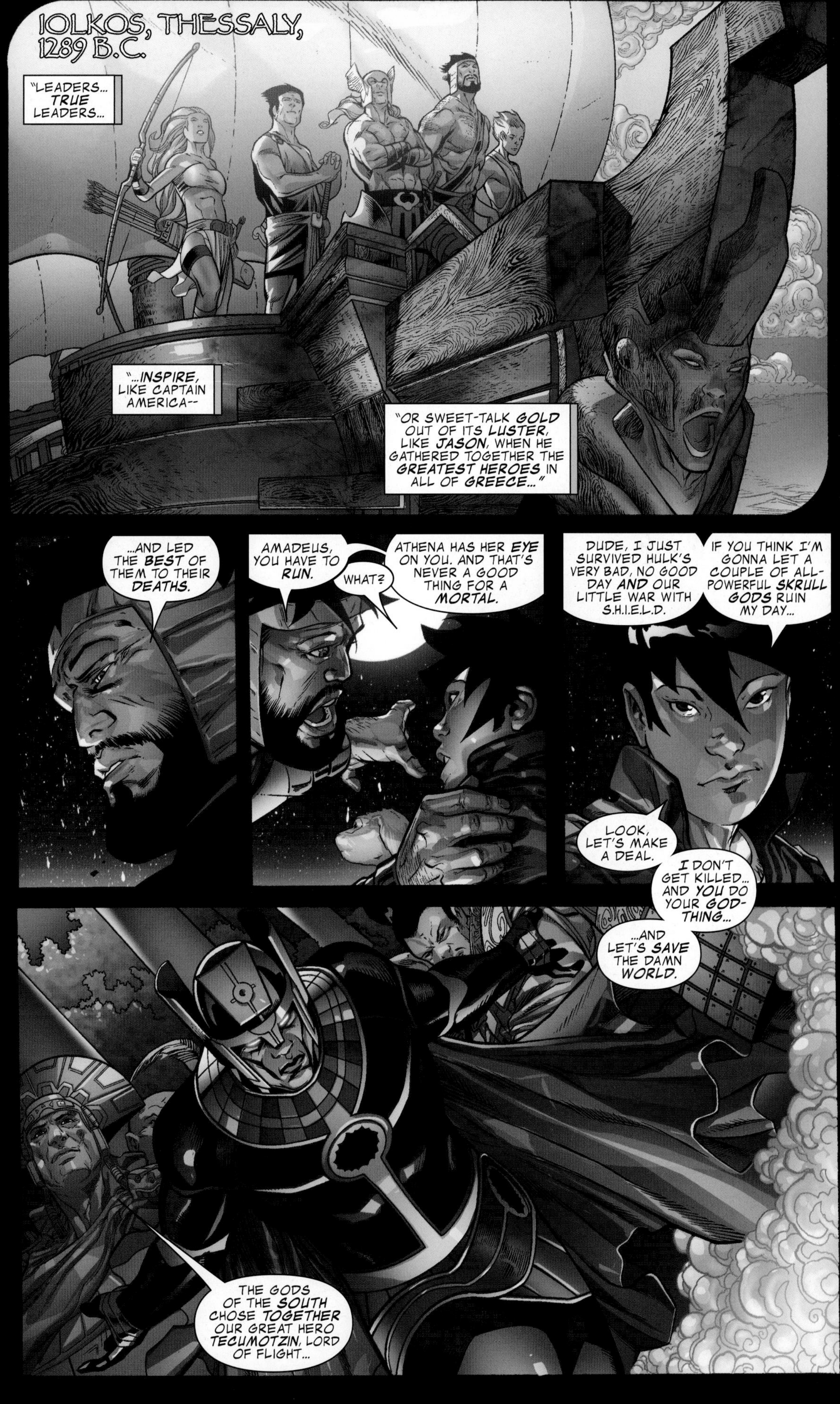
IOLKOS, THESSALY, 1289 B.C.
"LEADERS... TRUE LEADERS...
"...INSPIRE, LIKE CAPTAIN AMERICA--
"OR SWEET-TALK GOLD OUT OF ITS LUSTER, LIKE JASON, WHEN HE GATHERED TOGETHER THE GREATEST HEROES IN ALL OF GREECE..."
...AND LED THE BEST OF THEM TO THEIR DEATHS.
AMADEUS, YOU HAVE TO RUN.
WHAT?
ATHENA HAS HER EYE ON YOU. AND THAT'S NEVER A GOOD THING FOR A MORTAL.
DUDE, I JUST SURVIVED HULK'S VERY BAD, NO GOOD DAY AND OUR LITTLE WAR WITH S.H.I.E.L.D.
IF YOU THINK I'M GONNA LET A COUPLE OF ALL-POWERFUL SKRULL GODS RUIN MY DAY...
LOOK, LET'S MAKE A DEAL.
I DON'T GET KILLED... AND YOU DO YOUR GOD-THING...
...AND LET'S SAVE THE DAMN WORLD.
THE GODS OF THE SOUTH CHOSE TOGETHER OUR GREAT HERO TECUMOTZIN, LORD OF FLIGHT...

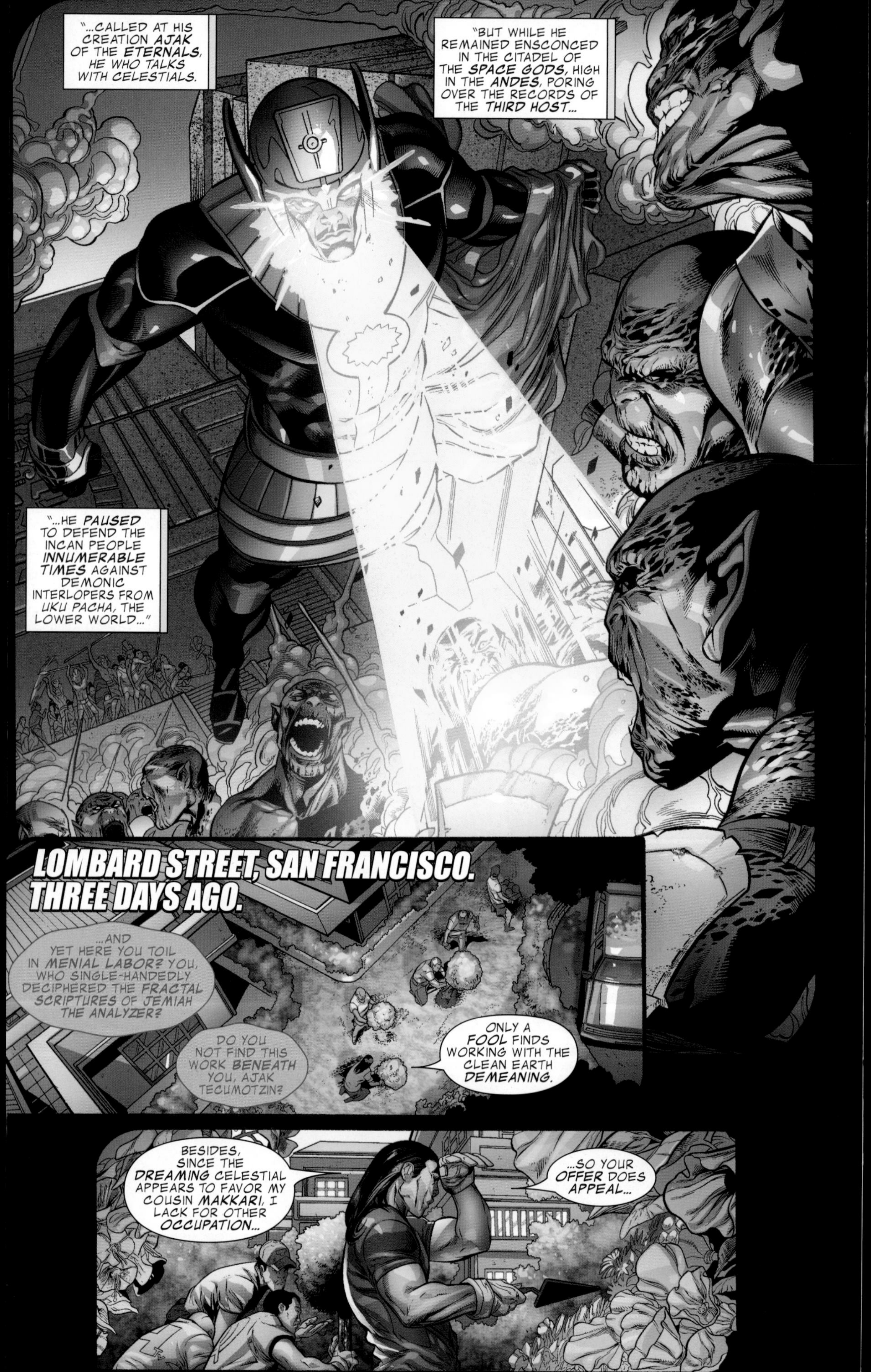
"...CALLED AT HIS CREATION AJAK OF THE ETERNALS, HE WHO TALKS WITH CELESTIALS.
"BUT WHILE HE REMAINED ENSCONCED IN THE CITADEL OF THE SPACE GODS, HIGH IN THE ANDES, PORING OVER THE RECORDS OF THE THIRD HOST...
"...HE PAUSED TO DEFEND THE INCAN PEOPLE INNUMERABLE TIMES AGAINST DEMONIC INTERLOPERS FROM UKU PACHA, THE LOWER WORLD..."
LOMBARD STREET, SAN FRANCISCO. THREE DAYS AGO.
...AND YET HERE YOU TOIL IN MENIAL LABOR? YOU, WHO SINGLE-HANDEDLY DECIPHERED THE FRACTAL SCRIPTURES OF JEMIAH THE ANALYZER?
DO YOU NOT FIND THIS WORK BENEATH YOU, AJAK TECUMOTZIN?
ONLY A FOOL FINDS WORKING WITH THE CLEAN EARTH DEMEANING.
BESIDES, SINCE THE DREAMING CELESTIAL APPEARS TO FAVOR MY COUSIN MAKKARI, I LACK FOR OTHER OCCUPATION...
...SO YOUR OFFER DOES APPEAL...

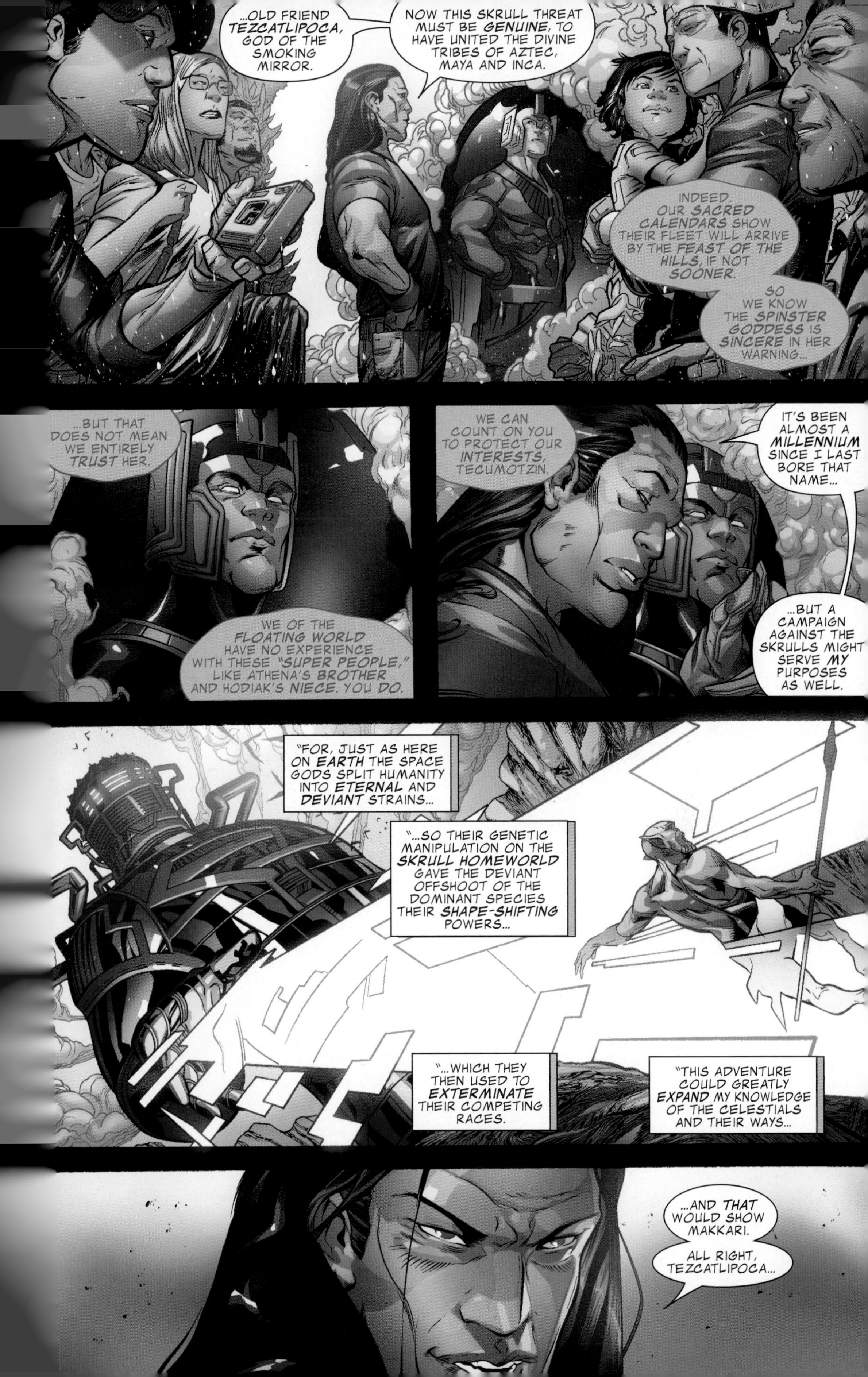

...OLD FRIEND TEZCATLIPOCA, GOD OF THE SMOKING MIRROR.
NOW THIS SKRULL THREAT MUST BE GENUINE, TO HAVE UNITED THE DIVINE TRIBES OF AZTEC, MAYA AND INCA.
INDEED. OUR SACRED CALENDARS SHOW THEIR FLEET WILL ARRIVE BY THE FEAST OF THE HILLS, IF NOT SOONER.
SO WE KNOW THE SPINSTER GODDESS IS SINCERE IN HER WARNING...
...BUT THAT DOES NOT MEAN WE ENTIRELY TRUST HER.
WE OF THE FLOATING WORLD HAVE NO EXPERIENCE WITH THESE "SUPER PEOPLE," LIKE ATHENA'S BROTHER AND HODIAK'S NIECE. YOU DO.
WE CAN COUNT ON YOU TO PROTECT OUR INTERESTS, TECUMOTZIN.
IT'S BEEN ALMOST A MILLENNIUM SINCE I LAST BORE THAT NAME...
...BUT A CAMPAIGN AGAINST THE SKRULLS MIGHT SERVE MY PURPOSES AS WELL.
"FOR, JUST AS HERE ON EARTH THE SPACE GODS SPLIT HUMANITY INTO ETERNAL AND DEVIANT STRAINS...
"...SO THEIR GENETIC MANIPULATION ON THE SKRULL HOMEWORLD GAVE THE DEVIANT OFFSHOOT OF THE DOMINANT SPECIES THEIR SHAPE-SHIFTING POWERS...
"...WHICH THEY THEN USED TO EXTERMINATE THEIR COMPETING RACES.
"THIS ADVENTURE COULD GREATLY EXPAND MY KNOWLEDGE OF THE CELESTIALS AND THEIR WAYS...
...AND THAT WOULD SHOW MAKKARI.
ALL RIGHT, TEZCATLIPOCA...

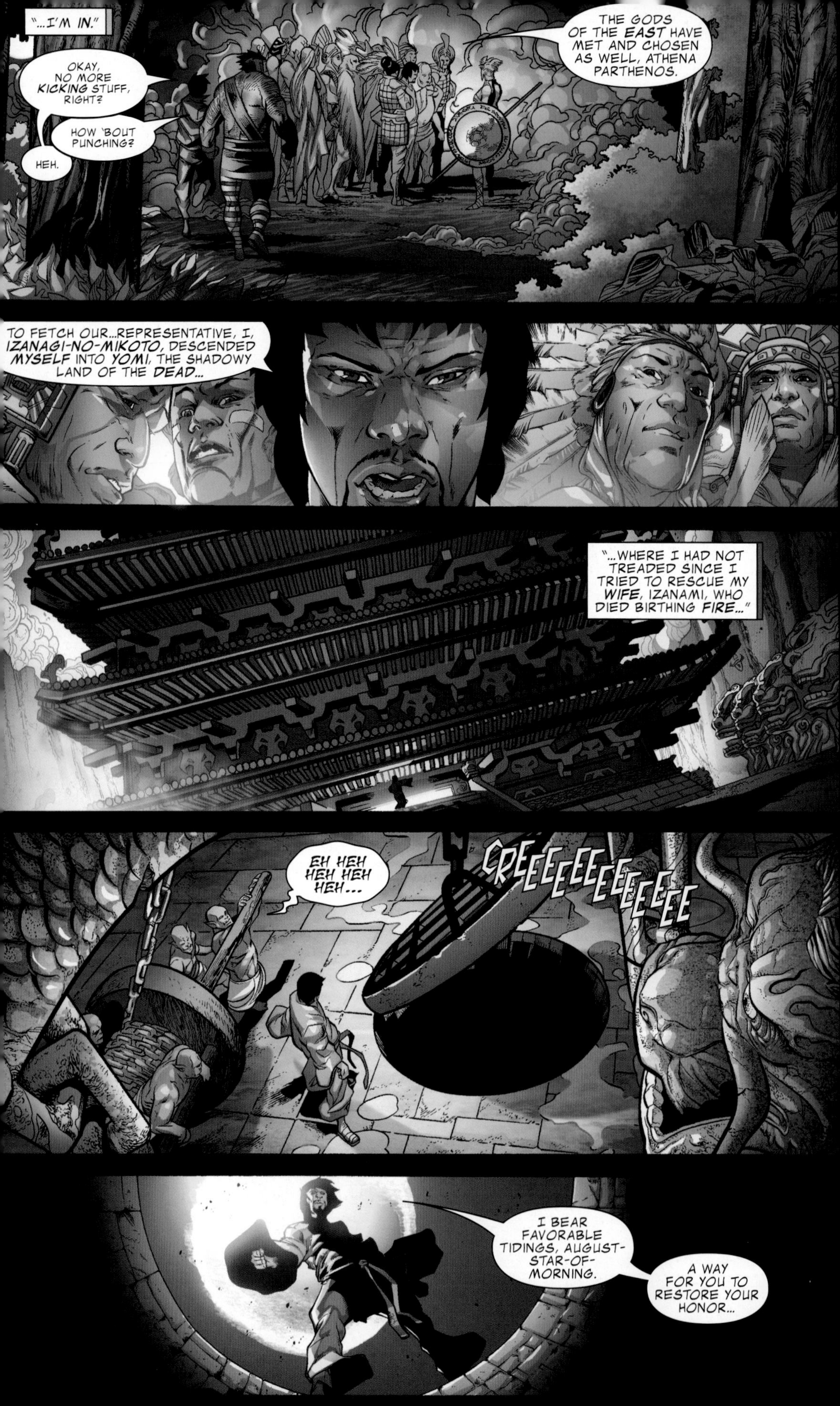
"...I'M IN."
OKAY, NO MORE KICKING STUFF, RIGHT?
HOW 'BOUT PUNCHING?
HEH.
THE GODS OF THE EAST HAVE MET AND CHOSEN AS WELL, ATHENA PARTHENOS.
TO FETCH OUR...REPRESENTATIVE, I, IZANAGI-NO-MIKOTO, DESCENDED MYSELF INTO YOMI, THE SHADOWY LAND OF THE DEAD...
"...WHERE I HAD NOT TREADED SINCE I TRIED TO RESCUE MY WIFE, IZANAMI, WHO DIED BIRTHING FIRE..."
EH HEH HEH HEH HEH...
CREEEEEEEEEEEEEE
I BEAR FAVORABLE TIDINGS, AUGUST-STAR-OF-MORNING.
A WAY FOR YOU TO RESTORE YOUR HONOR...

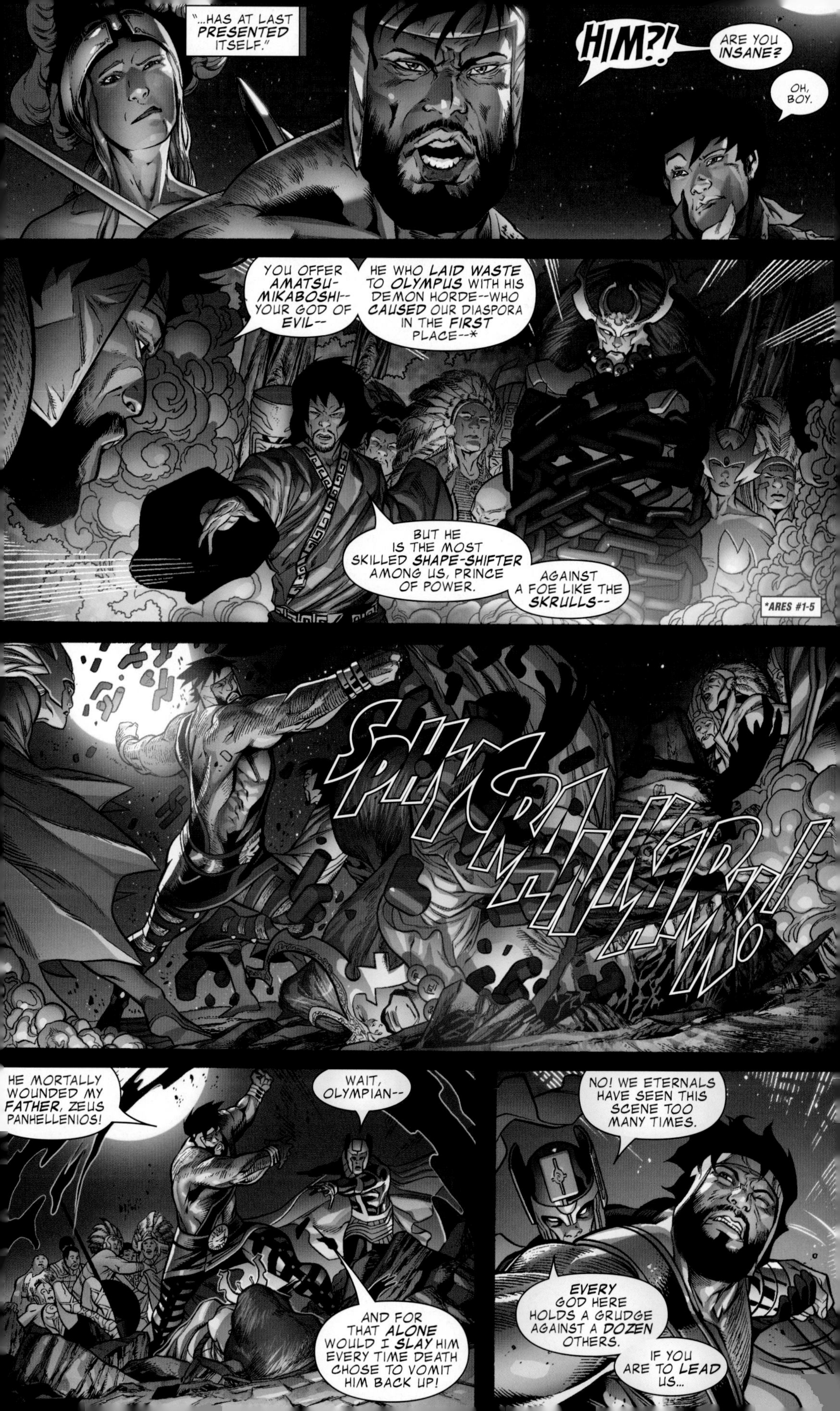
"...HAS AT LAST PRESENTED ITSELF."
HIM?!
ARE YOU INSANE?
OH, BOY.
YOU OFFER AMATSU-MIKABOSHI--YOUR GOD OF EVIL--
HE WHO LAID WASTE TO OLYMPUS WITH HIS DEMON HORDE--WHO CAUSED OUR DIASPORA IN THE FIRST PLACE--*
BUT HE IS THE MOST SKILLED SHAPE-SHIFTER AMONG US, PRINCE OF POWER.
AGAINST A FOE LIKE THE SKRULLS--
*ARES #1-5
SPHKRAAKKOOM!
HE MORTALLY WOUNDED MY FATHER, ZEUS PANHELLENIOS!
WAIT, OLYMPIAN--
AND FOR THAT ALONE WOULD I SLAY HIM EVERY TIME DEATH CHOSE TO VOMIT HIM BACK UP!
NO! WE ETERNALS HAVE SEEN THIS SCENE TOO MANY TIMES.
EVERY GOD HERE HOLDS A GRUDGE AGAINST A DOZEN OTHERS.
IF YOU ARE TO LEAD US...

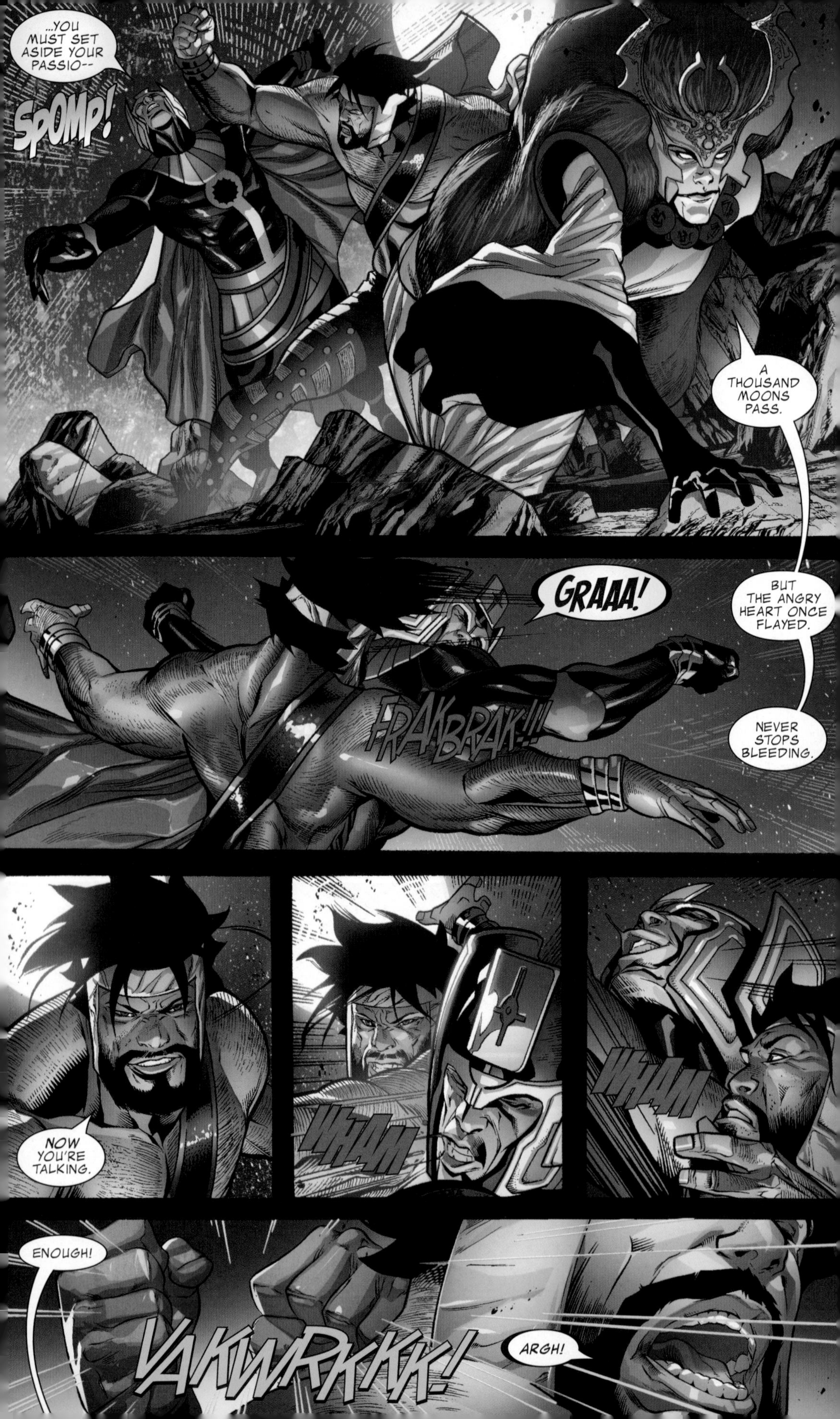
...YOU MUST SET ASIDE YOUR PASSIO--
SPOMP!
A THOUSAND MOONS PASS.
GRAAA!
BUT THE ANGRY HEART ONCE FLAYED.
FRAKBRAK!!!
NEVER STOPS BLEEDING.
NOW YOU'RE TALKING.
WHAM
WHAM
ENOUGH!
VAKWRKKK!
ARGH!

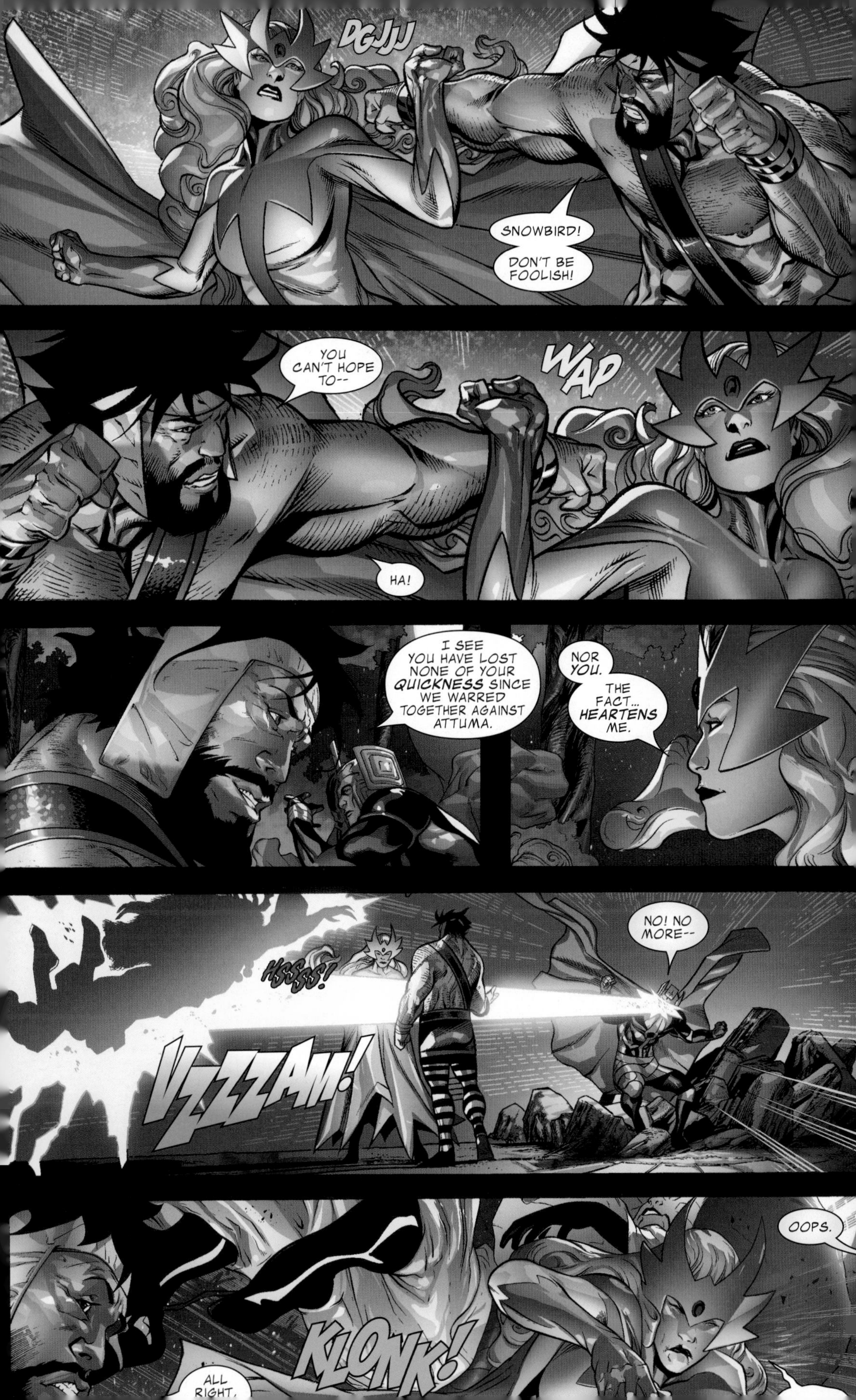
DGJJJ
SNOWBIRD!
DON'T BE FOOLISH!
YOU CAN'T HOPE TO--
WAP
HA!
I SEE YOU HAVE LOST NONE OF YOUR QUICKNESS SINCE WE WARRED TOGETHER AGAINST ATTUMA.
NOR YOU.
THE FACT... HEARTENS ME.
HSSSSS!
NO! NO MORE--
VZZZAM!
OOPS.
KLONK!
ALL RIGHT,

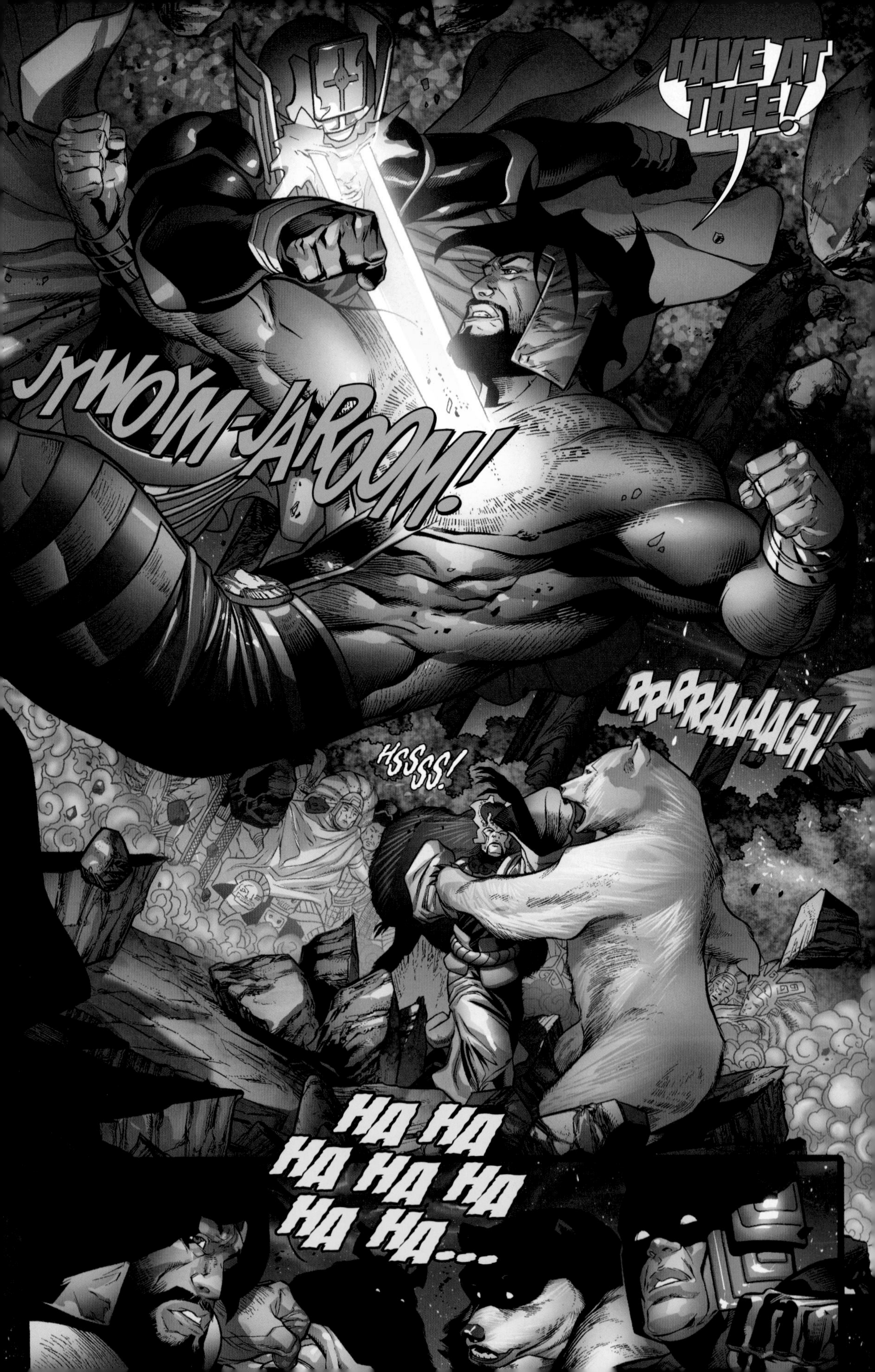
HAVE AT THEE!
JYWOYM-JAROOM!
RRRRAAAAAGH!
HSSSS!
HA HA HA HA HA HA HA...

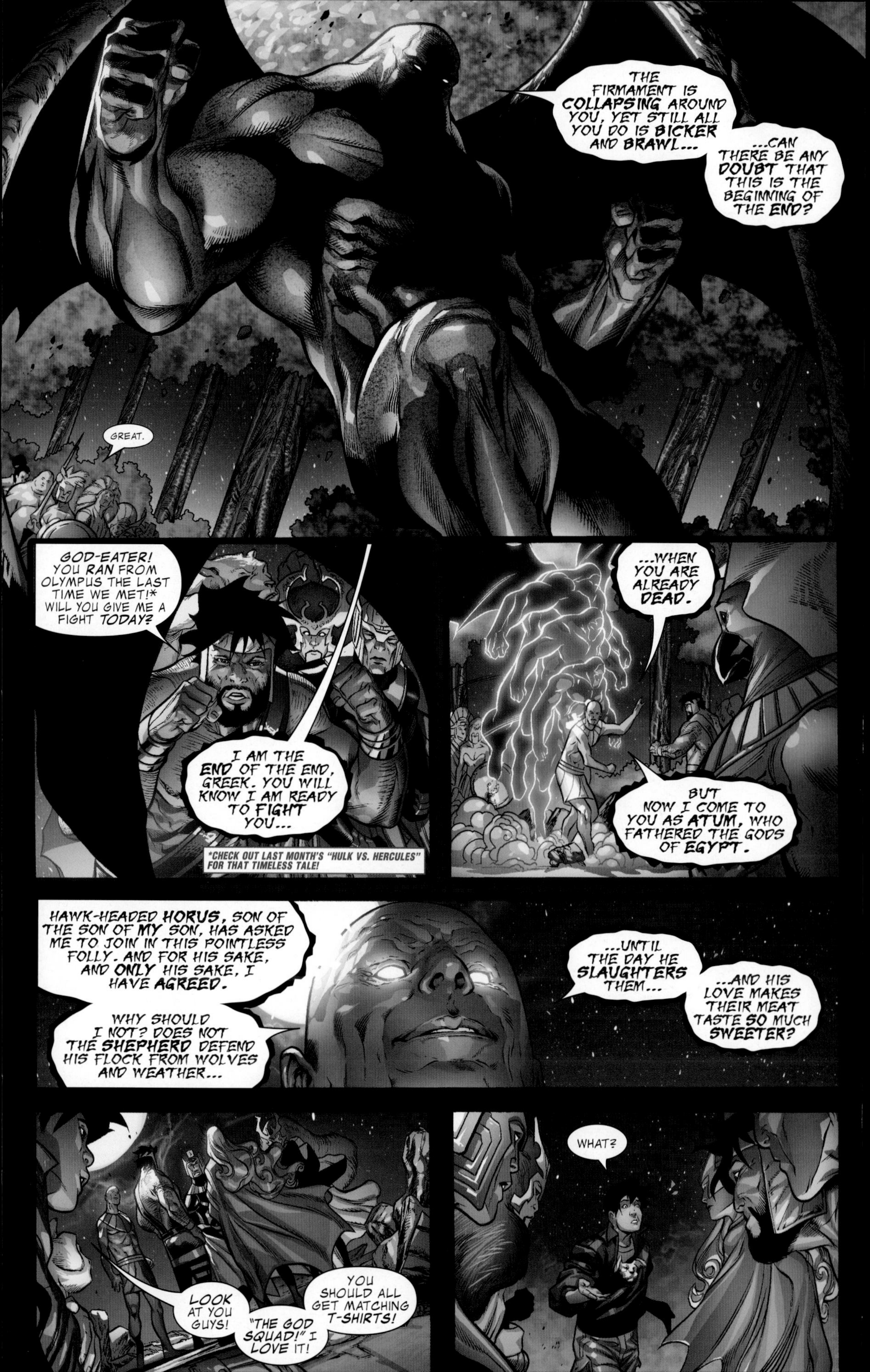
THE FIRMAMENT IS COLLAPSING AROUND YOU, YET STILL ALL YOU DO IS BICKER AND BRAWL...
...CAN THERE BE ANY DOUBT THAT THIS IS THE BEGINNING OF THE END?
GREAT.
GOD-EATER! YOU RAN FROM OLYMPUS THE LAST TIME WE MET!* WILL YOU GIVE ME A FIGHT TODAY?
I AM THE END OF THE END, GREEK. YOU WILL KNOW I AM READY TO FIGHT YOU...
*CHECK OUT LAST MONTH'S "HULK VS. HERCULES" FOR THAT TIMELESS TALE!
...WHEN YOU ARE ALREADY DEAD.
BUT NOW I COME TO YOU AS ATUM, WHO FATHERED THE GODS OF EGYPT.
HAWK-HEADED HORUS, SON OF THE SON OF MY SON, HAS ASKED ME TO JOIN IN THIS POINTLESS FOLLY. AND FOR HIS SAKE, AND ONLY HIS SAKE, I HAVE AGREED.
WHY SHOULD I NOT? DOES NOT THE SHEPHERD DEFEND HIS FLOCK FROM WOLVES AND WEATHER...
...UNTIL THE DAY HE SLAUGHTERS THEM...
...AND HIS LOVE MAKES THEIR MEAT TASTE SO MUCH SWEETER?
LOOK AT YOU GUYS!
"THE GOD SQUAD!" I LOVE IT!
YOU SHOULD ALL GET MATCHING T-SHIRTS!
WHAT?

I THANK YOU, GOD-HEROES...

...AND I OFFER YOU MY GIFT.

I, ALTJIRA, WHO CREATED THIS WORLD FROM THE DREAMTIME... CANNOT LEAVE IT.

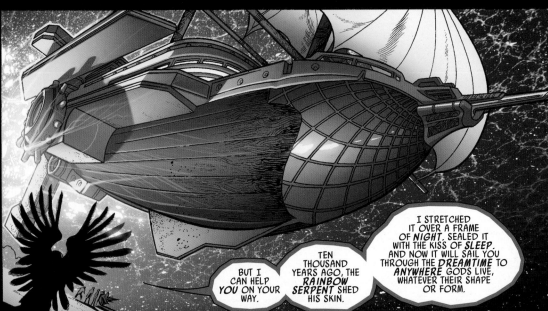

BUT I CAN HELP YOU ON YOUR WAY.

TEN THOUSAND YEARS AGO, THE RAINBOW SERPENT SHED HIS SKIN.

I STRETCHED IT OVER A FRAME OF NIGHT. SEALED IT WITH THE KISS OF SLEEP. AND NOW IT WILL SAIL YOU THROUGH THE DREAMTIME TO ANYWHERE GODS LIVE, WHATEVER THEIR SHAPE OR FORM.

DUDE! IT'S THE GODMOBILE!

SSSH!

ALTHOUGH... WHEN I CONSTRUCTED THE SHIP, I ASSUMED IT WOULD CARRY A MUCH LARGER FORCE.

AS DID I.

I HAVE ASSEMBLED THE PARAGONS AND DIVINITIES OF EVERY NATION AND CULTURE ON EARTH, AND THIS IS THE BEST YOU CAN DO?

FIVE WARRIORS? FIVE? TO STAND AGAINST AN ENTIRE EMPIRE?

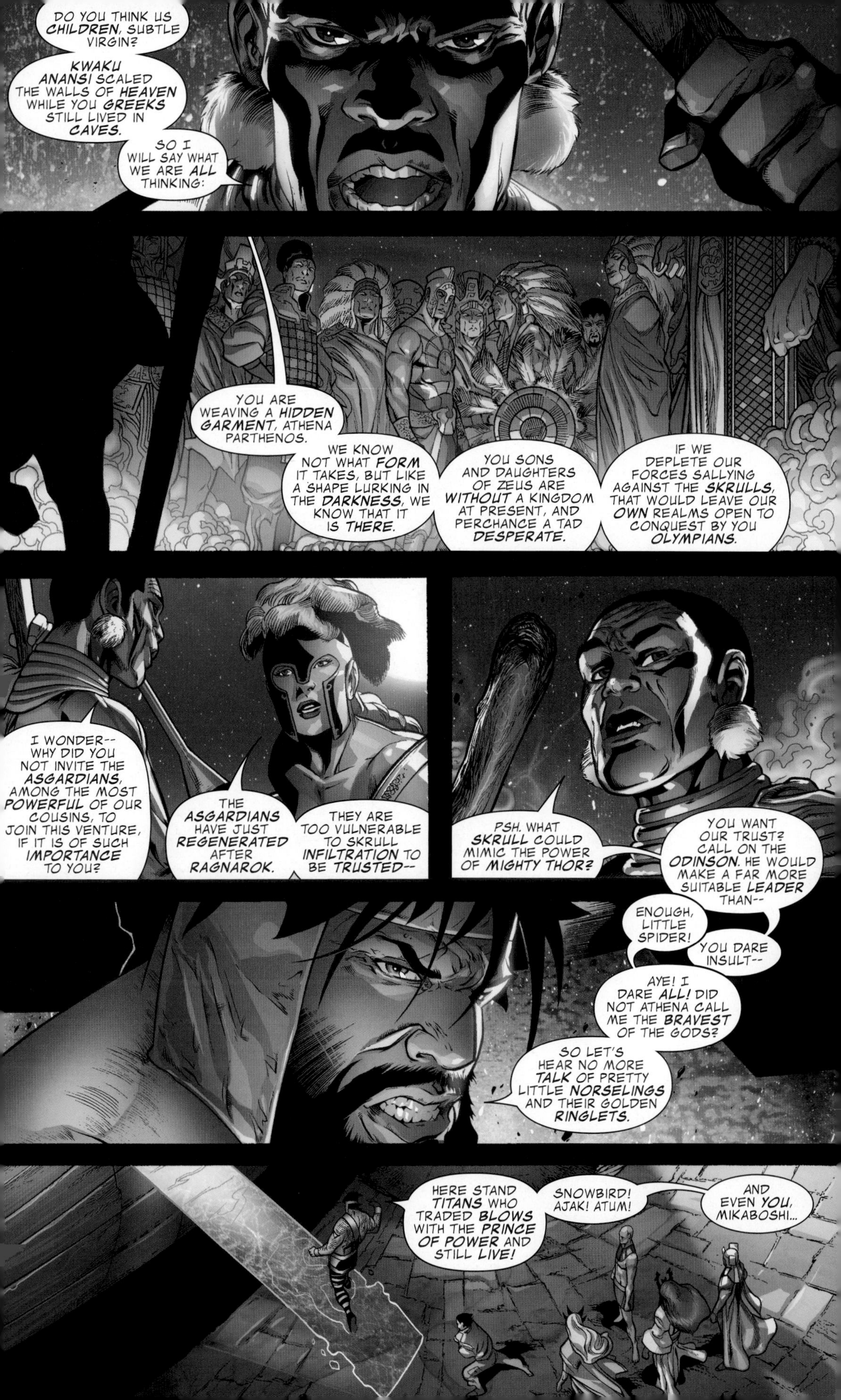

DO YOU THINK US CHILDREN, SUBTLE VIRGIN?
KWAKU ANANSI SCALED THE WALLS OF HEAVEN WHILE YOU GREEKS STILL LIVED IN CAVES.
SO I WILL SAY WHAT WE ARE ALL THINKING:
YOU ARE WEAVING A HIDDEN GARMENT, ATHENA PARTHENOS.
WE KNOW NOT WHAT FORM IT TAKES, BUT LIKE A SHAPE LURKING IN THE DARKNESS, WE KNOW THAT IT IS THERE.
YOU SONS AND DAUGHTERS OF ZEUS ARE WITHOUT A KINGDOM AT PRESENT, AND PERCHANCE A TAD DESPERATE.
IF WE DEPLETE OUR FORCES SALLYING AGAINST THE SKRULLS, THAT WOULD LEAVE OUR OWN REALMS OPEN TO CONQUEST BY YOU OLYMPIANS.
I WONDER-- WHY DID YOU NOT INVITE THE ASGARDIANS, AMONG THE MOST POWERFUL OF OUR COUSINS, TO JOIN THIS VENTURE, IF IT IS OF SUCH IMPORTANCE TO YOU?
THE ASGARDIANS HAVE JUST REGENERATED AFTER RAGNAROK.
THEY ARE TOO VULNERABLE TO SKRULL INFILTRATION TO BE TRUSTED--
PSH. WHAT SKRULL COULD MIMIC THE POWER OF MIGHTY THOR?
YOU WANT OUR TRUST? CALL ON THE ODINSON. HE WOULD MAKE A FAR MORE SUITABLE LEADER THAN--
ENOUGH, LITTLE SPIDER!
YOU DARE INSULT--
AYE! I DARE ALL! DID NOT ATHENA CALL ME THE BRAVEST OF THE GODS?
SO LET'S HEAR NO MORE TALK OF PRETTY LITTLE NORSELINGS AND THEIR GOLDEN RINGLETS.
HERE STAND TITANS WHO TRADED BLOWS WITH THE PRINCE OF POWER AND STILL LIVE!
SNOWBIRD! AJAK! ATUM!
AND EVEN YOU, MIKABOSHI...

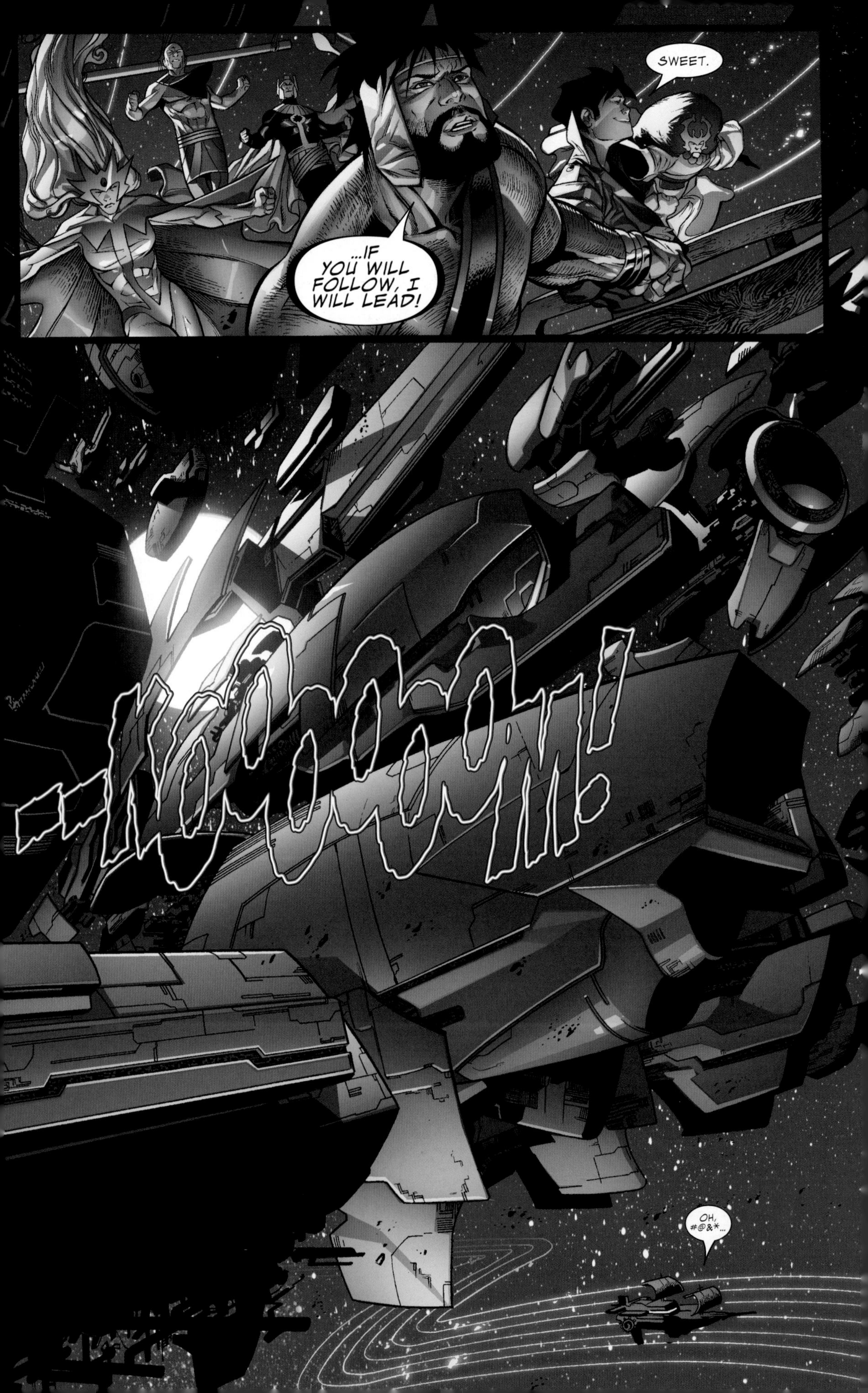
...IF YOU WILL FOLLOW, I WILL LEAD!
SWEET.
OH, #@&*...

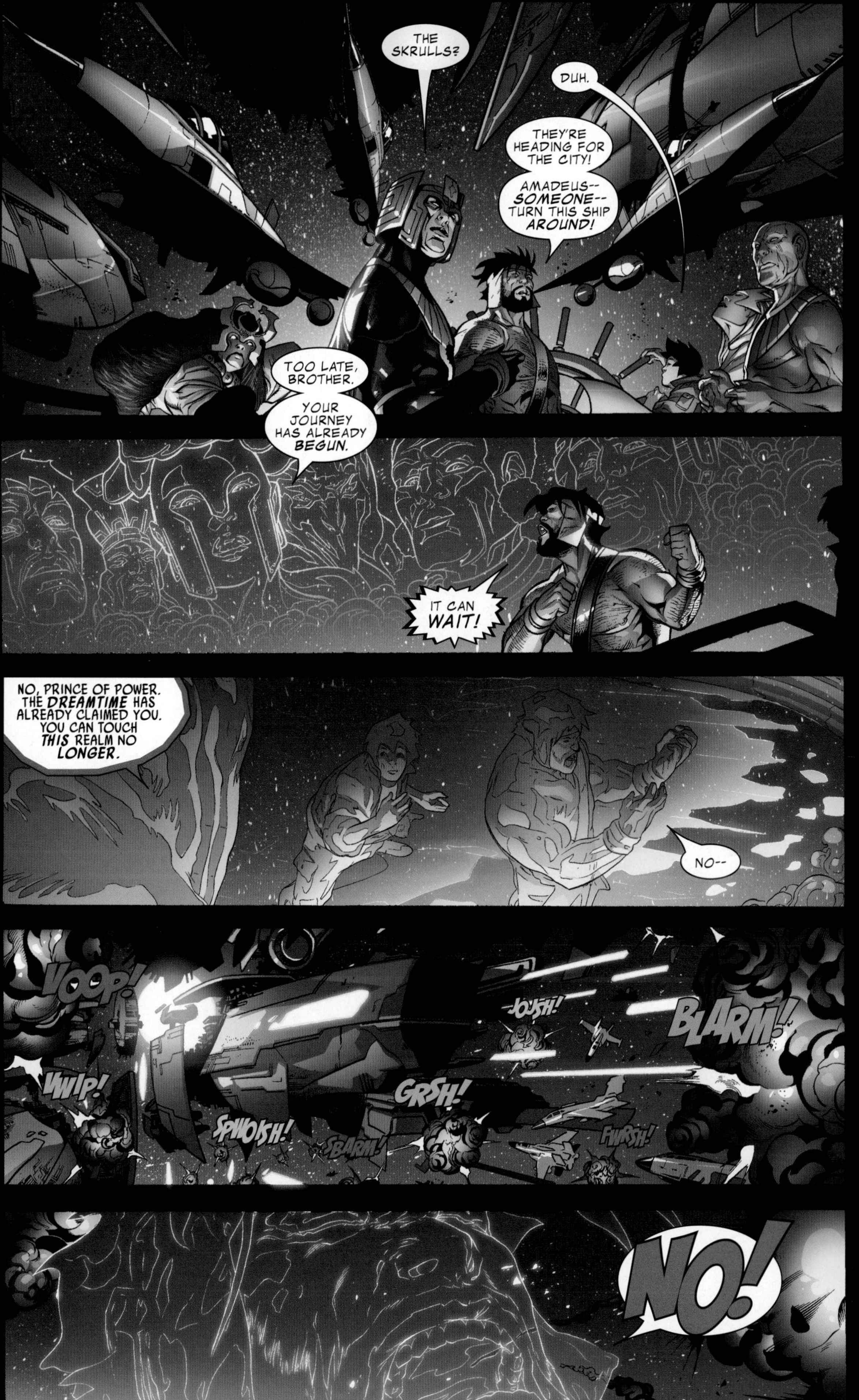
THE SKRULLS?
DUH.
THEY'RE HEADING FOR THE CITY!
AMADEUS-- SOMEONE-- TURN THIS SHIP AROUND!
TOO LATE, BROTHER.
YOUR JOURNEY HAS ALREADY BEGUN.
IT CAN WAIT!
NO, PRINCE OF POWER. THE DREAMTIME HAS ALREADY CLAIMED YOU. YOU CAN TOUCH THIS REALM NO LONGER.
NO--
VOOP!
JOOSH!
BLARM!!
VWIP!
GRSH!
SPWOOSH!
SBARM!
FWRSH!
NO!

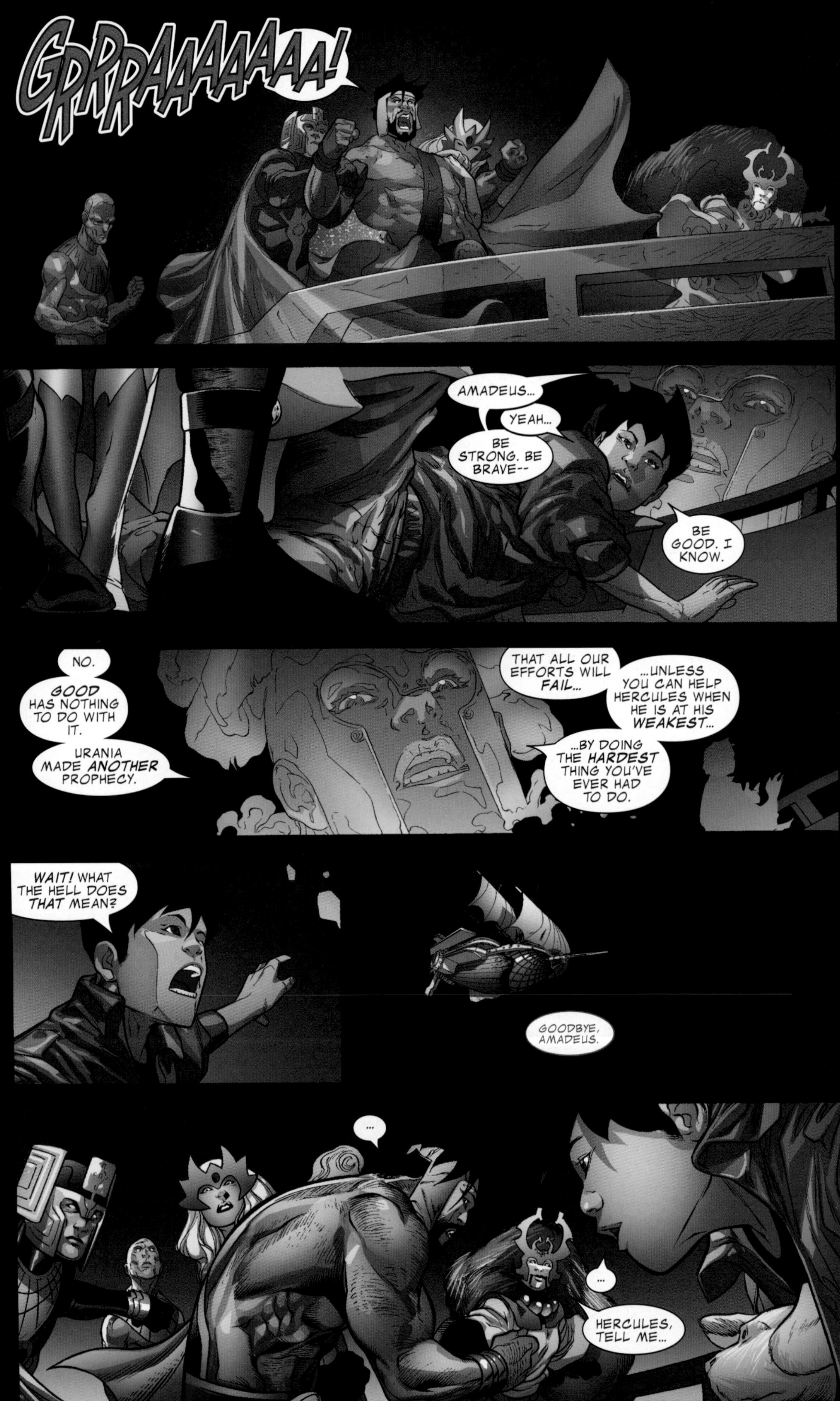
GRRRAAAAAAA!
AMADEUS...
YEAH...
BE STRONG. BE BRAVE--
BE GOOD. I KNOW.
NO.
GOOD HAS NOTHING TO DO WITH IT.
URANIA MADE ANOTHER PROPHECY.
THAT ALL OUR EFFORTS WILL FAIL...
...UNLESS YOU CAN HELP HERCULES WHEN HE IS AT HIS WEAKEST...
...BY DOING THE HARDEST THING YOU'VE EVER HAD TO DO.
WAIT! WHAT THE HELL DOES THAT MEAN?
GOODBYE, AMADEUS.
...
...
HERCULES, TELL ME...

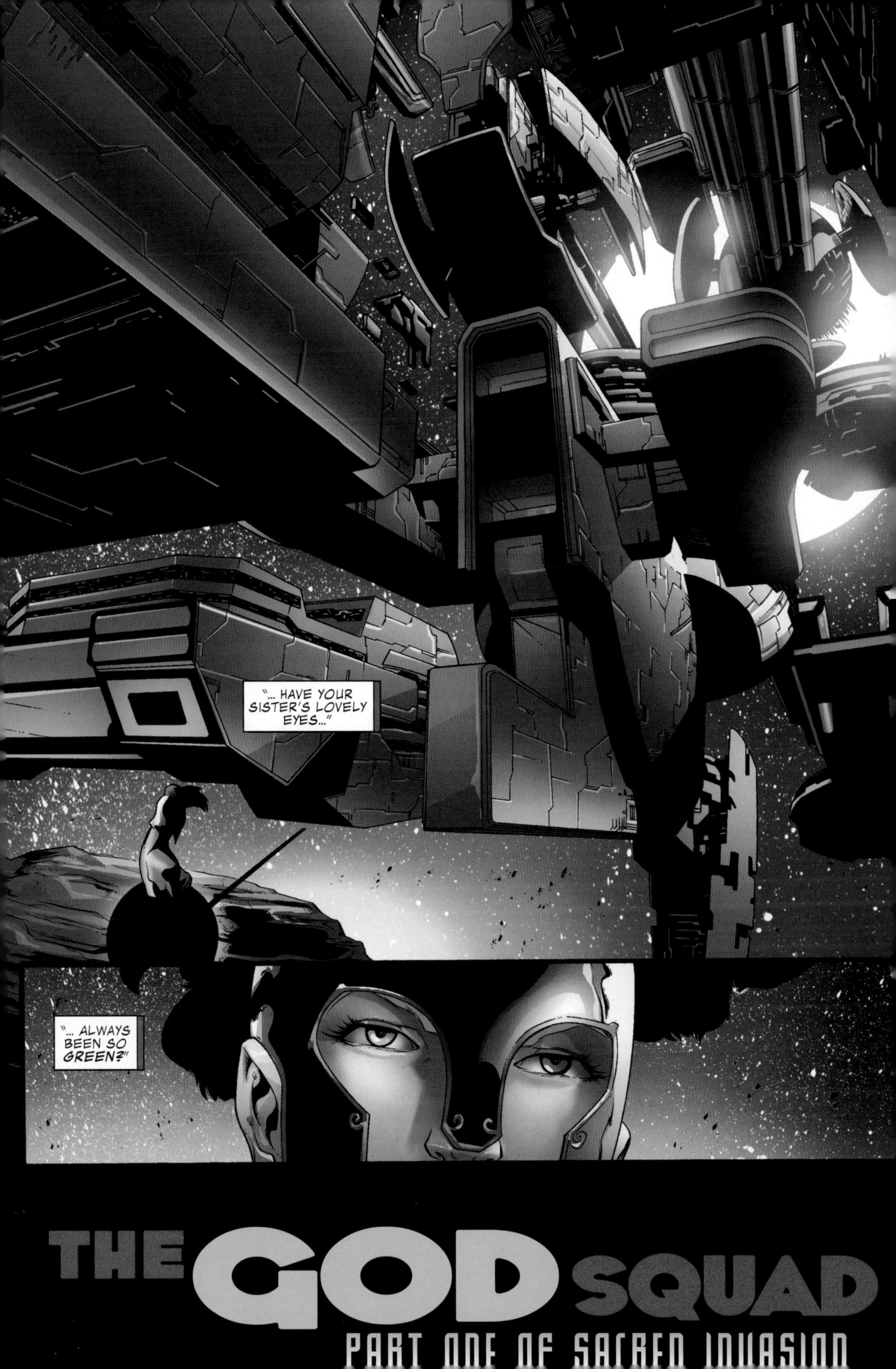
"... HAVE YOUR SISTER'S LOVELY EYES..."
"... ALWAYS BEEN SO GREEN?"
THE GOD SQUAD
PART ONE OF SACRED INVASION

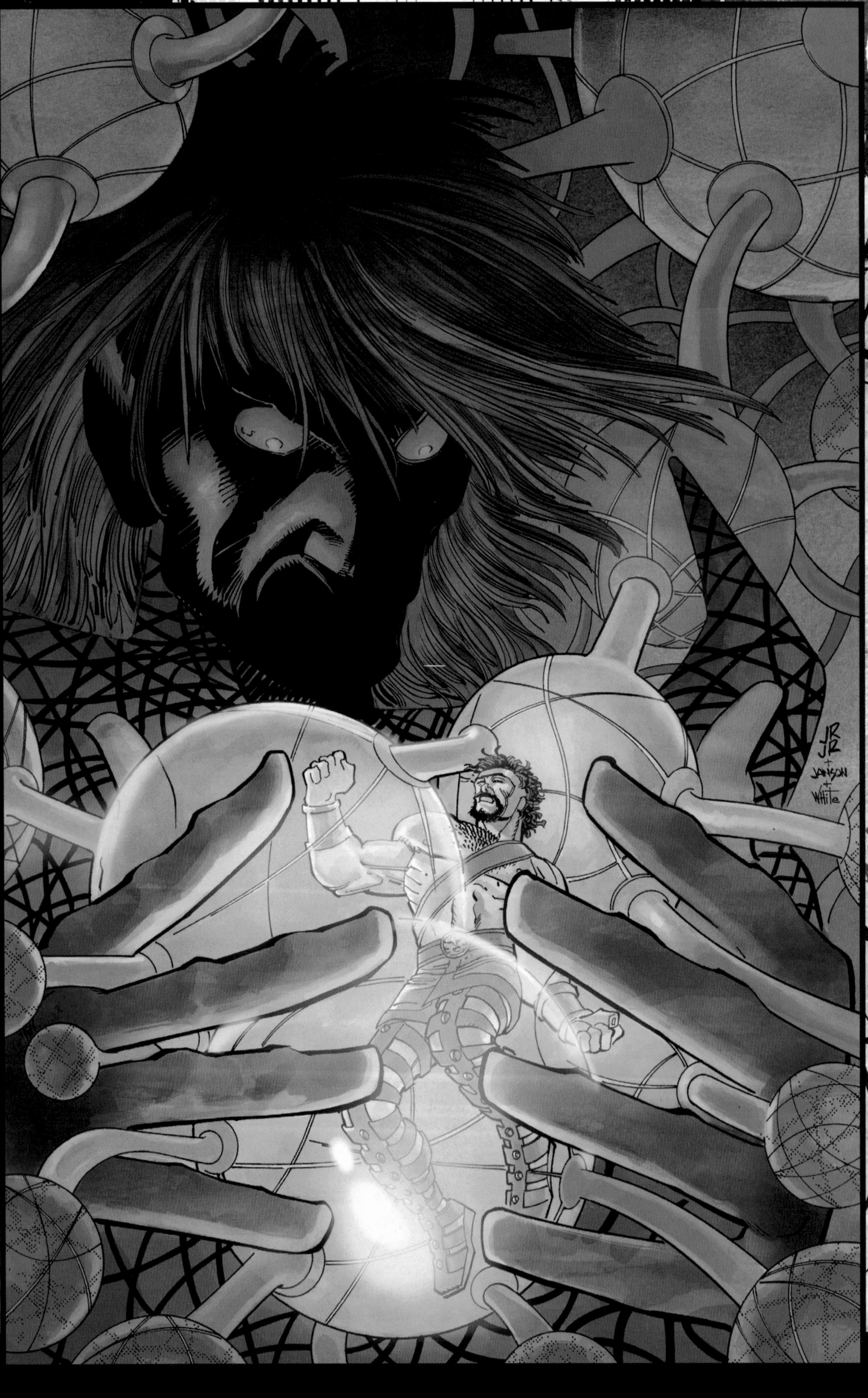
JR JR
+
JANSON
+
WHITE

AND NOW!

YON STARTING LINEUP FOR *THY*

GOD SQUAD!

COLLECTETH ALL VI!

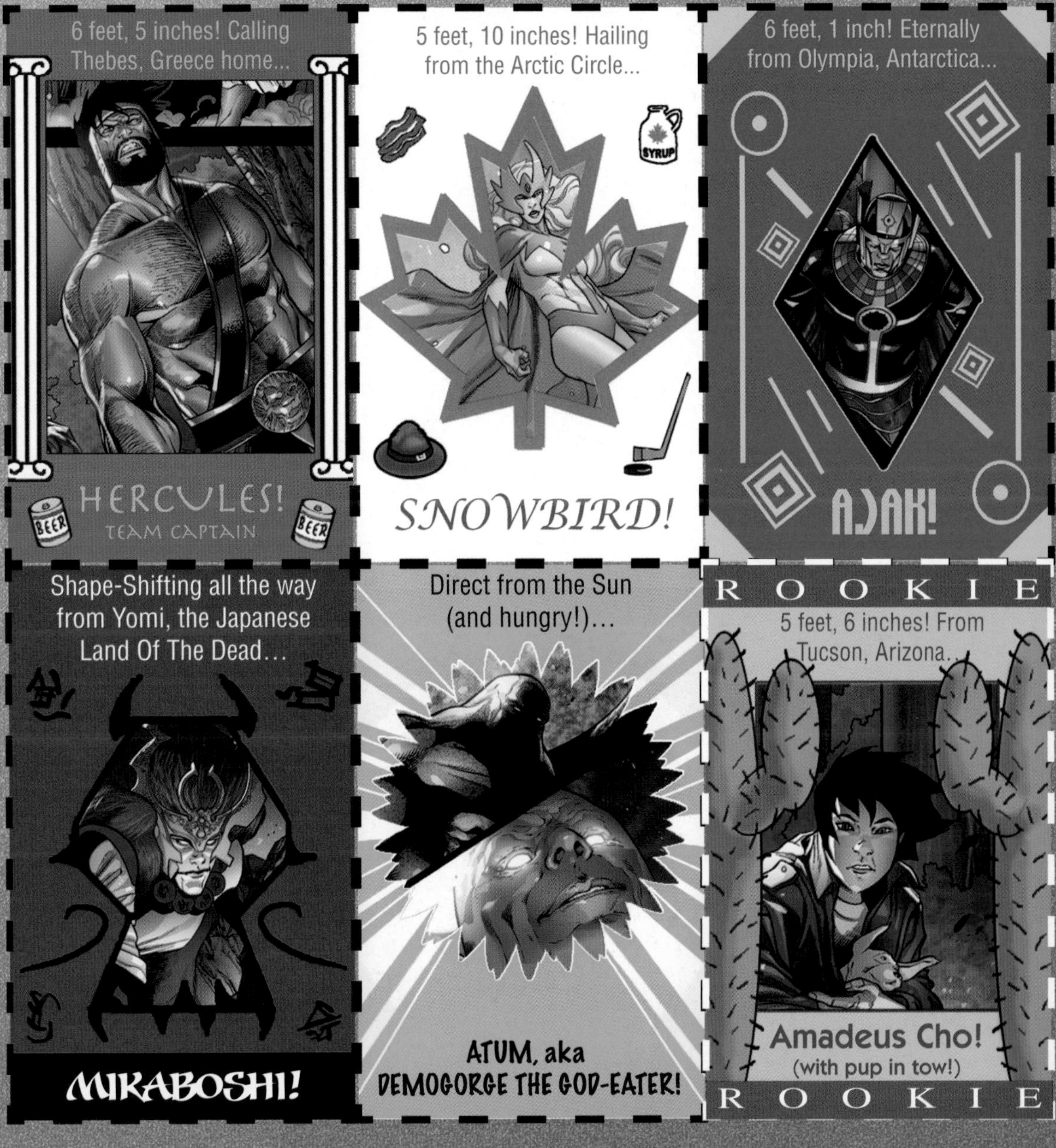
6 feet, 5 inches! Calling Thebes, Greece home...
BEER
BEER
HERCULES!
TEAM CAPTAIN
5 feet, 10 inches! Hailing from the Arctic Circle...
SYRUP
SNOWBIRD!
6 feet, 1 inch! Eternally from Olympia, Antarctica...
AJAK!
Shape-Shifting all the way from Yomi, the Japanese Land Of The Dead...
MIKABOSHI!
Direct from the Sun (and hungry!)...
ATUM, aka
DEMOGORGE THE GOD-EATER!
ROOKIE
5 feet, 6 inches! From Tucson, Arizona...
Amadeus Cho!
(with pup in tow!)
ROOKIE

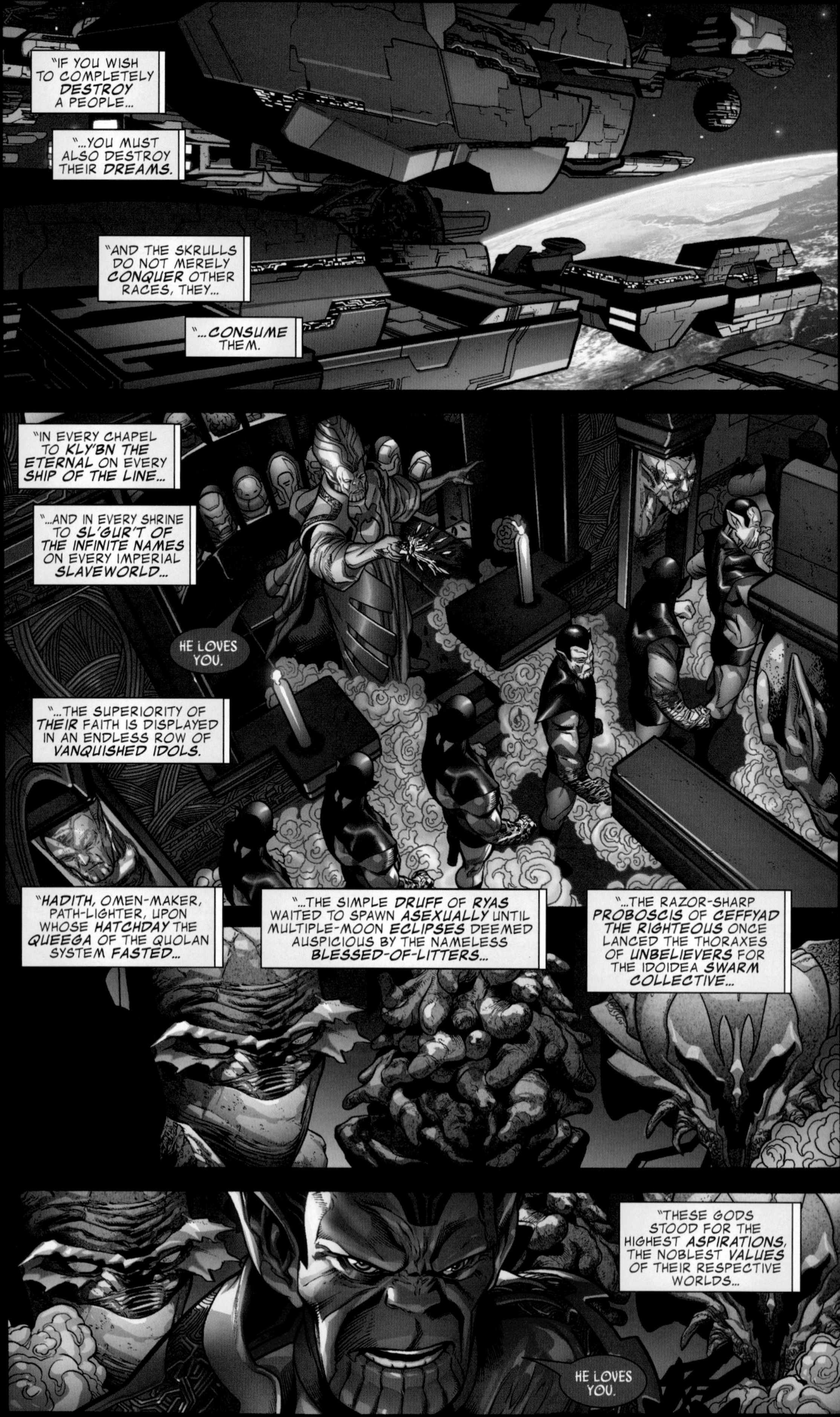

"IF YOU WISH TO COMPLETELY DESTROY A PEOPLE...
"...YOU MUST ALSO DESTROY THEIR DREAMS.
"AND THE SKRULLS DO NOT MERELY CONQUER OTHER RACES, THEY...
"...CONSUME THEM.
"IN EVERY CHAPEL TO KLY'BN THE ETERNAL ON EVERY SHIP OF THE LINE...
"...AND IN EVERY SHRINE TO SL'GUR'T OF THE INFINITE NAMES ON EVERY IMPERIAL SLAVEWORLD...
HE LOVES YOU.
"...THE SUPERIORITY OF THEIR FAITH IS DISPLAYED IN AN ENDLESS ROW OF VANQUISHED IDOLS.
"HADITH, OMEN-MAKER, PATH-LIGHTER, UPON WHOSE HATCHDAY THE QUEEGA OF THE QUOLAN SYSTEM FASTED...
"...THE SIMPLE DRUFF OF RYAS WAITED TO SPAWN ASEXUALLY UNTIL MULTIPLE-MOON ECLIPSES DEEMED AUSPICIOUS BY THE NAMELESS BLESSED-OF-LITTERS...
"...THE RAZOR-SHARP PROBOSCIS OF CEFFYAD THE RIGHTEOUS ONCE LANCED THE THORAXES OF UNBELIEVERS FOR THE IDOIDEA SWARM COLLECTIVE...
"THESE GODS STOOD FOR THE HIGHEST ASPIRATIONS, THE NOBLEST VALUES OF THEIR RESPECTIVE WORLDS...
HE LOVES YOU.

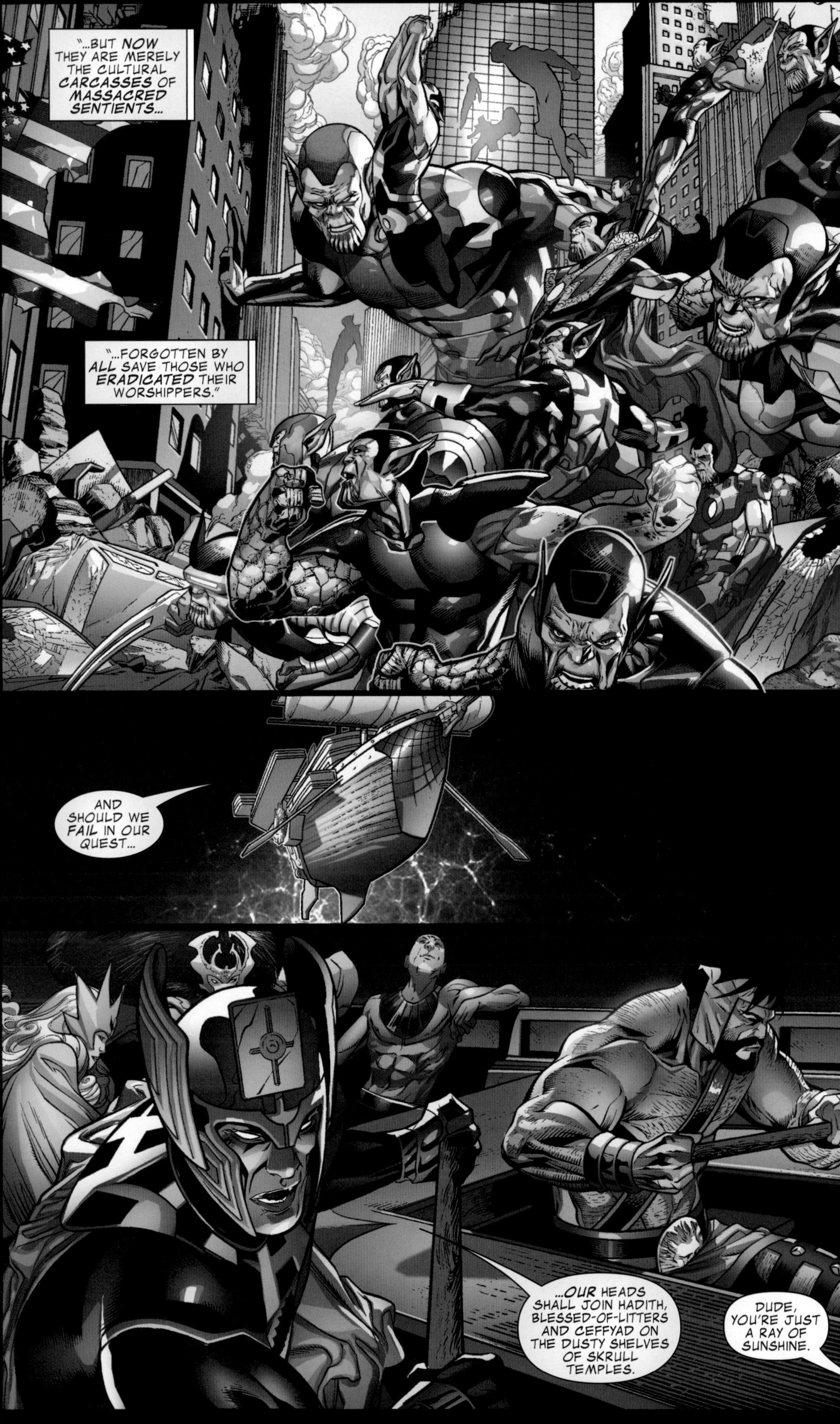
"...BUT NOW THEY ARE MERELY THE CULTURAL CARCASSES OF MASSACRED SENTIENTS...
"...FORGOTTEN BY ALL SAVE THOSE WHO ERADICATED THEIR WORSHIPPERS."
AND SHOULD WE FAIL IN OUR QUEST...
...OUR HEADS SHALL JOIN HADITH, BLESSED-OF-LITTERS AND CEFFYAD ON THE DUSTY SHELVES OF SKRULL TEMPLES.
DUDE, YOU'RE JUST A RAY OF SUNSHINE.

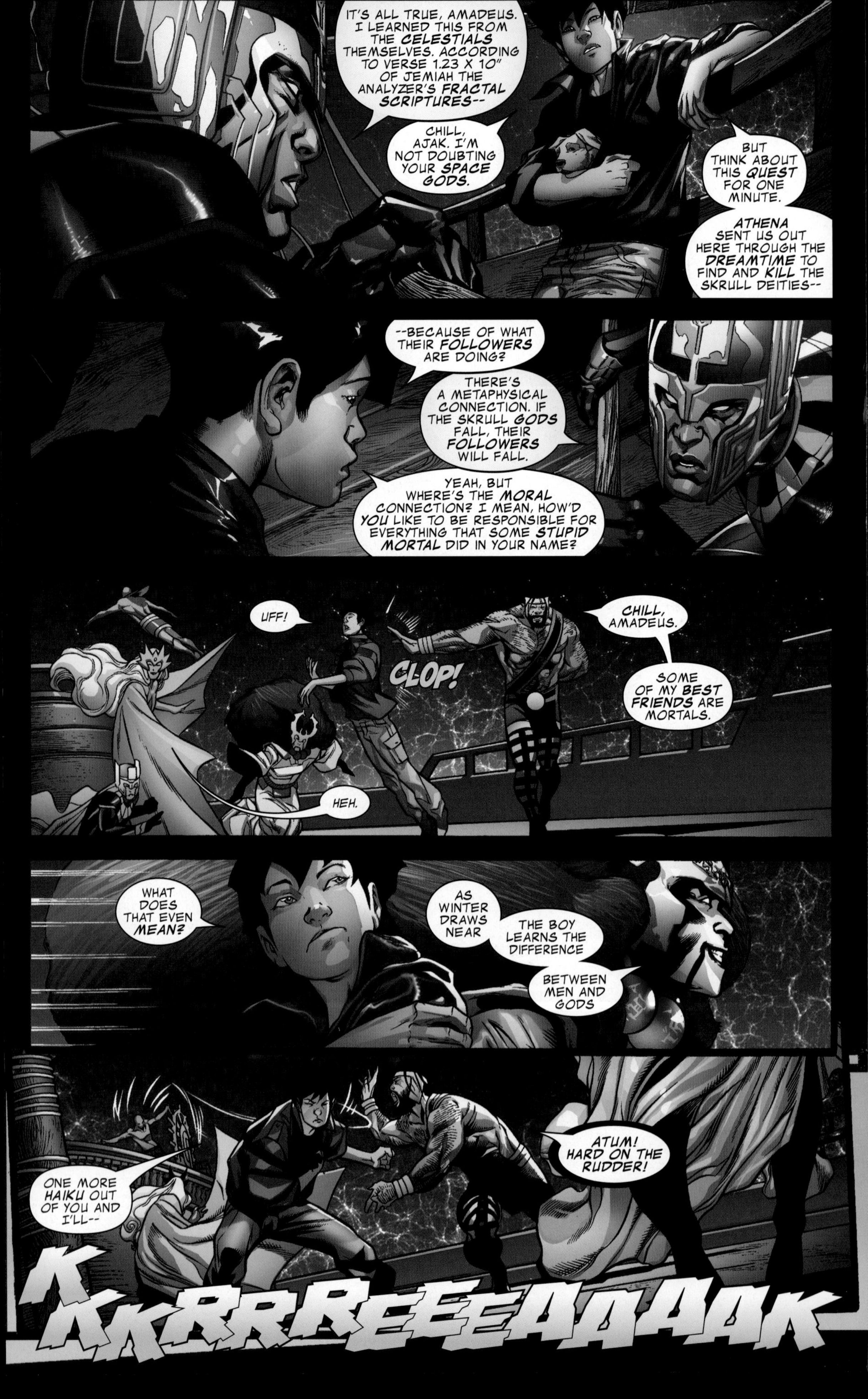

IT'S ALL TRUE, AMADEUS. I LEARNED THIS FROM THE CELESTIALS THEMSELVES. ACCORDING TO VERSE 1.23 X 10" OF JEMIAH THE ANALYZER'S FRACTAL SCRIPTURES--
CHILL, AJAK. I'M NOT DOUBTING YOUR SPACE GODS.
BUT THINK ABOUT THIS QUEST FOR ONE MINUTE.
ATHENA SENT US OUT HERE THROUGH THE DREAMTIME TO FIND AND KILL THE SKRULL DEITIES--
--BECAUSE OF WHAT THEIR FOLLOWERS ARE DOING?
THERE'S A METAPHYSICAL CONNECTION. IF THE SKRULL GODS FALL, THEIR FOLLOWERS WILL FALL.
YEAH, BUT WHERE'S THE MORAL CONNECTION? I MEAN, HOW'D YOU LIKE TO BE RESPONSIBLE FOR EVERYTHING THAT SOME STUPID MORTAL DID IN YOUR NAME?
UFF!
CLOP!
CHILL, AMADEUS.
SOME OF MY BEST FRIENDS ARE MORTALS.
HEH.
WHAT DOES THAT EVEN MEAN?
AS WINTER DRAWS NEAR
THE BOY LEARNS THE DIFFERENCE
BETWEEN MEN AND GODS
ONE MORE HAIKU OUT OF YOU AND I'LL--
ATUM! HARD ON THE RUDDER!
KKRRRREEEAAAAK

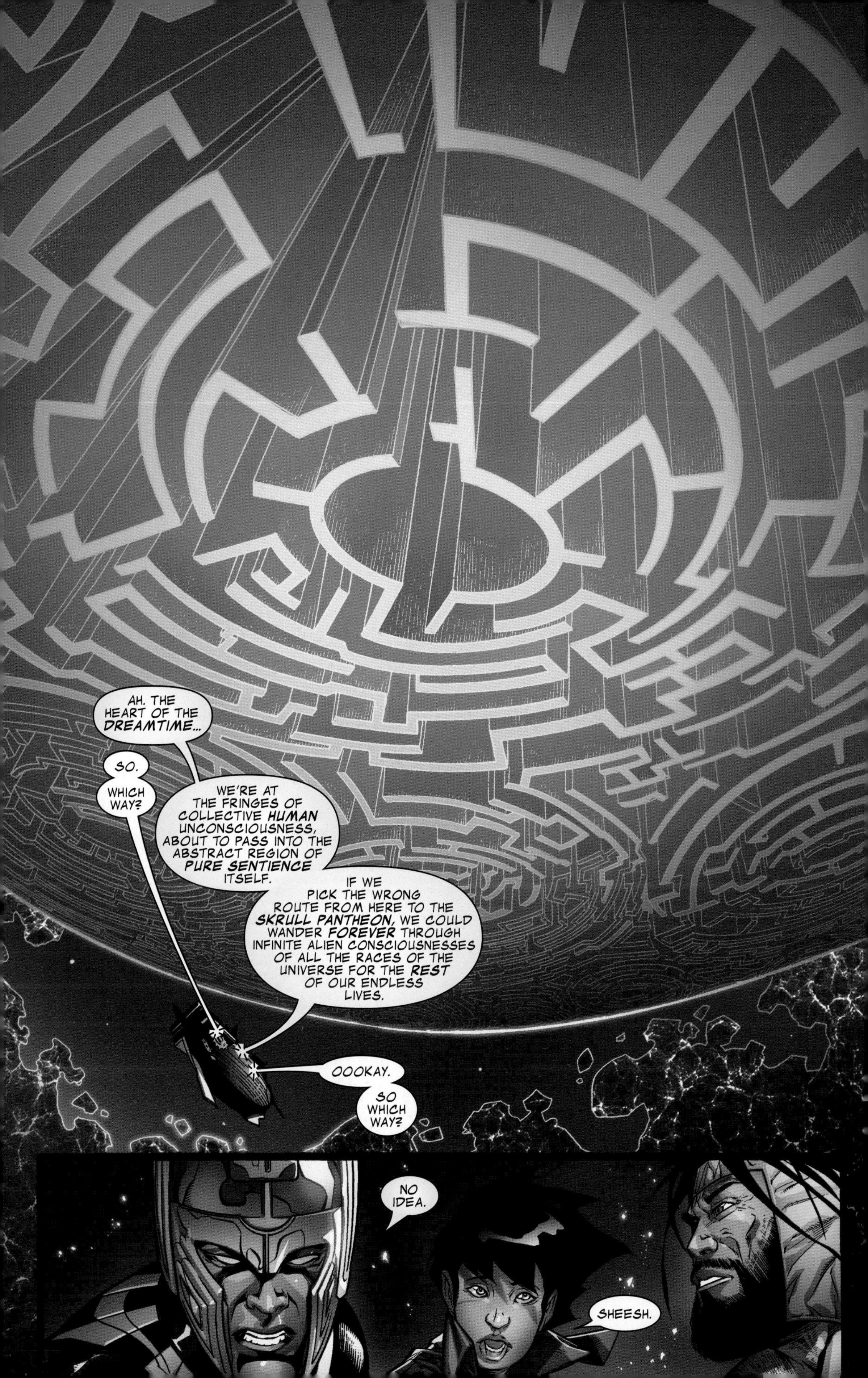
AH. THE HEART OF THE DREAMTIME...
SO.
WHICH WAY?
WE'RE AT THE FRINGES OF COLLECTIVE HUMAN UNCONSCIOUSNESS, ABOUT TO PASS INTO THE ABSTRACT REGION OF PURE SENTIENCE ITSELF.
IF WE PICK THE WRONG ROUTE FROM HERE TO THE SKRULL PANTHEON, WE COULD WANDER FOREVER THROUGH INFINITE ALIEN CONSCIOUSNESSES OF ALL THE RACES OF THE UNIVERSE FOR THE REST OF OUR ENDLESS LIVES.
OOOKAY.
SO WHICH WAY?
NO IDEA.
SHEESH.

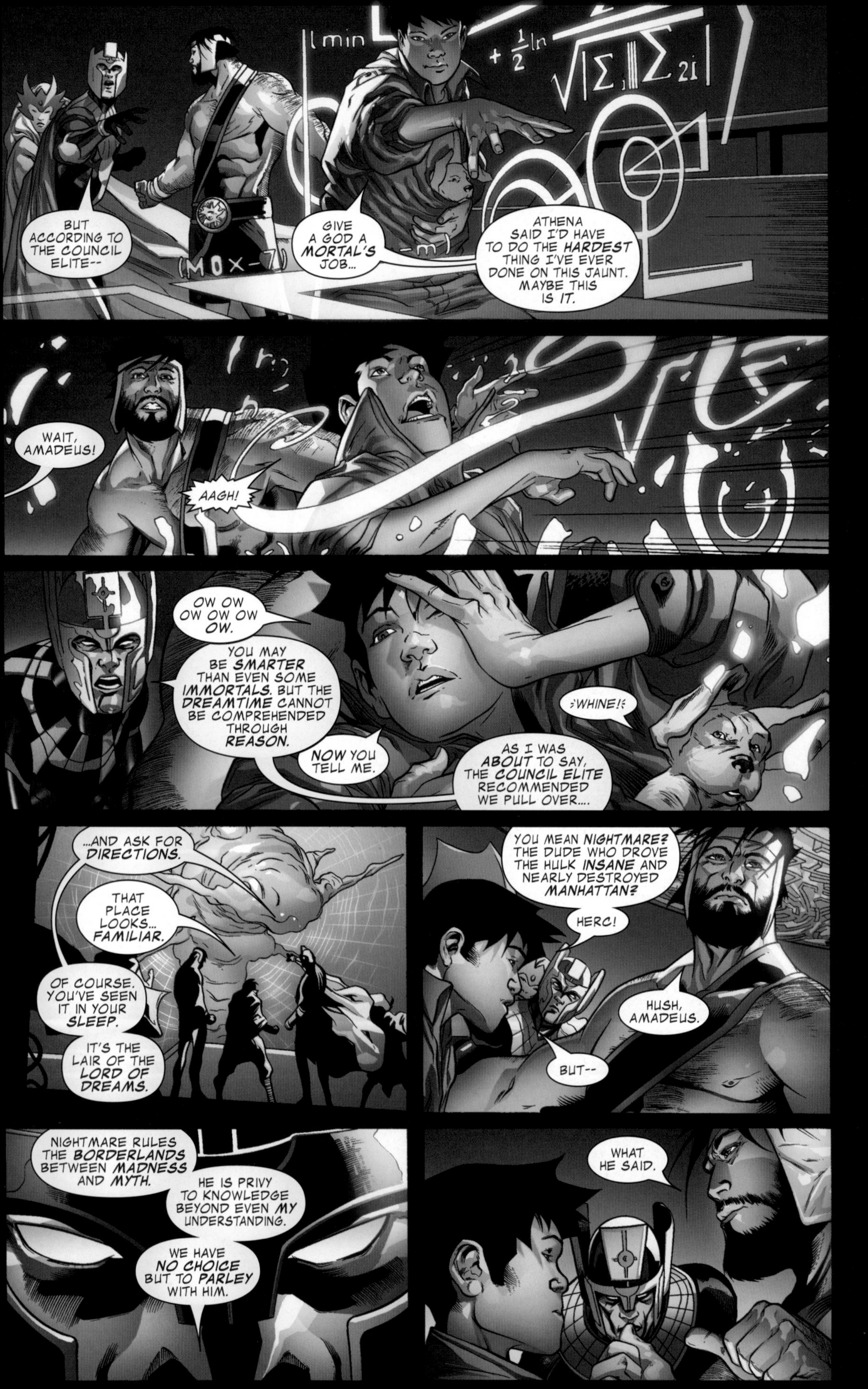
BUT ACCORDING TO THE COUNCIL ELITE--
GIVE A GOD A MORTAL'S JOB...
ATHENA SAID I'D HAVE TO DO THE HARDEST THING I'VE EVER DONE ON THIS JAUNT. MAYBE THIS IS IT.
WAIT, AMADEUS!
AAGH!
OW OW OW OW OW OW.
YOU MAY BE SMARTER THAN EVEN SOME IMMORTALS. BUT THE DREAMTIME CANNOT BE COMPREHENDED THROUGH REASON.
NOW YOU TELL ME.
WHINE!
AS I WAS ABOUT TO SAY, THE COUNCIL ELITE RECOMMENDED WE PULL OVER....
...AND ASK FOR DIRECTIONS.
THAT PLACE LOOKS... FAMILIAR.
OF COURSE. YOU'VE SEEN IT IN YOUR SLEEP.
IT'S THE LAIR OF THE LORD OF DREAMS.
YOU MEAN NIGHTMARE? THE DUDE WHO DROVE THE HULK INSANE AND NEARLY DESTROYED MANHATTAN?
HERC!
HUSH, AMADEUS.
BUT--
NIGHTMARE RULES THE BORDERLANDS BETWEEN MADNESS AND MYTH.
HE IS PRIVY TO KNOWLEDGE BEYOND EVEN MY UNDERSTANDING.
WE HAVE NO CHOICE BUT TO PARLEY WITH HIM.
WHAT HE SAID.

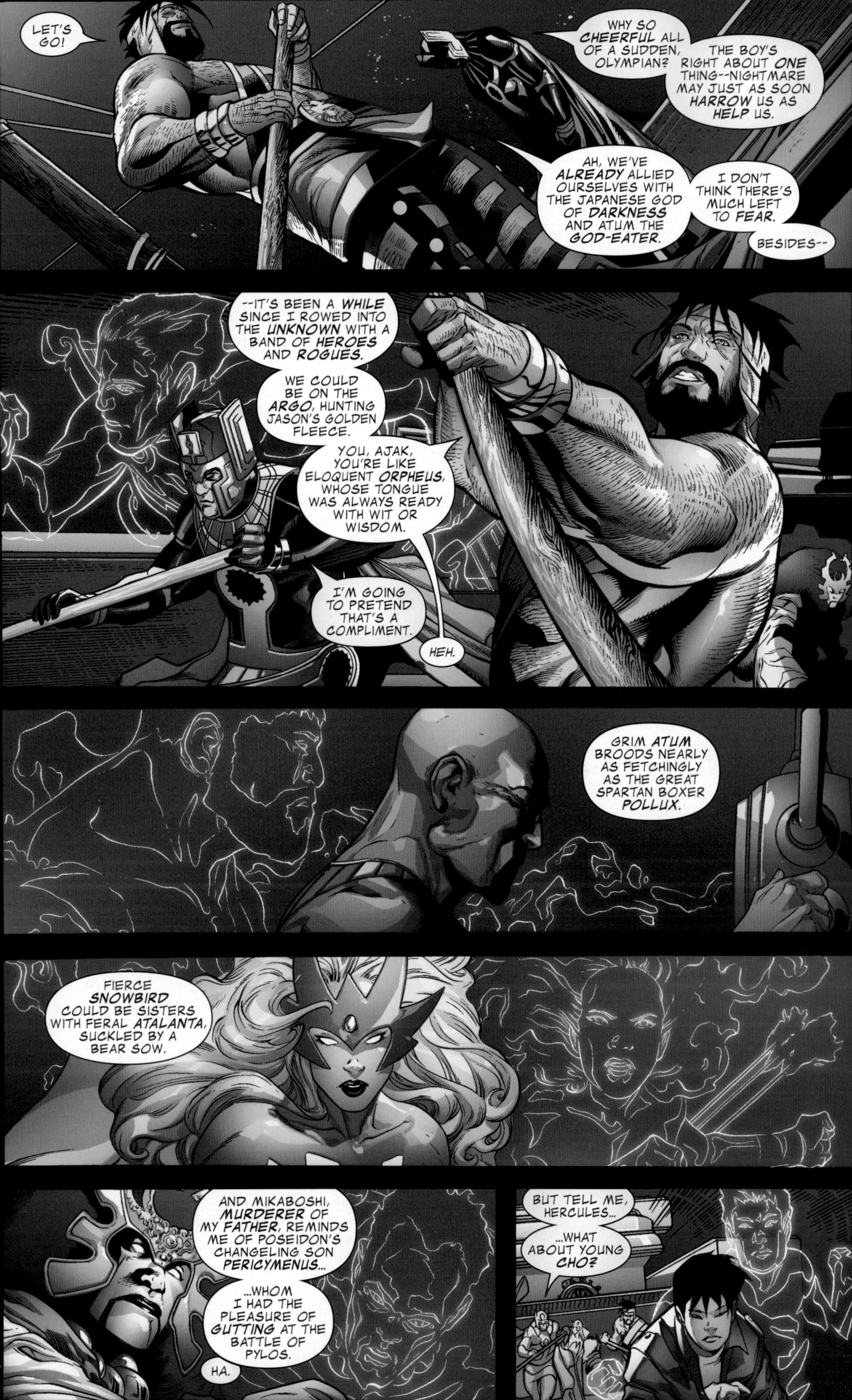
LET'S GO!
WHY SO CHEERFUL ALL OF A SUDDEN, OLYMPIAN?
THE BOY'S RIGHT ABOUT ONE THING--NIGHTMARE MAY JUST AS SOON HARROW US AS HELP US.
AH, WE'VE ALREADY ALLIED OURSELVES WITH THE JAPANESE GOD OF DARKNESS AND ATUM THE GOD-EATER.
I DON'T THINK THERE'S MUCH LEFT TO FEAR.
BESIDES--
--IT'S BEEN A WHILE SINCE I ROWED INTO THE UNKNOWN WITH A BAND OF HEROES AND ROGUES.
WE COULD BE ON THE ARGO, HUNTING JASON'S GOLDEN FLEECE.
YOU, AJAK, YOU'RE LIKE ELOQUENT ORPHEUS, WHOSE TONGUE WAS ALWAYS READY WITH WIT OR WISDOM.
I'M GOING TO PRETEND THAT'S A COMPLIMENT.
HEH.
GRIM ATUM BROODS NEARLY AS FETCHINGLY AS THE GREAT SPARTAN BOXER POLLUX.
FIERCE SNOWBIRD COULD BE SISTERS WITH FERAL ATALANTA, SUCKLED BY A BEAR SOW.
AND MIKABOSHI, MURDERER OF MY FATHER, REMINDS ME OF POSEIDON'S CHANGELING SON PERICYMENUS...
...WHOM I HAD THE PLEASURE OF GUTTING AT THE BATTLE OF PYLOS.
HA.
BUT TELL ME, HERCULES...
...WHAT ABOUT YOUNG CHO?

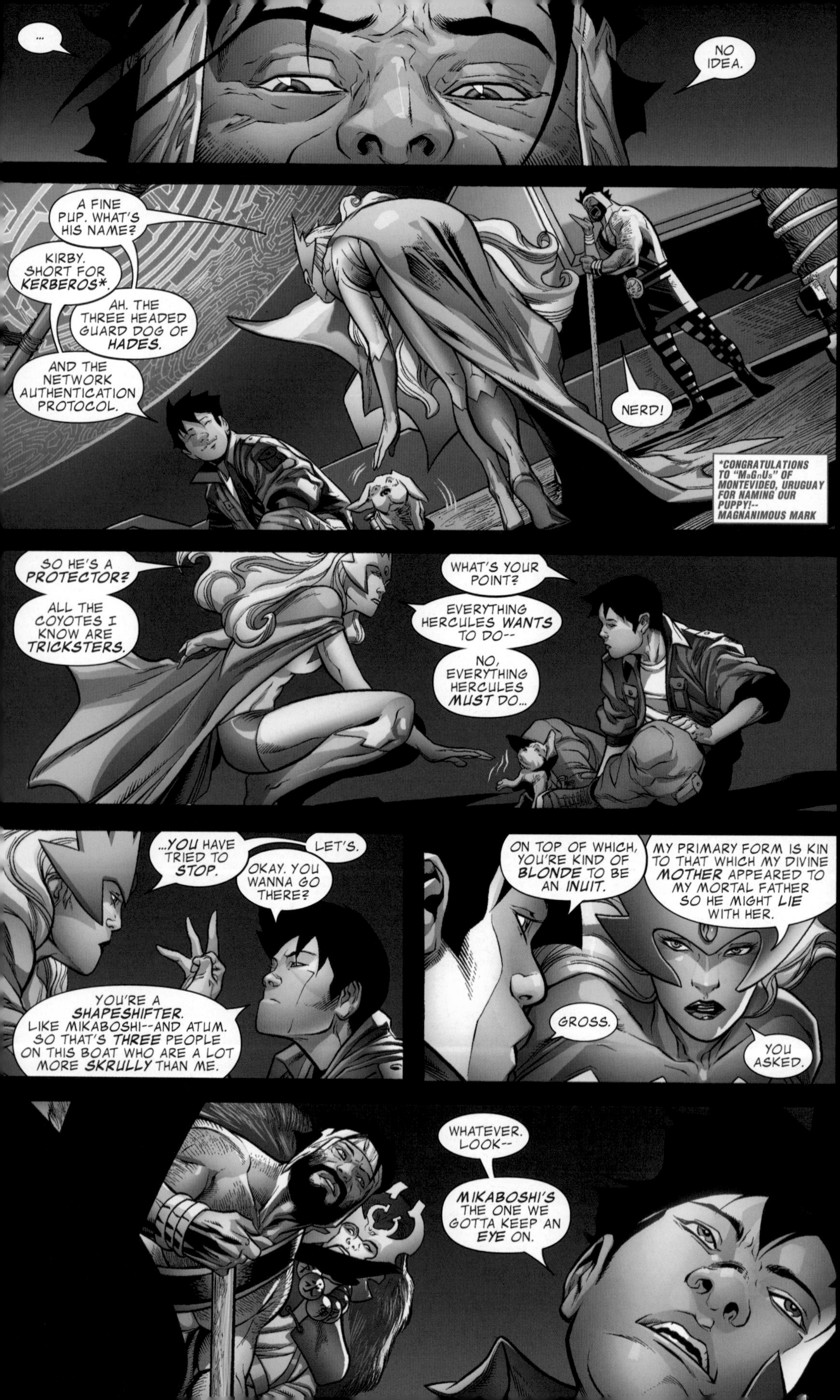
...
NO IDEA.
A FINE PUP. WHAT'S HIS NAME?
KIRBY. SHORT FOR KERBEROS*.
AH. THE THREE HEADED GUARD DOG OF HADES.
AND THE NETWORK AUTHENTICATION PROTOCOL.
NERD!
*CONGRATULATIONS TO "MaGnUs" OF MONTEVIDEO, URUGUAY FOR NAMING OUR PUPPY!-- MAGNANIMOUS MARK
SO HE'S A PROTECTOR?
ALL THE COYOTES I KNOW ARE TRICKSTERS.
WHAT'S YOUR POINT?
EVERYTHING HERCULES WANTS TO DO--
NO, EVERYTHING HERCULES MUST DO...
...YOU HAVE TRIED TO STOP.
LET'S.
OKAY. YOU WANNA GO THERE?
YOU'RE A SHAPESHIFTER. LIKE MIKABOSHI--AND ATUM. SO THAT'S THREE PEOPLE ON THIS BOAT WHO ARE A LOT MORE SKRULLY THAN ME.
ON TOP OF WHICH, YOU'RE KIND OF BLONDE TO BE AN INUIT.
MY PRIMARY FORM IS KIN TO THAT WHICH MY DIVINE MOTHER APPEARED TO MY MORTAL FATHER SO HE MIGHT LIE WITH HER.
GROSS.
YOU ASKED.
WHATEVER. LOOK--
MIKABOSHI'S THE ONE WE GOTTA KEEP AN EYE ON.

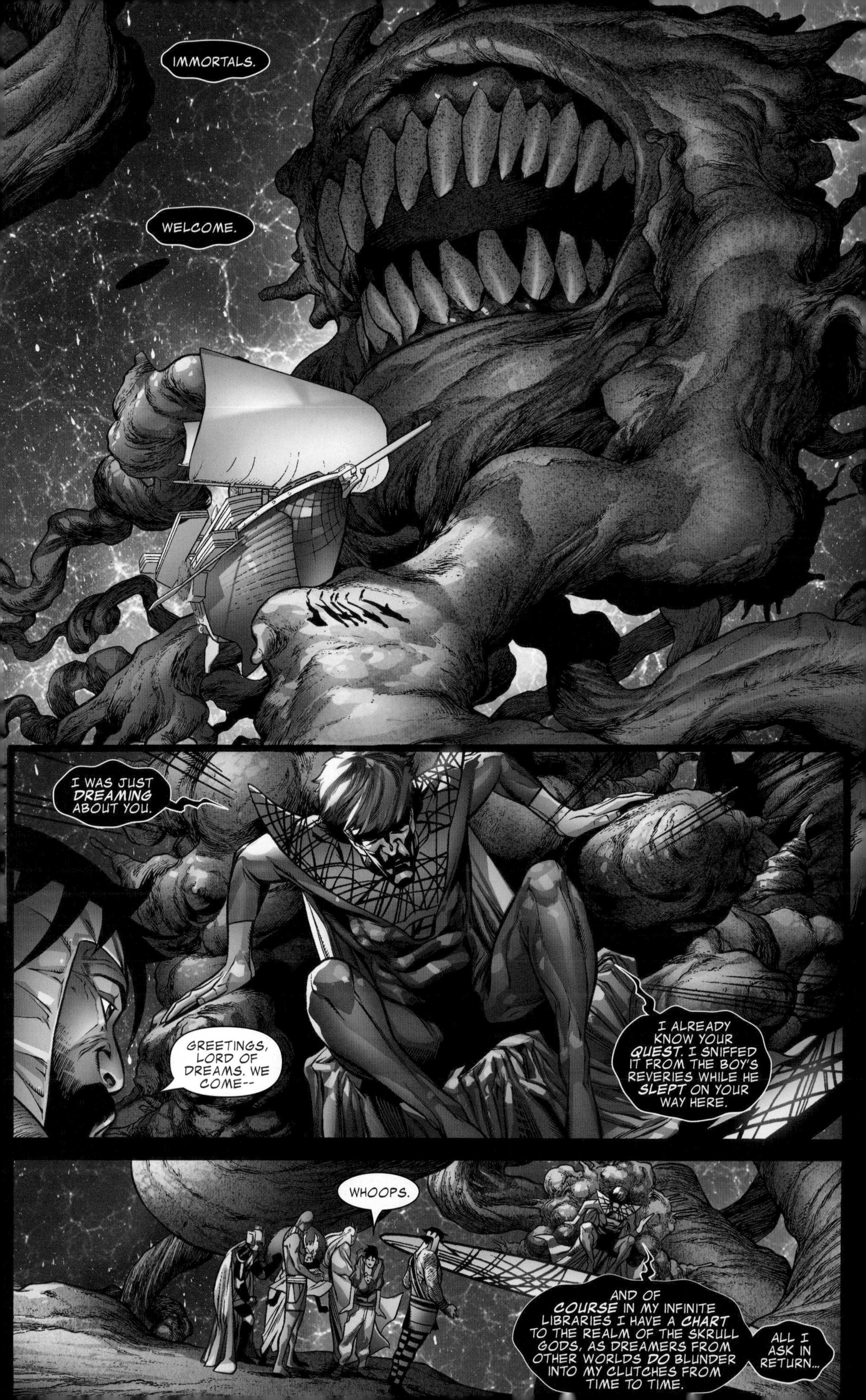
IMMORTALS.
WELCOME.
I WAS JUST DREAMING ABOUT YOU.
GREETINGS, LORD OF DREAMS. WE COME--
I ALREADY KNOW YOUR QUEST. I SNIFFED IT FROM THE BOY'S REVERIES WHILE HE SLEPT ON YOUR WAY HERE.
WHOOPS.
AND OF COURSE IN MY INFINITE LIBRARIES I HAVE A CHART TO THE REALM OF THE SKRULL GODS, AS DREAMERS FROM OTHER WORLDS DO BLUNDER INTO MY CLUTCHES FROM TIME TO TIME.
ALL I ASK IN RETURN...

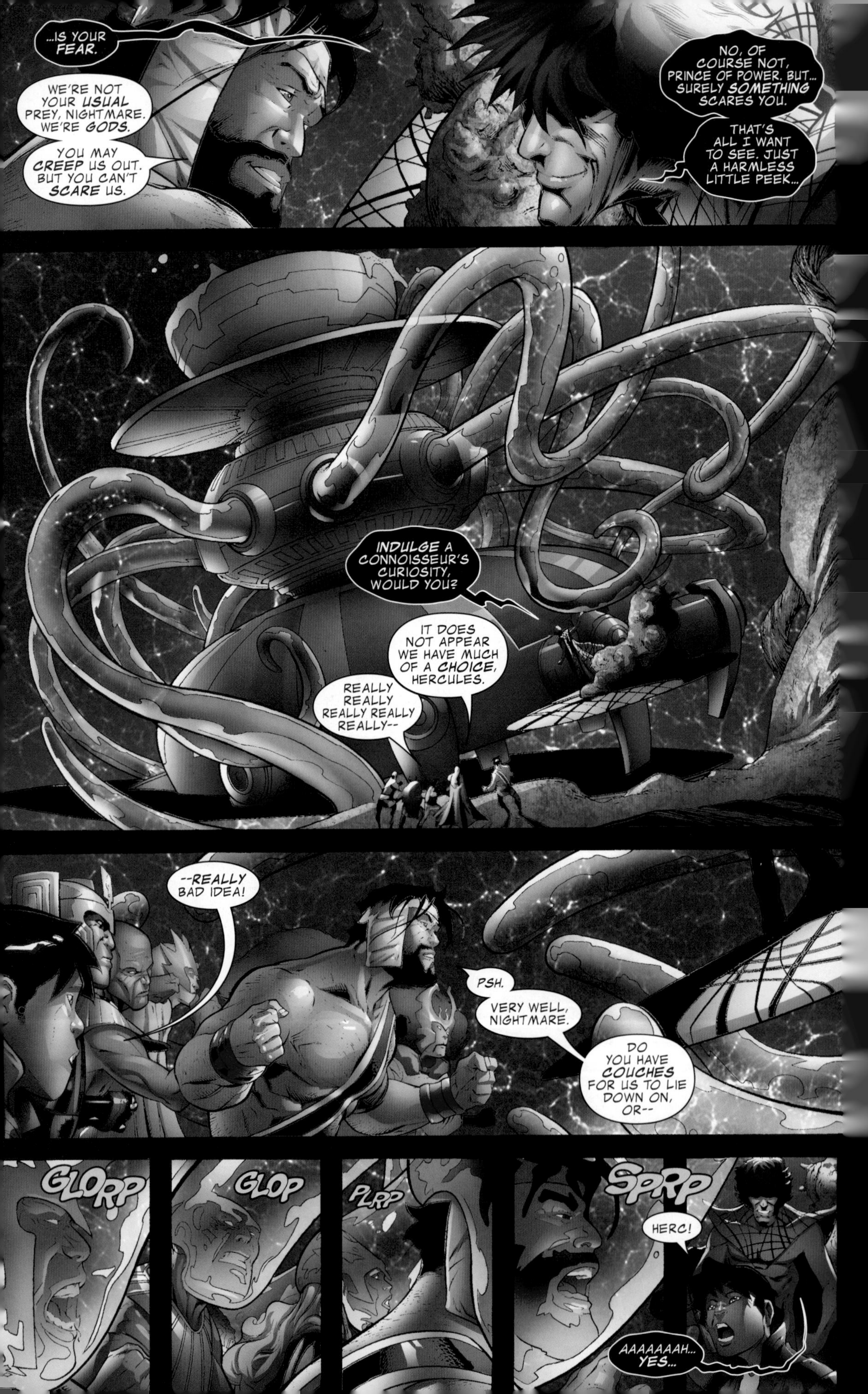
...IS YOUR FEAR.
WE'RE NOT YOUR USUAL PREY, NIGHTMARE. WE'RE GODS.
YOU MAY CREEP US OUT. BUT YOU CAN'T SCARE US.
NO, OF COURSE NOT, PRINCE OF POWER. BUT... SURELY SOMETHING SCARES YOU.
THAT'S ALL I WANT TO SEE. JUST A HARMLESS LITTLE PEEK...
INDULGE A CONNOISSEUR'S CURIOSITY, WOULD YOU?
IT DOES NOT APPEAR WE HAVE MUCH OF A CHOICE, HERCULES.
REALLY REALLY REALLY REALLY REALLY--
--REALLY BAD IDEA!
PSH.
VERY WELL, NIGHTMARE.
DO YOU HAVE COUCHES FOR US TO LIE DOWN ON, OR--
GLORP
GLOP
PLRP
SPRP
HERC!
AAAAAAAH... YES...

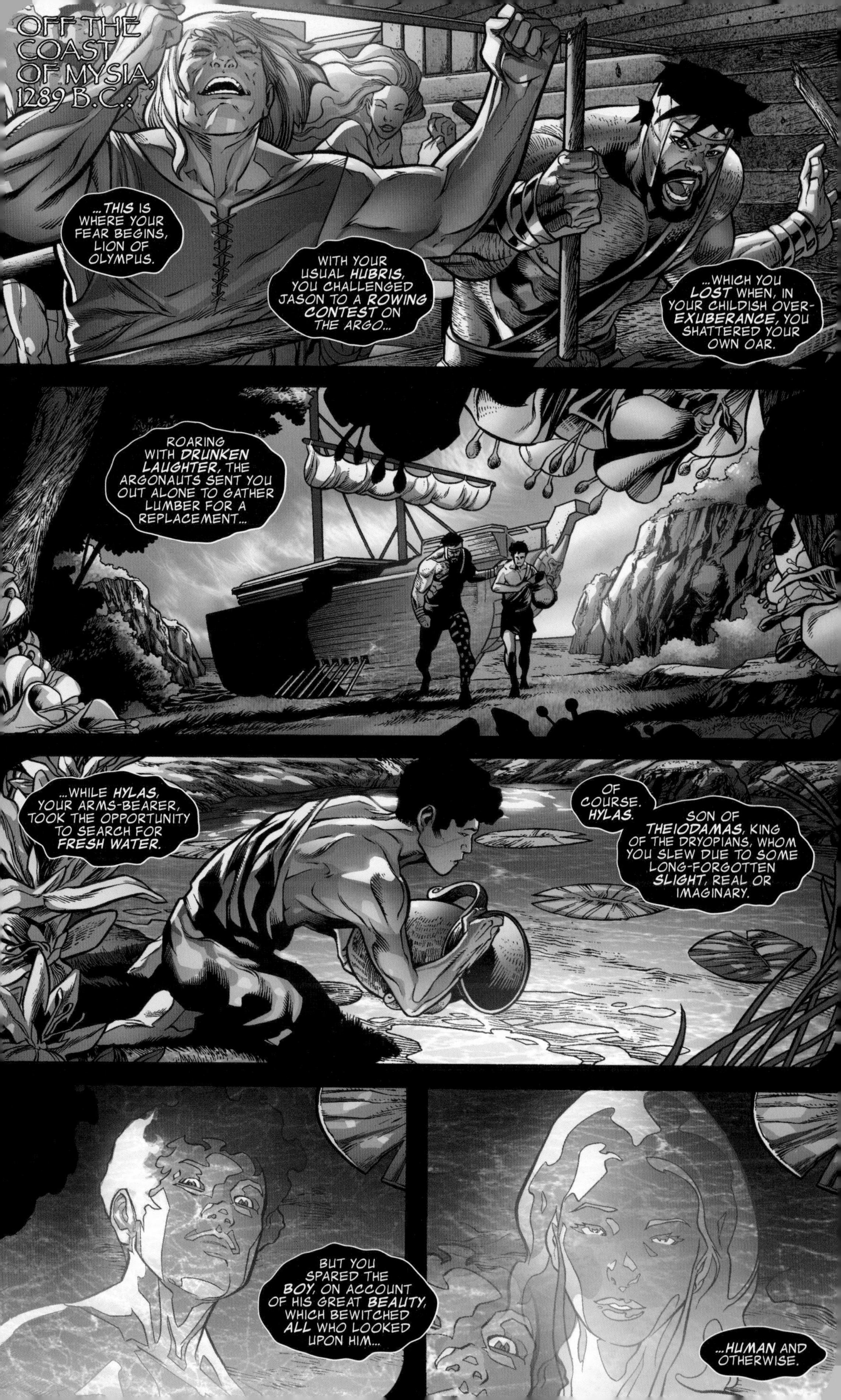
OFF THE COAST OF MYSIA, 1289 B.C.:
...THIS IS WHERE YOUR FEAR BEGINS, LION OF OLYMPUS.
WITH YOUR USUAL HUBRIS, YOU CHALLENGED JASON TO A ROWING CONTEST ON THE ARGO...
...WHICH YOU LOST WHEN, IN YOUR CHILDISH OVER-EXUBERANCE, YOU SHATTERED YOUR OWN OAR.
ROARING WITH DRUNKEN LAUGHTER, THE ARGONAUTS SENT YOU OUT ALONE TO GATHER LUMBER FOR A REPLACEMENT...
...WHILE HYLAS, YOUR ARMS-BEARER, TOOK THE OPPORTUNITY TO SEARCH FOR FRESH WATER.
OF COURSE. HYLAS.
SON OF THEIODAMAS, KING OF THE DRYOPIANS, WHOM YOU SLEW DUE TO SOME LONG-FORGOTTEN SLIGHT, REAL OR IMAGINARY.
BUT YOU SPARED THE BOY, ON ACCOUNT OF HIS GREAT BEAUTY, WHICH BEWITCHED ALL WHO LOOKED UPON HIM...
...HUMAN AND OTHERWISE.

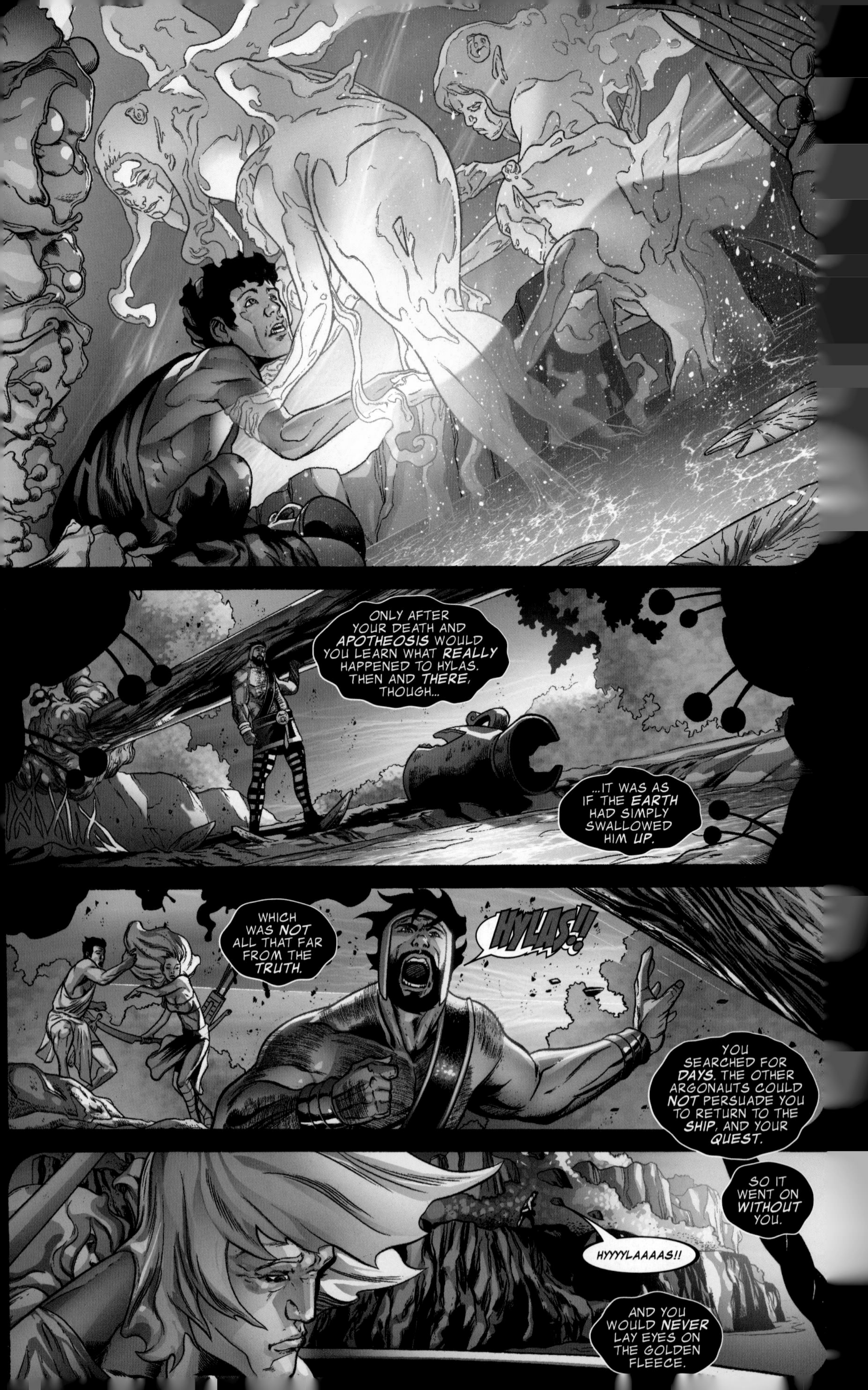
ONLY AFTER YOUR DEATH AND APOTHEOSIS WOULD YOU LEARN WHAT REALLY HAPPENED TO HYLAS. THEN AND THERE, THOUGH...
...IT WAS AS IF THE EARTH HAD SIMPLY SWALLOWED HIM UP.
WHICH WAS NOT ALL THAT FAR FROM THE TRUTH.
HYLAS!!
YOU SEARCHED FOR DAYS. THE OTHER ARGONAUTS COULD NOT PERSUADE YOU TO RETURN TO THE SHIP, AND YOUR QUEST.
SO IT WENT ON WITHOUT YOU.
HYYYYLAAAAS!!
AND YOU WOULD NEVER LAY EYES ON THE GOLDEN FLEECE.

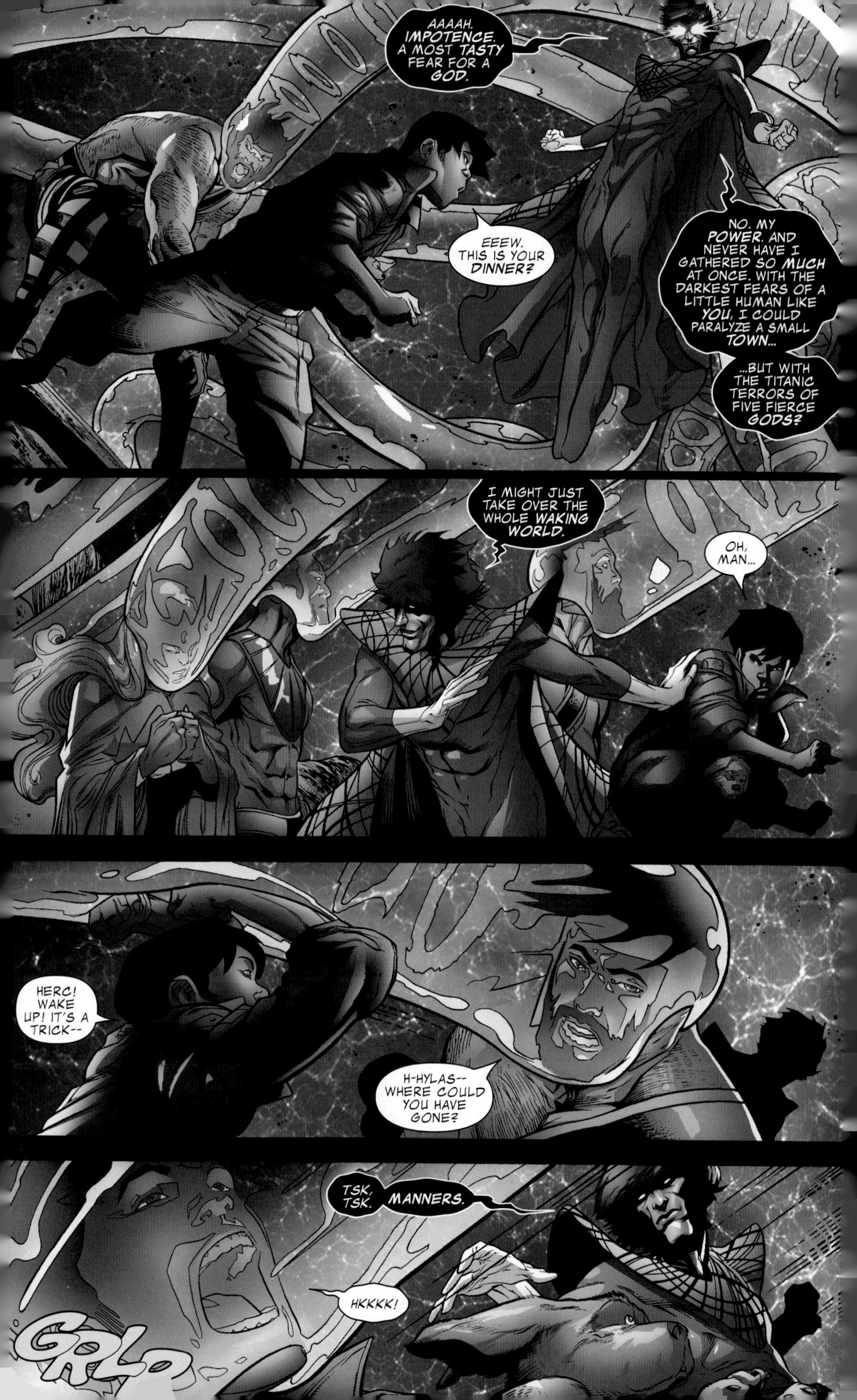
AAAAH. IMPOTENCE. A MOST TASTY FEAR FOR A GOD.
EEEW. THIS IS YOUR DINNER?
NO. MY POWER. AND NEVER HAVE I GATHERED SO MUCH AT ONCE. WITH THE DARKEST FEARS OF A LITTLE HUMAN LIKE YOU, I COULD PARALYZE A SMALL TOWN...
...BUT WITH THE TITANIC TERRORS OF FIVE FIERCE GODS?
I MIGHT JUST TAKE OVER THE WHOLE WAKING WORLD.
OH, MAN...
HERC! WAKE UP! IT'S A TRICK--
H-HYLAS-- WHERE COULD YOU HAVE GONE?
TSK, TSK.
MANNERS.
HKKKK!
GRLO

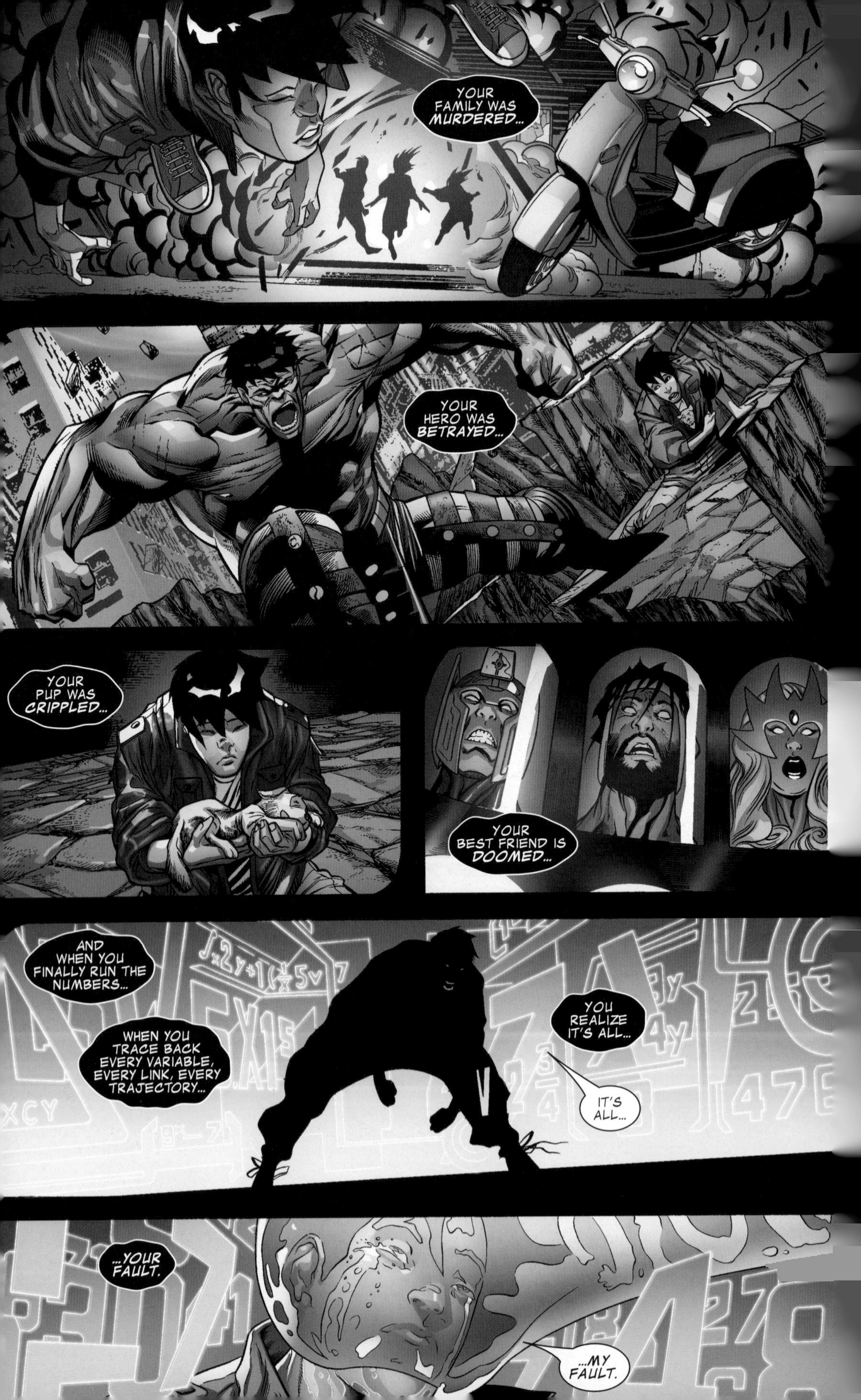
YOUR FAMILY WAS MURDERED...
YOUR HERO WAS BETRAYED...
YOUR PUP WAS CRIPPLED...
YOUR BEST FRIEND IS DOOMED...
AND WHEN YOU FINALLY RUN THE NUMBERS...
WHEN YOU TRACE BACK EVERY VARIABLE, EVERY LINK, EVERY TRAJECTORY...
YOU REALIZE IT'S ALL...
IT'S ALL...
...YOUR FAULT.
...MY FAULT.

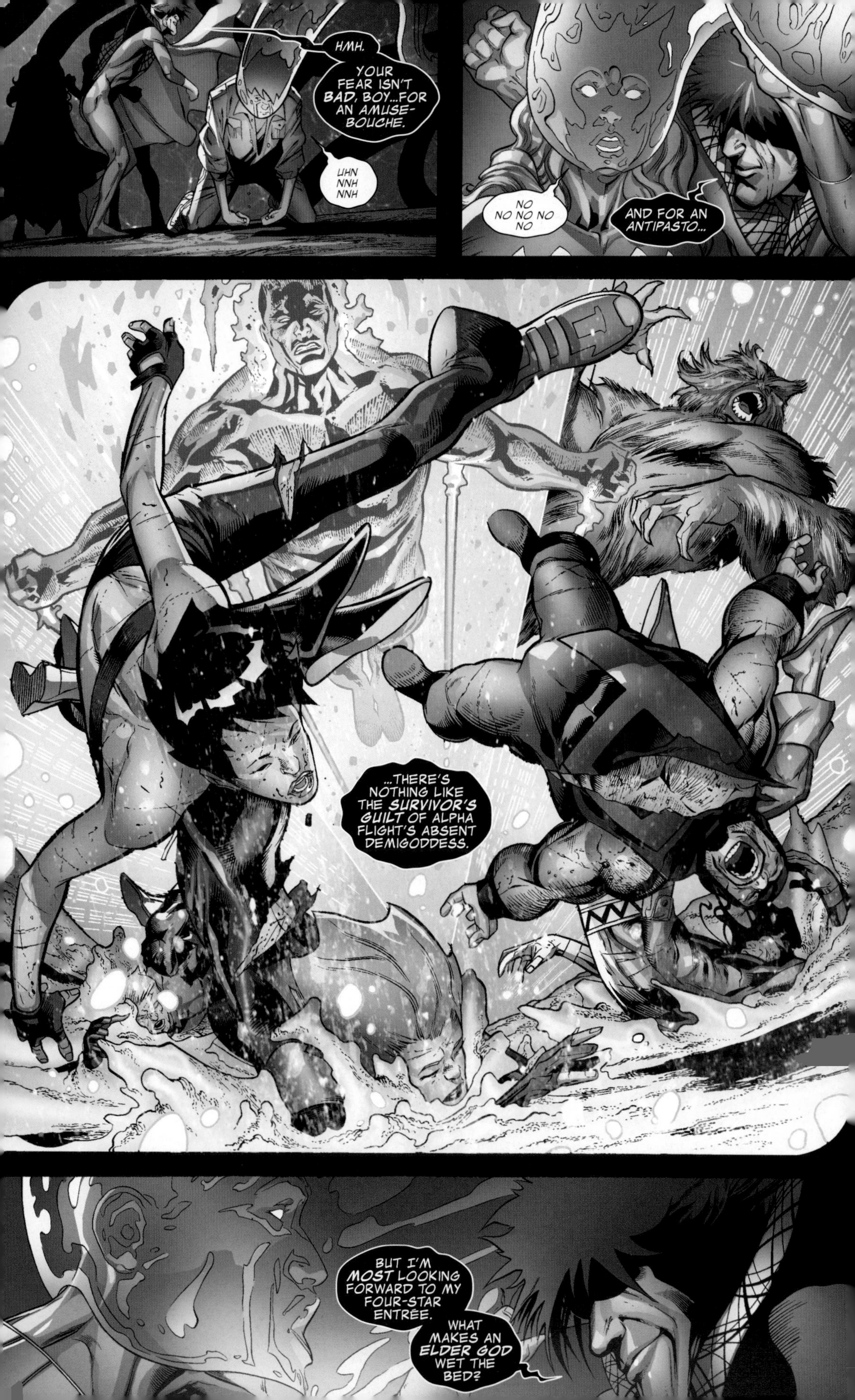
HMH.
YOUR FEAR ISN'T BAD, BOY...FOR AN AMUSE-BOUCHE.
UHN NNH NNH
NO NO NO NO NO
AND FOR AN ANTIPASTO...
...THERE'S NOTHING LIKE THE SURVIVOR'S GUILT OF ALPHA FLIGHT'S ABSENT DEMIGODDESS.
BUT I'M MOST LOOKING FORWARD TO MY FOUR-STAR ENTRÉE.
WHAT MAKES AN ELDER GOD WET THE BED?

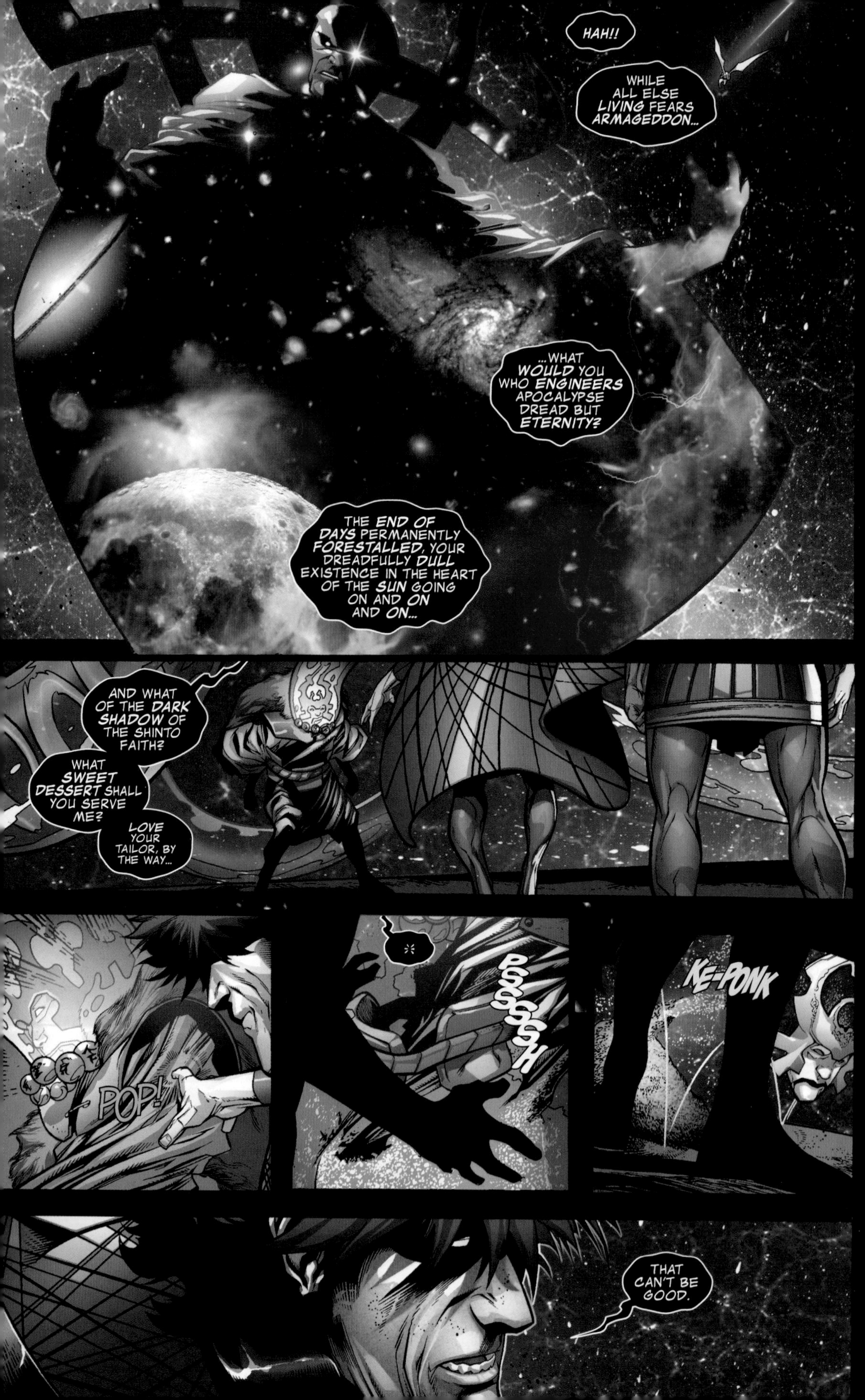
HAH!!
WHILE ALL ELSE LIVING FEARS ARMAGEDDON...
...WHAT WOULD YOU WHO ENGINEERS APOCALYPSE DREAD BUT ETERNITY?
THE END OF DAYS PERMANENTLY FORESTALLED, YOUR DREADFULLY DULL EXISTENCE IN THE HEART OF THE SUN GOING ON AND ON AND ON...
AND WHAT OF THE DARK SHADOW OF THE SHINTO FAITH?
WHAT SWEET DESSERT SHALL YOU SERVE ME?
LOVE YOUR TAILOR, BY THE WAY...
POP!
PSSSSH
KE-PONK
THAT CAN'T BE GOOD.

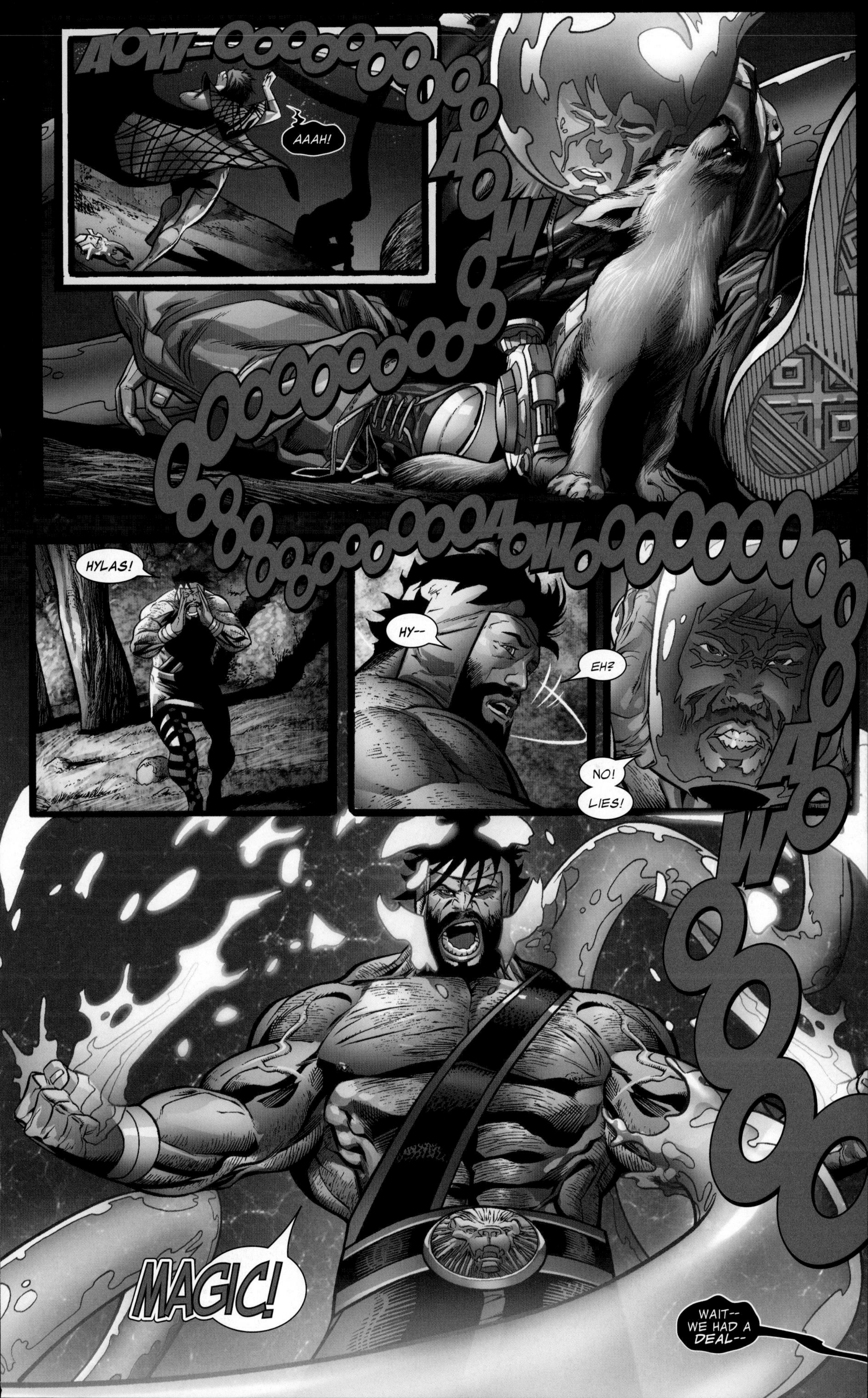
AOW-OOOOOOOOOOOOO
AAAH!
AOWOOOOOOOOOOOOOOOOOOOOOOOOOOOAOWOOOOOOOOOOOOOOOOOOOO
HYLAS!
HY--
EH?
NO! LIES!
MAGIC!
WAIT-- WE HAD A DEAL--

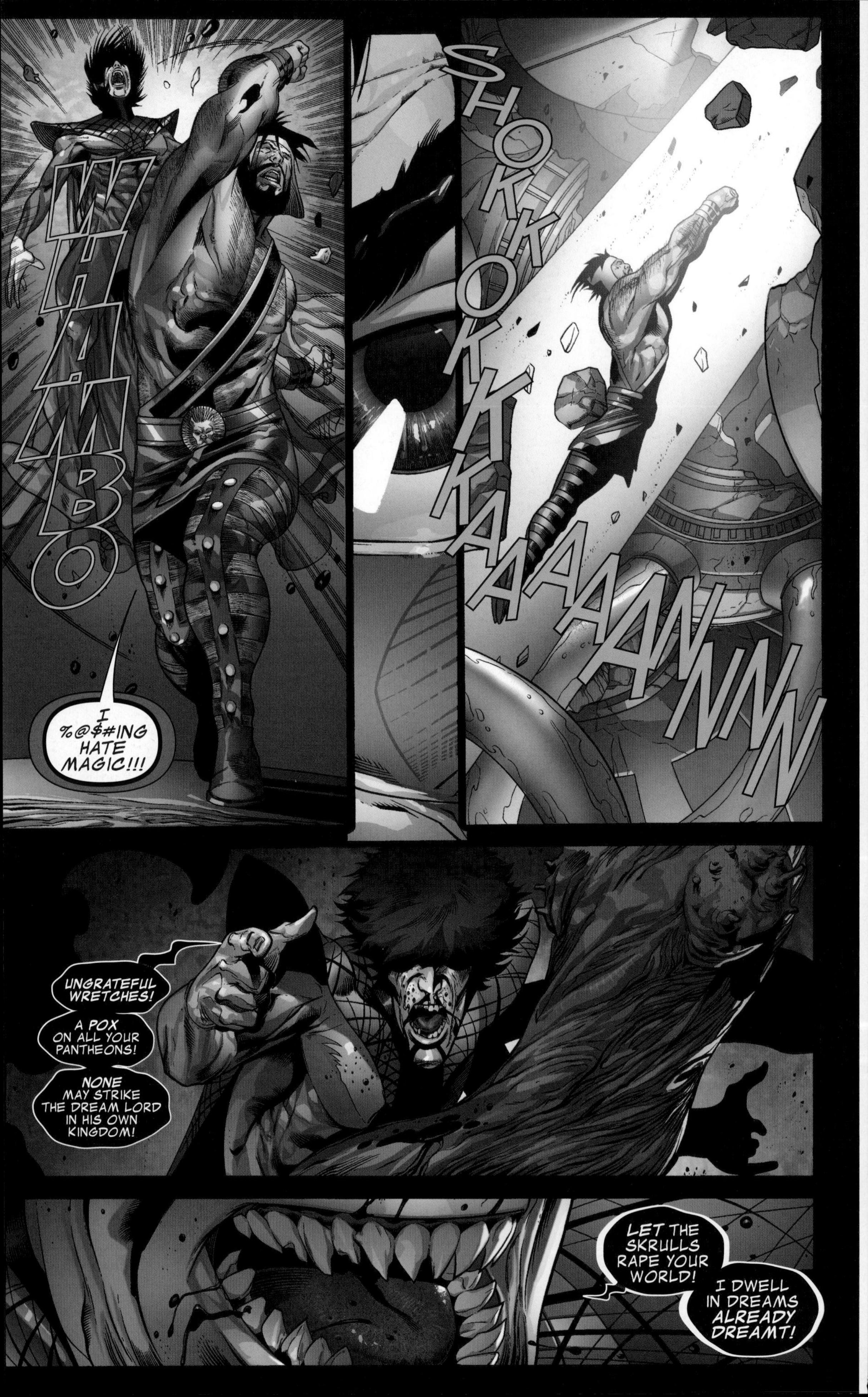
WHAMBO
I %@$#ING HATE MAGIC!!!
SHOKKOKKAAAAANNNN
UNGRATEFUL WRETCHES!
A POX ON ALL YOUR PANTHEONS!
NONE MAY STRIKE THE DREAM LORD IN HIS OWN KINGDOM!
LET THE SKRULLS RAPE YOUR WORLD!
I DWELL IN DREAMS ALREADY DREAMT!

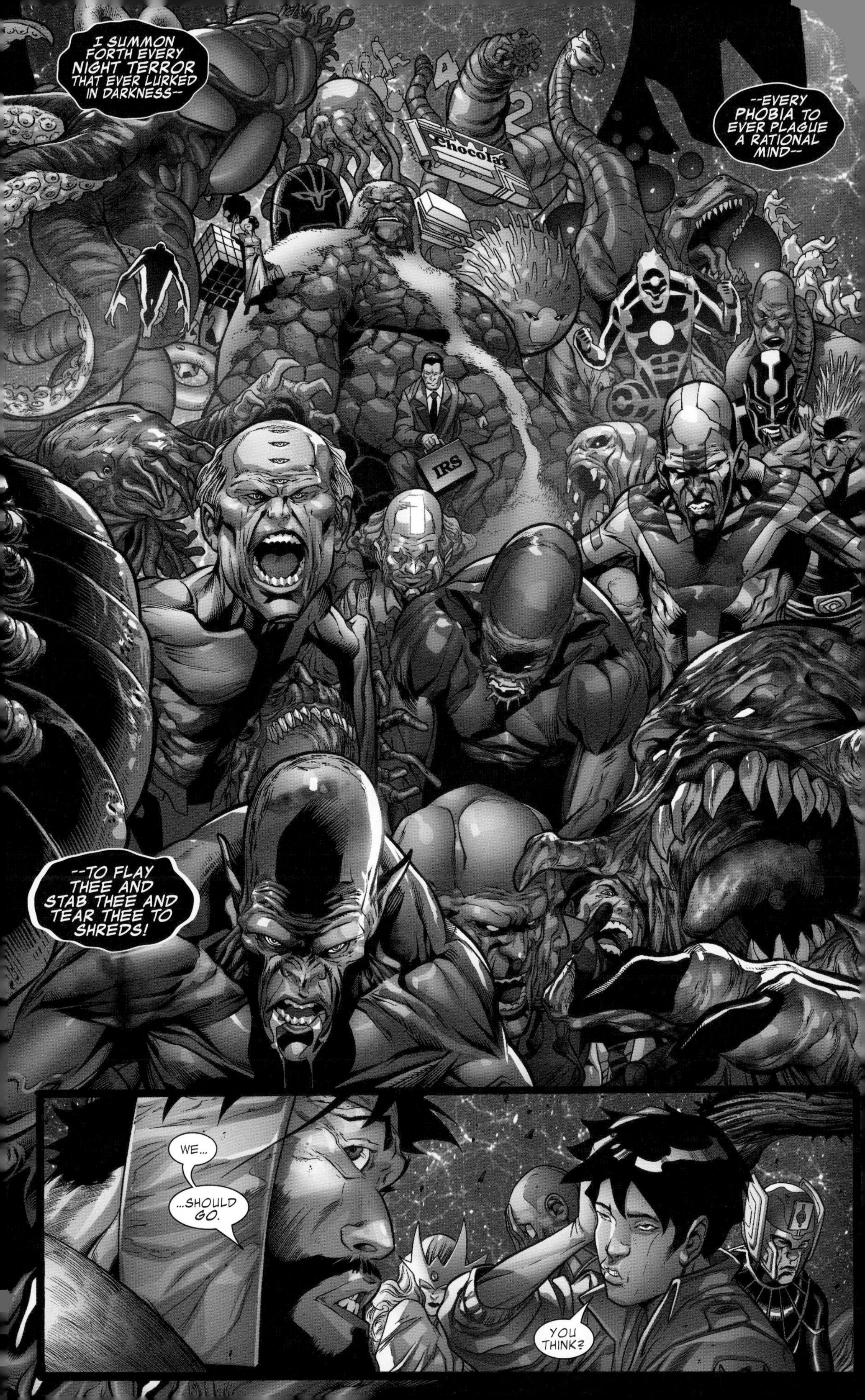
I SUMMON FORTH EVERY NIGHT TERROR THAT EVER LURKED IN DARKNESS--
--EVERY PHOBIA TO EVER PLAGUE A RATIONAL MIND--
Chocolat
IRS
--TO FLAY THEE AND STAB THEE AND TEAR THEE TO SHREDS!
WE...
...SHOULD GO.
YOU THINK?

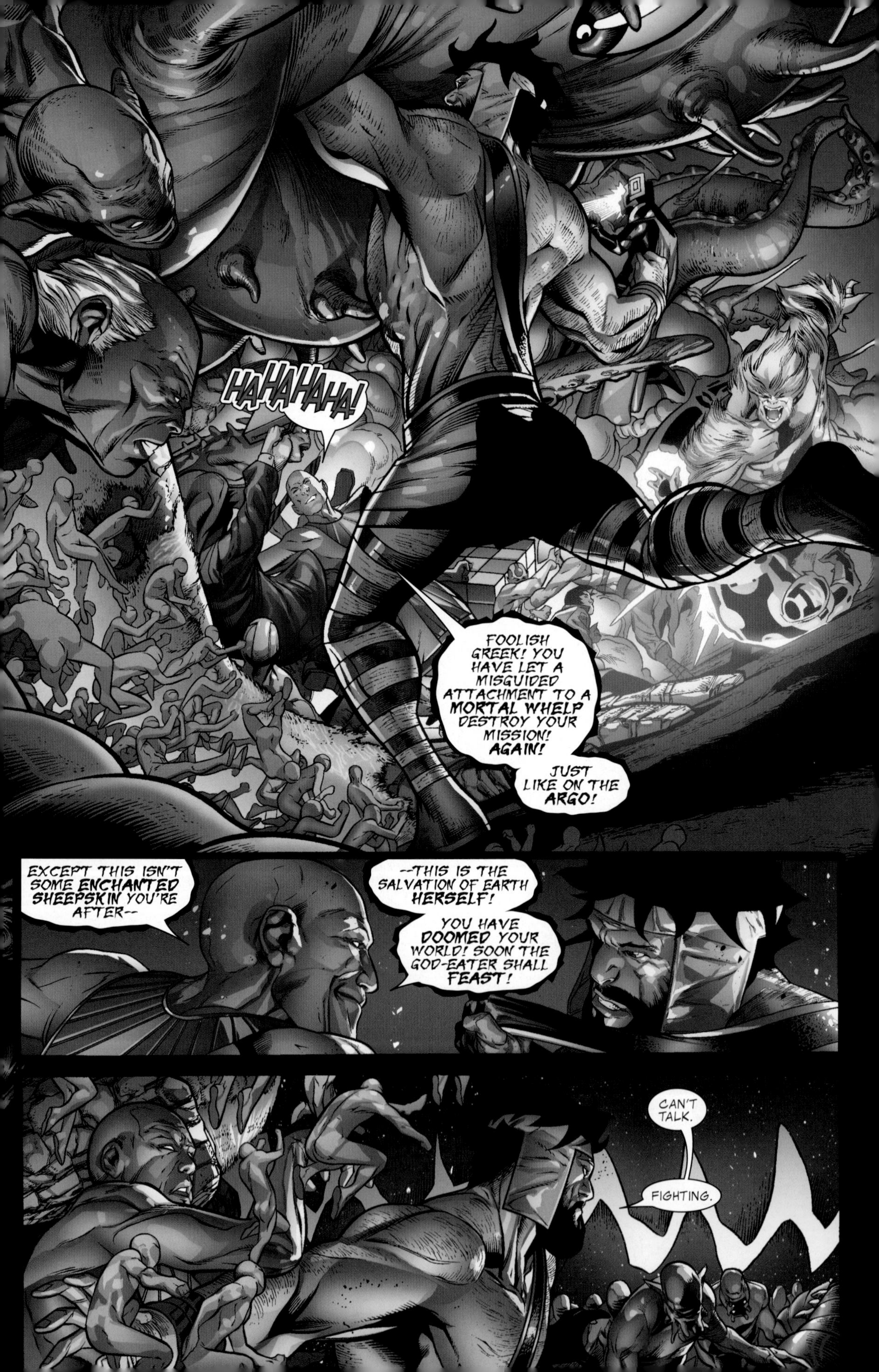
HAHAHAHA!
FOOLISH GREEK! YOU HAVE LET A MISGUIDED ATTACHMENT TO A MORTAL WHELP DESTROY YOUR MISSION! AGAIN!
JUST LIKE ON THE ARGO!
EXCEPT THIS ISN'T SOME ENCHANTED SHEEPSKIN YOU'RE AFTER--
--THIS IS THE SALVATION OF EARTH HERSELF!
YOU HAVE DOOMED YOUR WORLD! SOON THE GOD-EATER SHALL FEAST!
CAN'T TALK.
FIGHTING.

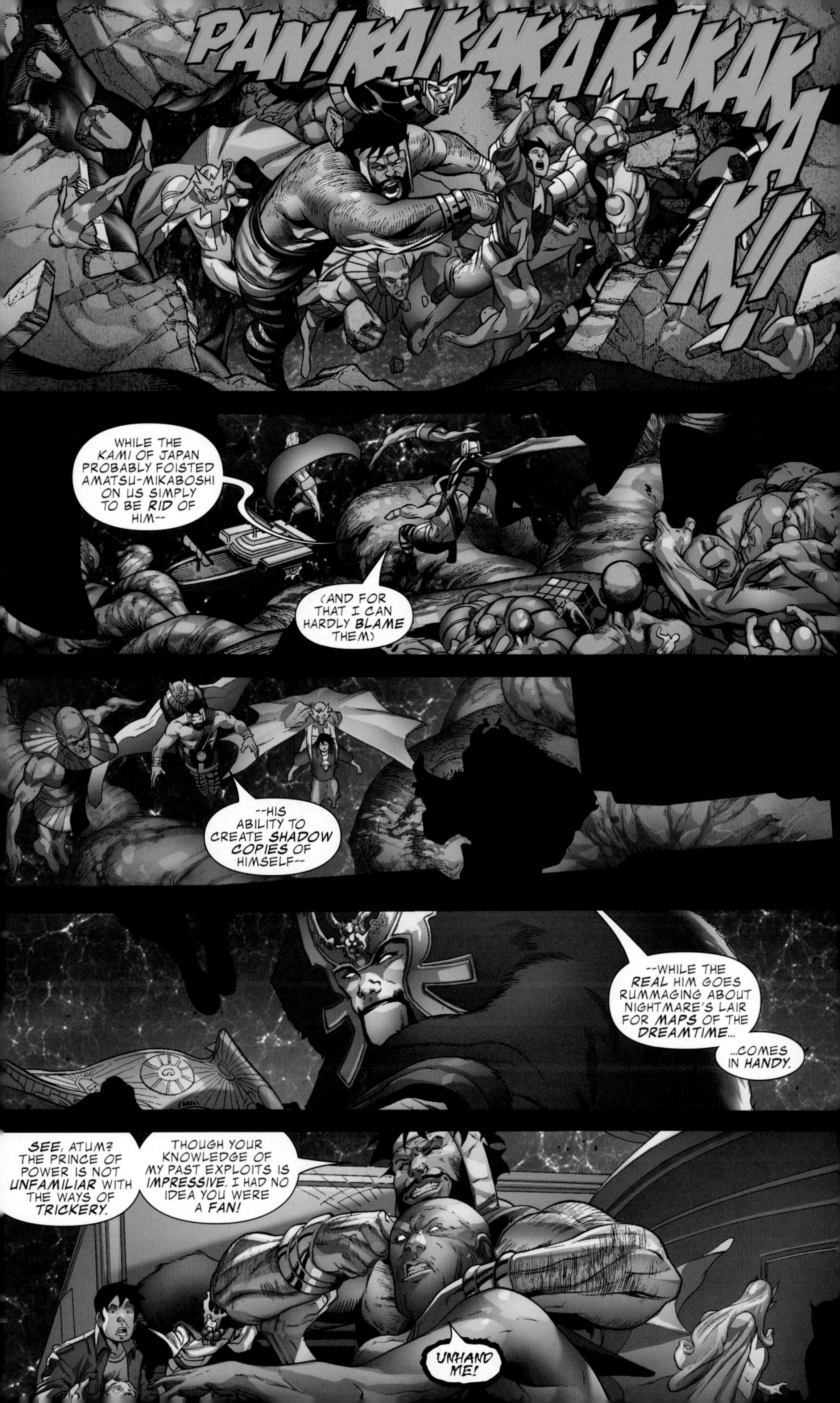
PANIKAKAKAKAKAKAKAKAK!!
WHILE THE KAMI OF JAPAN PROBABLY FOISTED AMATSU-MIKABOSHI ON US SIMPLY TO BE RID OF HIM--
(AND FOR THAT I CAN HARDLY BLAME THEM)
--HIS ABILITY TO CREATE SHADOW COPIES OF HIMSELF--
--WHILE THE REAL HIM GOES RUMMAGING ABOUT NIGHTMARE'S LAIR FOR MAPS OF THE DREAMTIME...
...COMES IN HANDY.
SEE, ATUM? THE PRINCE OF POWER IS NOT UNFAMILIAR WITH THE WAYS OF TRICKERY.
THOUGH YOUR KNOWLEDGE OF MY PAST EXPLOITS IS IMPRESSIVE. I HAD NO IDEA YOU WERE A FAN!
UNHAND ME!

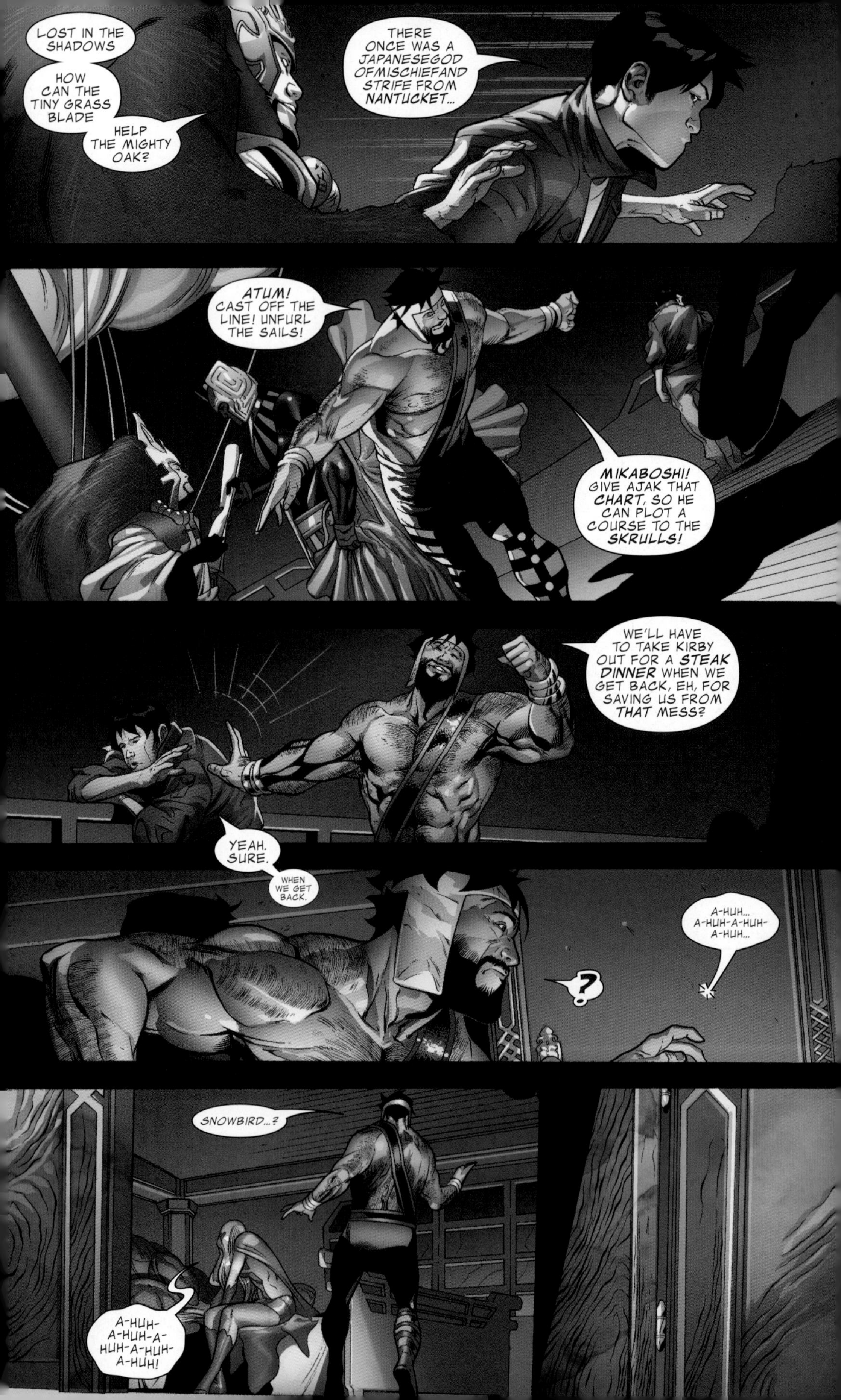

LOST IN THE SHADOWS
HOW CAN THE TINY GRASS BLADE
HELP THE MIGHTY OAK?
THERE ONCE WAS A JAPANESEGOD OFMISCHIEFAND STRIFE FROM NANTUCKET...
ATUM! CAST OFF THE LINE! UNFURL THE SAILS!
MIKABOSHI! GIVE AJAK THAT CHART, SO HE CAN PLOT A COURSE TO THE SKRULLS!
WE'LL HAVE TO TAKE KIRBY OUT FOR A STEAK DINNER WHEN WE GET BACK, EH, FOR SAVING US FROM THAT MESS?
YEAH. SURE.
WHEN WE GET BACK.
A-HUH... A-HUH-A-HUH-A-HUH...
?
SNOWBIRD...?
A-HUH-A-HUH-A-HUH-A-HUH-A-HUH!

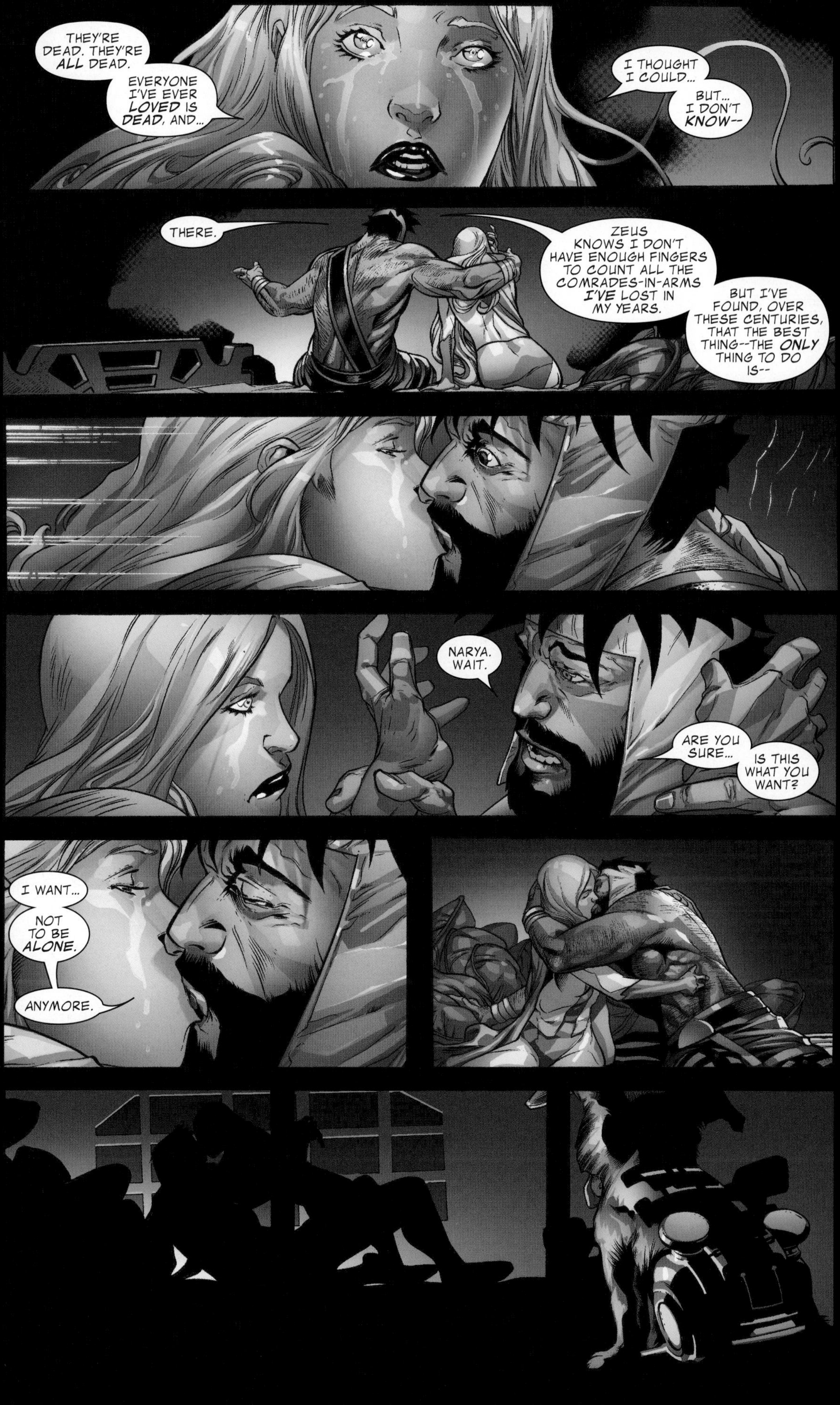
THEY'RE DEAD. THEY'RE *ALL* DEAD.
EVERYONE I'VE EVER *LOVED* IS *DEAD*, AND...
I THOUGHT I COULD...
BUT... I DON'T *KNOW*--
THERE.
ZEUS KNOWS I DON'T HAVE ENOUGH FINGERS TO COUNT ALL THE COMRADES-IN-ARMS *I'VE* LOST IN MY YEARS.
BUT I'VE FOUND, OVER THESE CENTURIES, THAT THE BEST THING--THE *ONLY* THING TO DO IS--
NARYA. WAIT.
ARE YOU SURE...
IS THIS WHAT YOU WANT?
I WANT...
NOT TO BE *ALONE*.
ANYMORE.

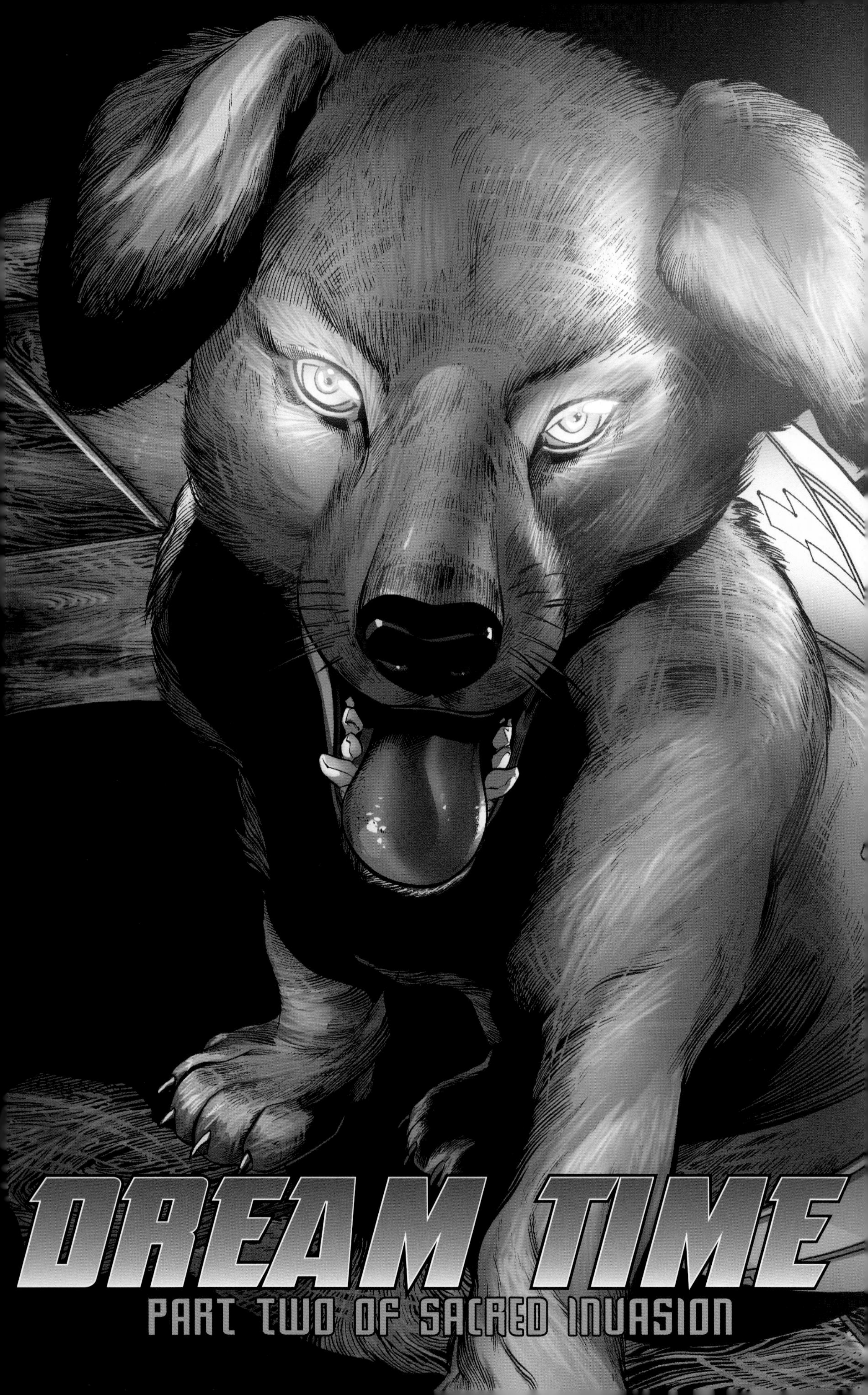
DREAM TIME
PART TWO OF SACRED INVASION

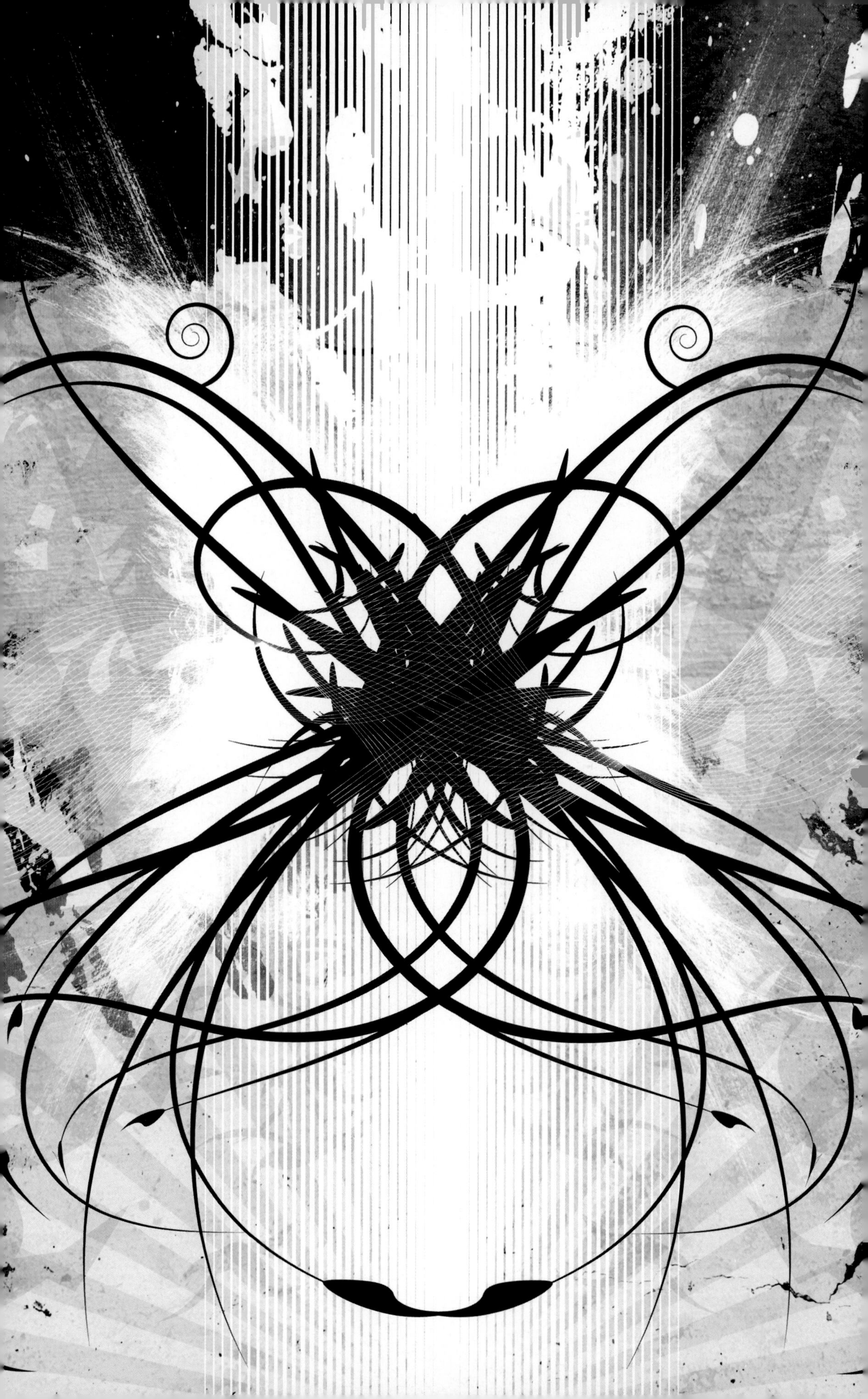

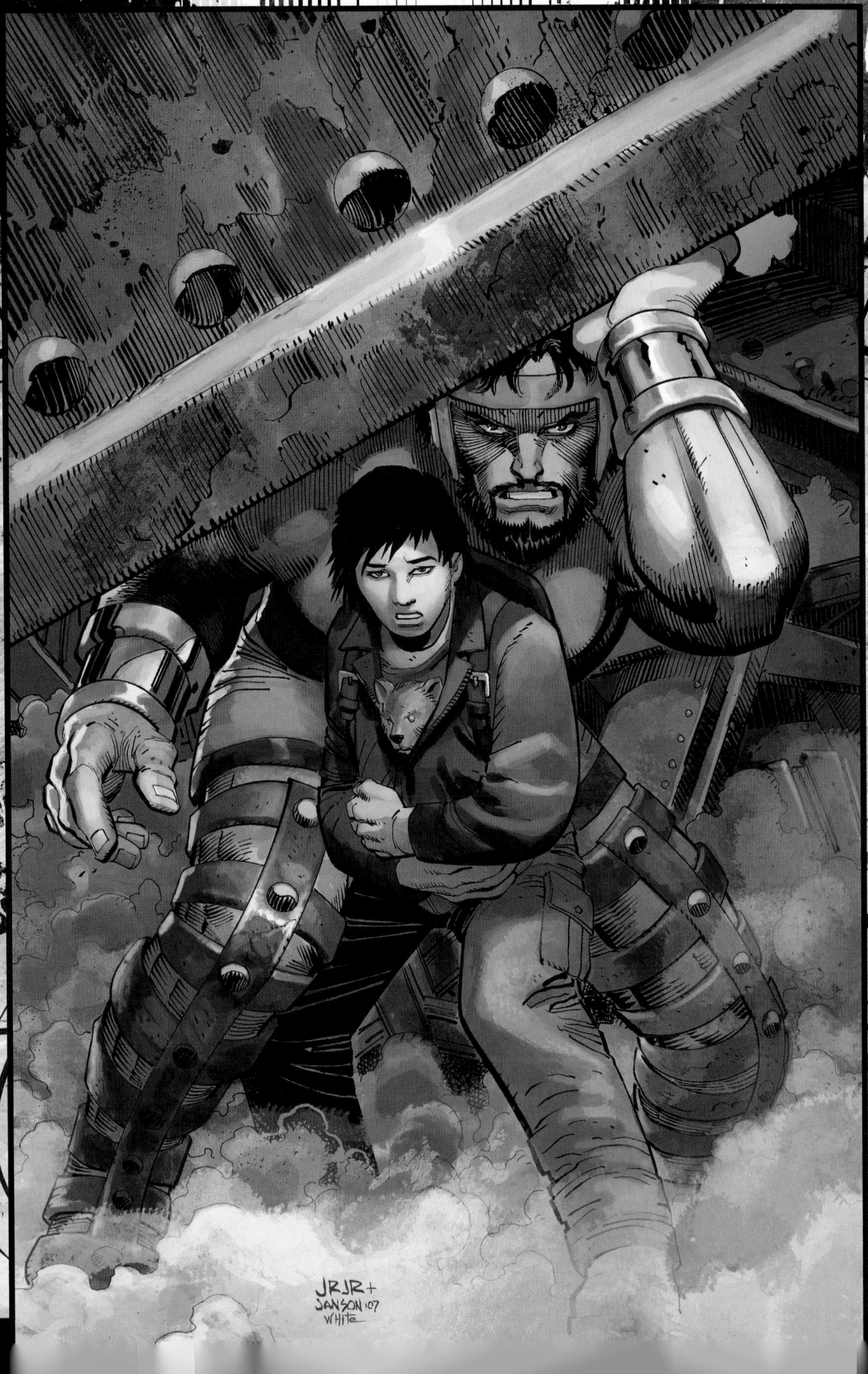
JRJR+
JANSON '07
WHITE

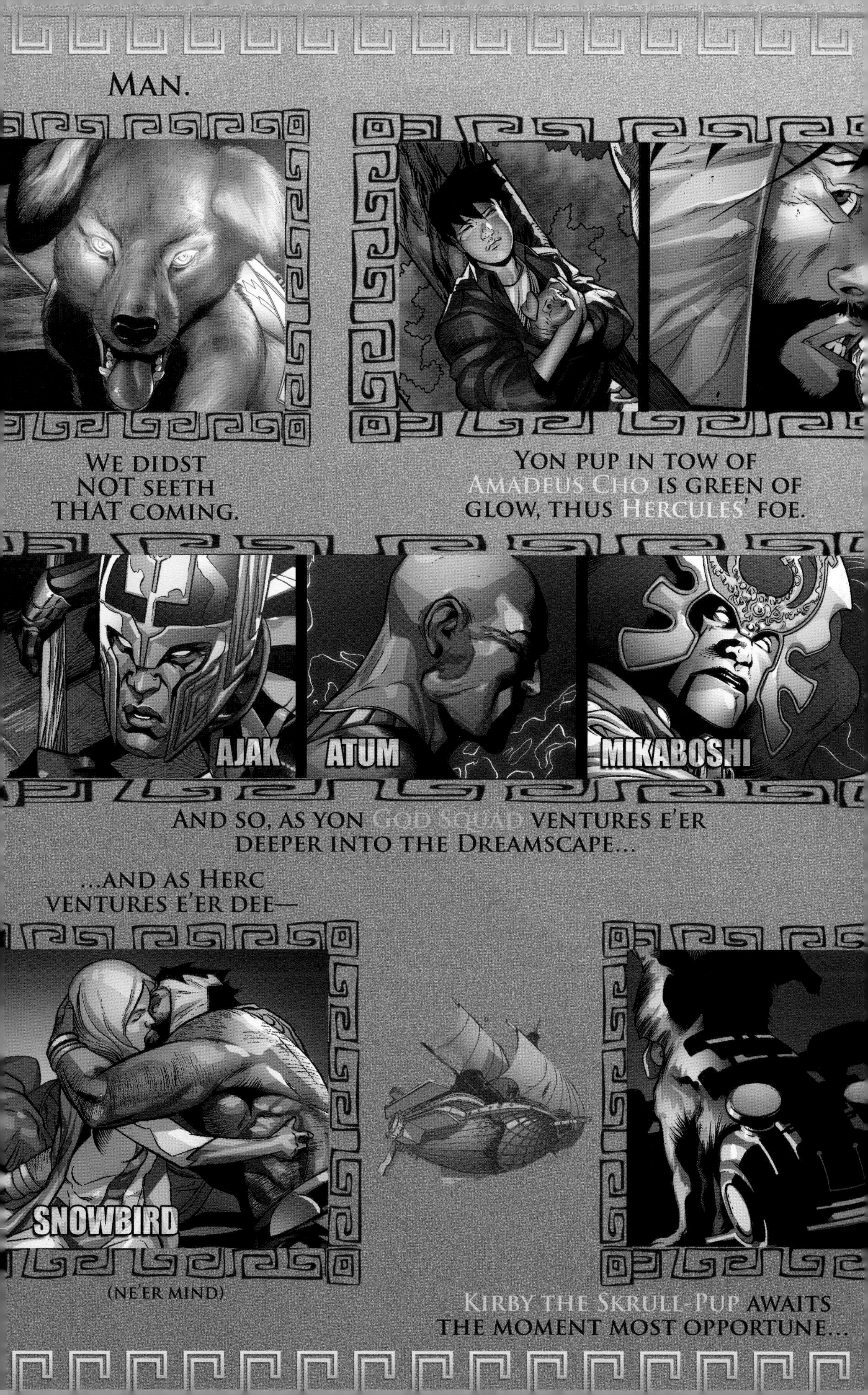
MAN.
WE DIDST NOT SEETH THAT COMING.
YON PUP IN TOW OF AMADEUS CHO IS GREEN OF GLOW, THUS HERCULES' FOE.
AJAK
ATUM
MIKABOSHI
AND SO, AS YON GOD SQUAD VENTURES E'ER DEEPER INTO THE DREAMSCAPE...
...AND AS HERC VENTURES E'ER DEE—
SNOWBIRD
(NE'ER MIND)
KIRBY THE SKRULL-PUP AWAITS THE MOMENT MOST OPPORTUNE...

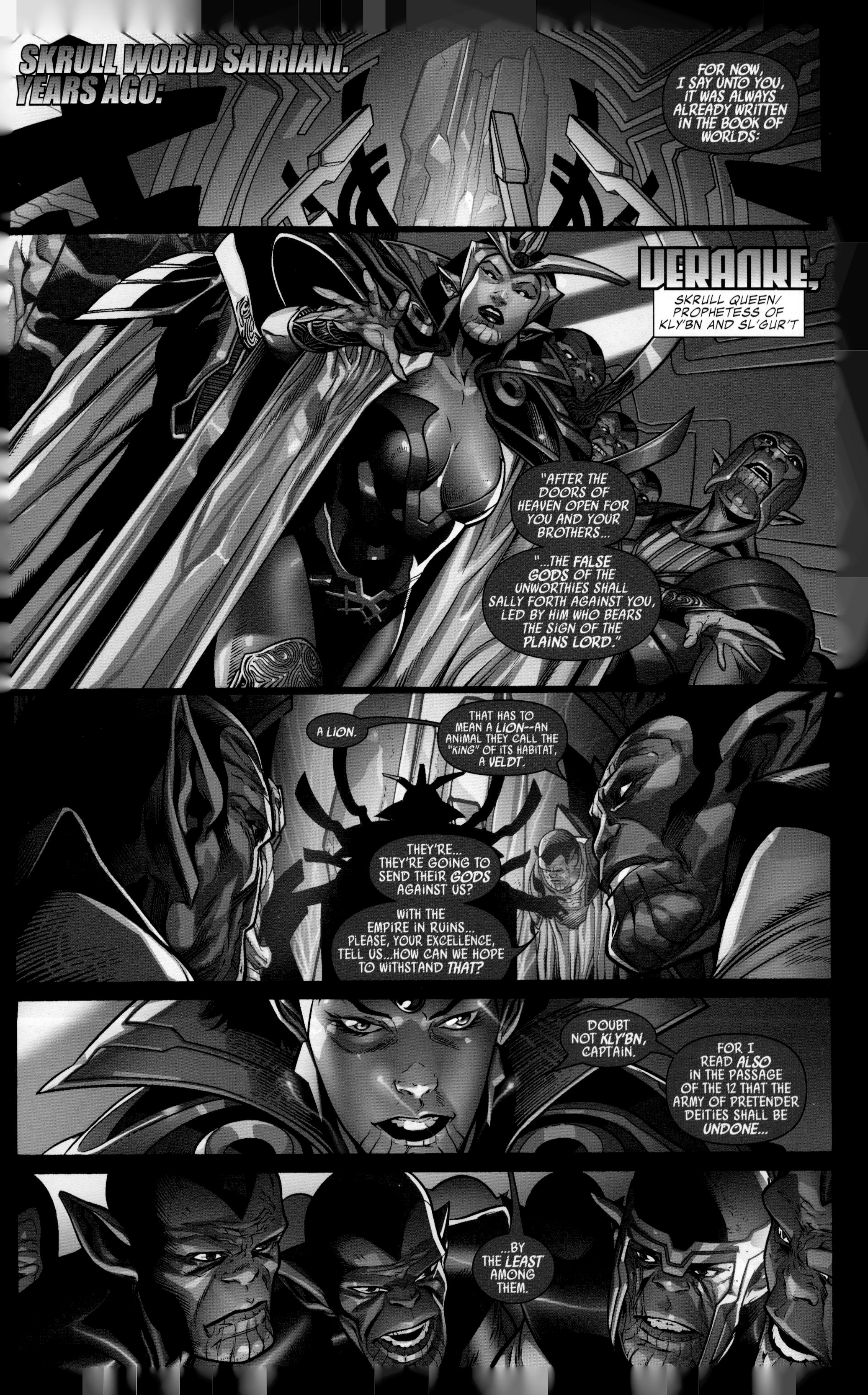
SKRULL WORLD SATRIANI. YEARS AGO:
FOR NOW, I SAY UNTO YOU, IT WAS ALWAYS ALREADY WRITTEN IN THE BOOK OF WORLDS:
VERANKE,
SKRULL QUEEN/ PROPHETESS OF KLY'BN AND SL'GUR'T
"AFTER THE DOORS OF HEAVEN OPEN FOR YOU AND YOUR BROTHERS...
"...THE FALSE GODS OF THE UNWORTHIES SHALL SALLY FORTH AGAINST YOU, LED BY HIM WHO BEARS THE SIGN OF THE PLAINS LORD."
A LION.
THAT HAS TO MEAN A LION--AN ANIMAL THEY CALL THE "KING" OF ITS HABITAT, A VELDT.
THEY'RE... THEY'RE GOING TO SEND THEIR GODS AGAINST US?
WITH THE EMPIRE IN RUINS... PLEASE, YOUR EXCELLENCE, TELL US...HOW CAN WE HOPE TO WITHSTAND THAT?
DOUBT NOT KLY'BN, CAPTAIN.
FOR I READ ALSO IN THE PASSAGE OF THE 12 THAT THE ARMY OF PRETENDER DEITIES SHALL BE UNDONE...
...BY THE LEAST AMONG THEM.

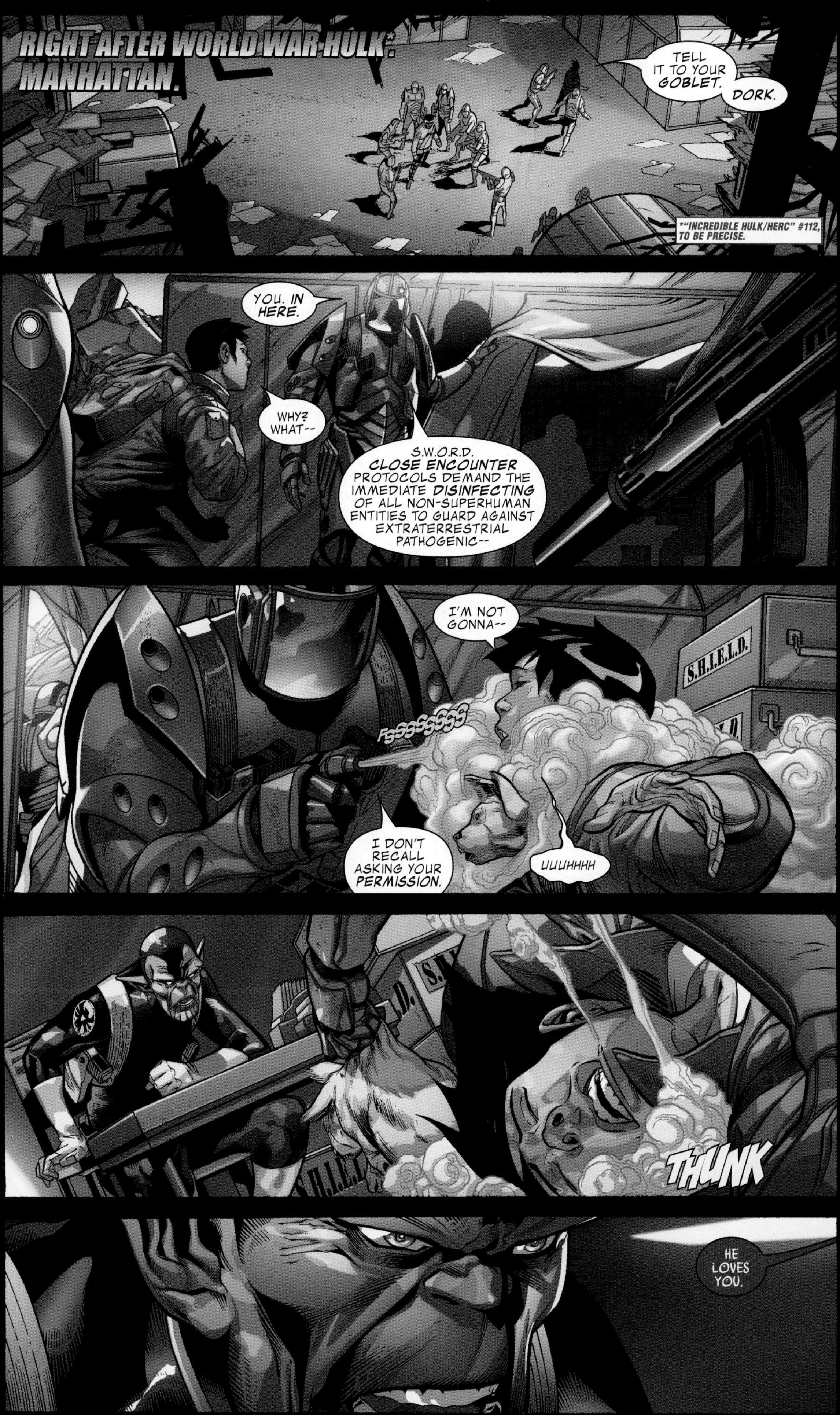
RIGHT AFTER WORLD WAR HULK*: MANHATTAN.
TELL IT TO YOUR GOBLET.
DORK.
*"INCREDIBLE HULK/HERC" #112, TO BE PRECISE.
YOU. IN HERE.
WHY? WHAT--
S.W.O.R.D. CLOSE ENCOUNTER PROTOCOLS DEMAND THE IMMEDIATE DISINFECTING OF ALL NON-SUPERHUMAN ENTITIES TO GUARD AGAINST EXTRATERRESTRIAL PATHOGENIC--
I'M NOT GONNA--
S.H.I.E.L.D.
FSSSSSSSS
I DON'T RECALL ASKING YOUR PERMISSION.
UUUHHHH
THUNK
HE LOVES YOU.

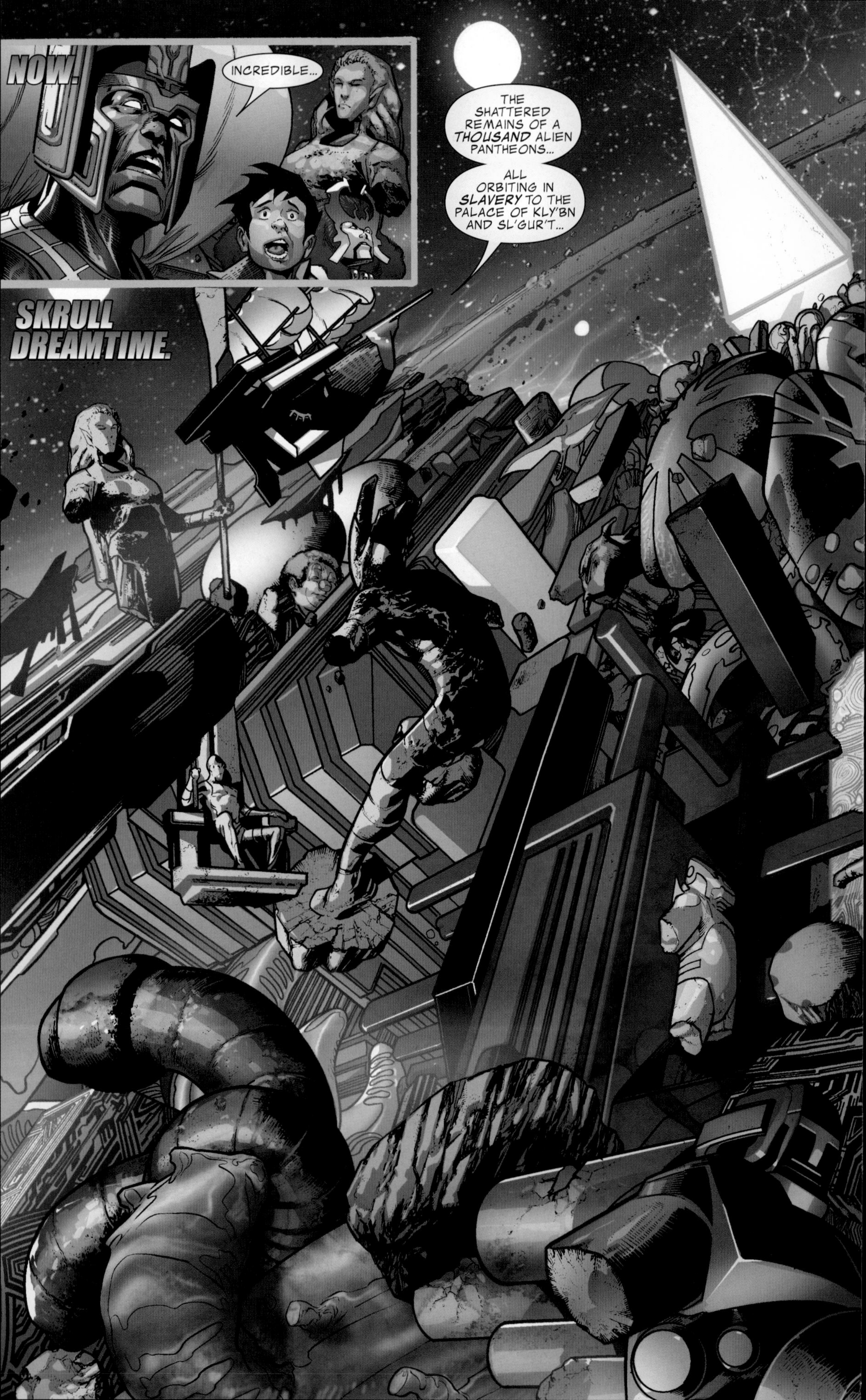
NOW.
INCREDIBLE...
THE SHATTERED REMAINS OF A THOUSAND ALIEN PANTHEONS...
ALL ORBITING IN SLAVERY TO THE PALACE OF KLY'BN AND SL'GUR'T...
SKRULL DREAMTIME.

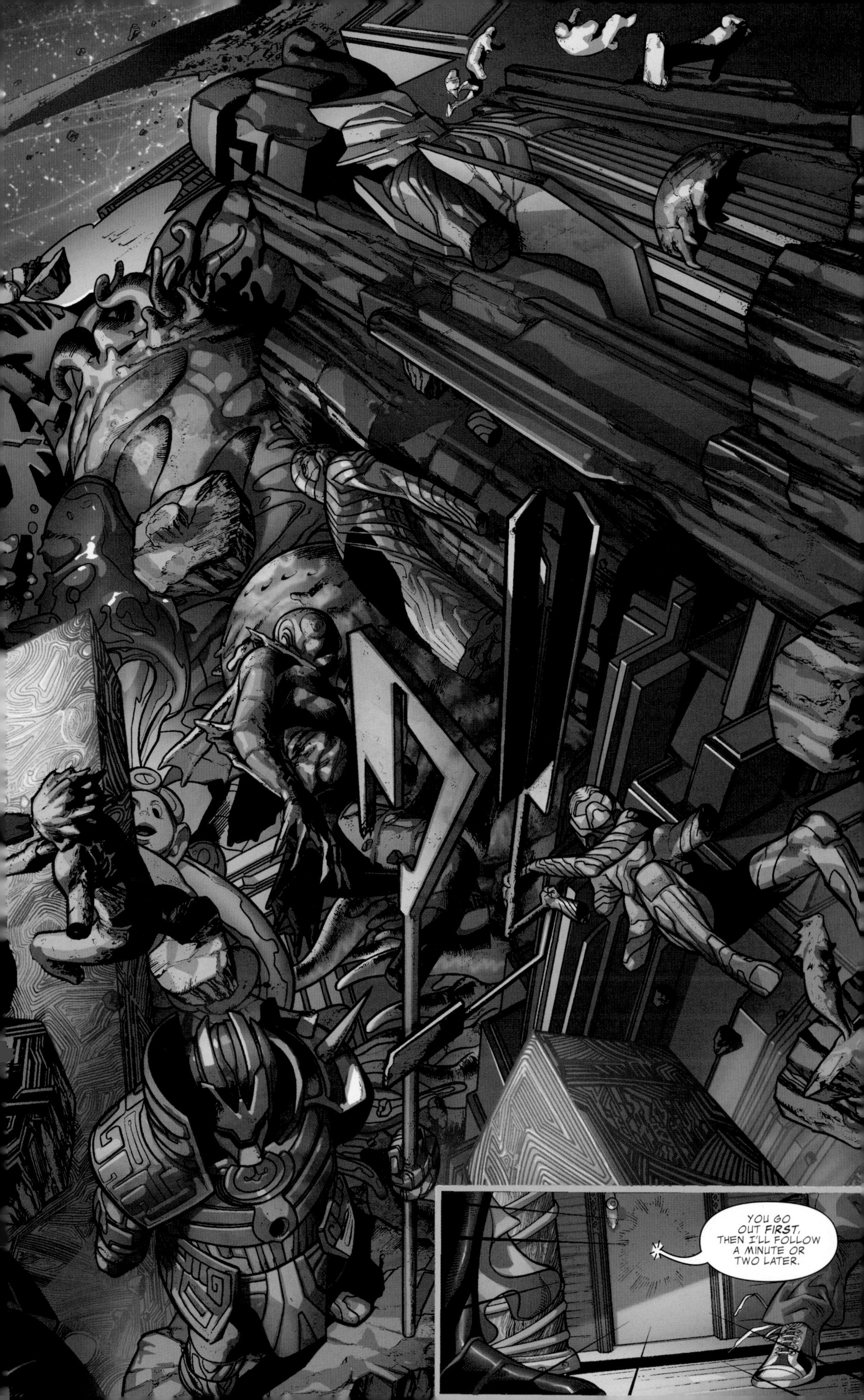
YOU GO OUT FIRST, THEN I'LL FOLLOW A MINUTE OR TWO LATER.

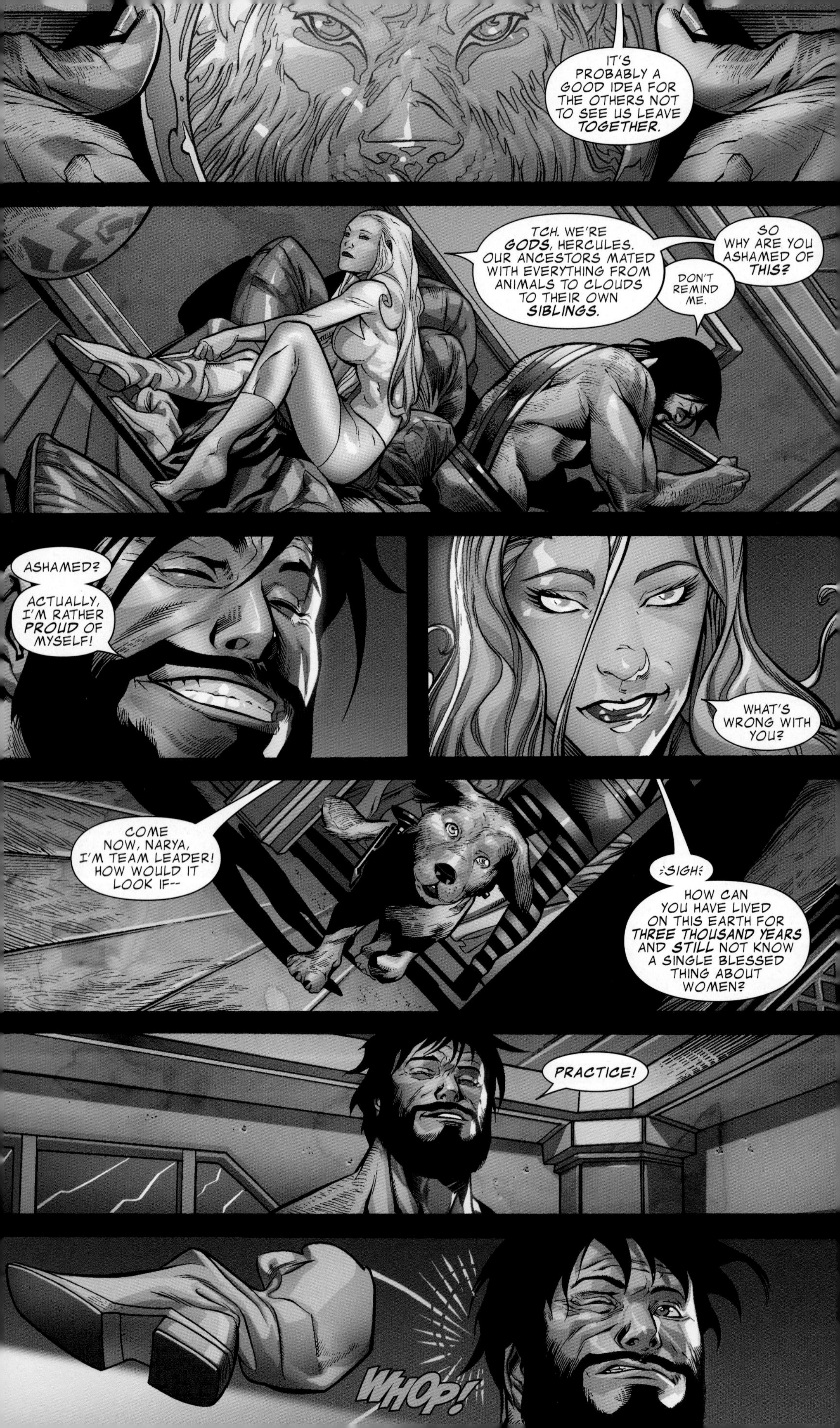

IT'S PROBABLY A GOOD IDEA FOR THE OTHERS NOT TO SEE US LEAVE TOGETHER.
TCH. WE'RE GODS, HERCULES. OUR ANCESTORS MATED WITH EVERYTHING FROM ANIMALS TO CLOUDS TO THEIR OWN SIBLINGS.
DON'T REMIND ME.
SO WHY ARE YOU ASHAMED OF THIS?
ASHAMED?
ACTUALLY, I'M RATHER PROUD OF MYSELF!
WHAT'S WRONG WITH YOU?
COME NOW, NARYA, I'M TEAM LEADER! HOW WOULD IT LOOK IF--
SIGH
HOW CAN YOU HAVE LIVED ON THIS EARTH FOR THREE THOUSAND YEARS AND STILL NOT KNOW A SINGLE BLESSED THING ABOUT WOMEN?
PRACTICE!
WHOP!

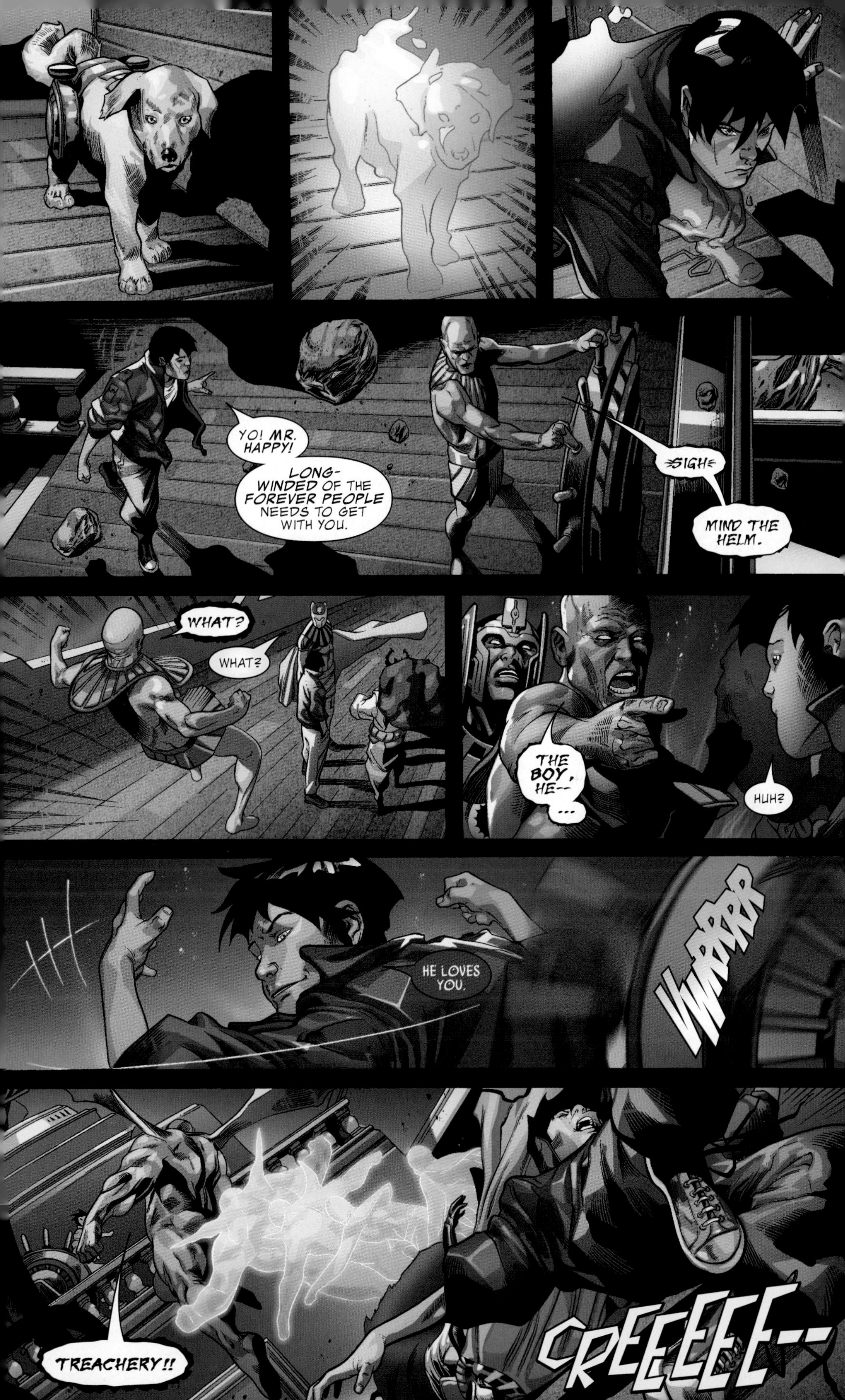
YO! MR. HAPPY!
LONG-WINDED OF THE FOREVER PEOPLE NEEDS TO GET WITH YOU.
SIGH
MIND THE HELM.
WHAT?
WHAT?
THE BOY, HE-- ...
HUH?
HE LOVES YOU.
WHRRRR
TREACHERY!!
CREEEEEE--

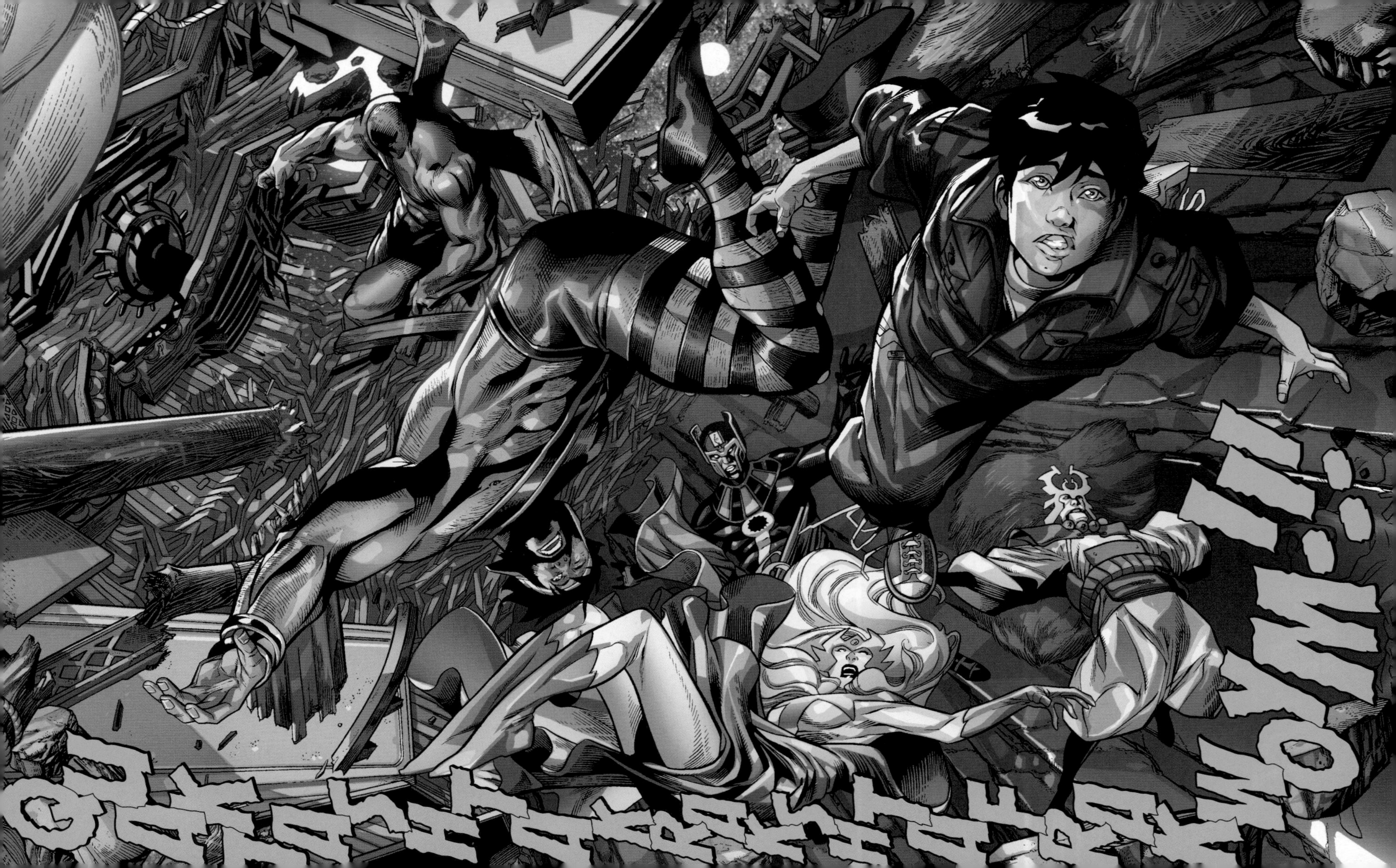
QUAKTOASHTOAKRAKSHTOAFROAKWOYM!!!

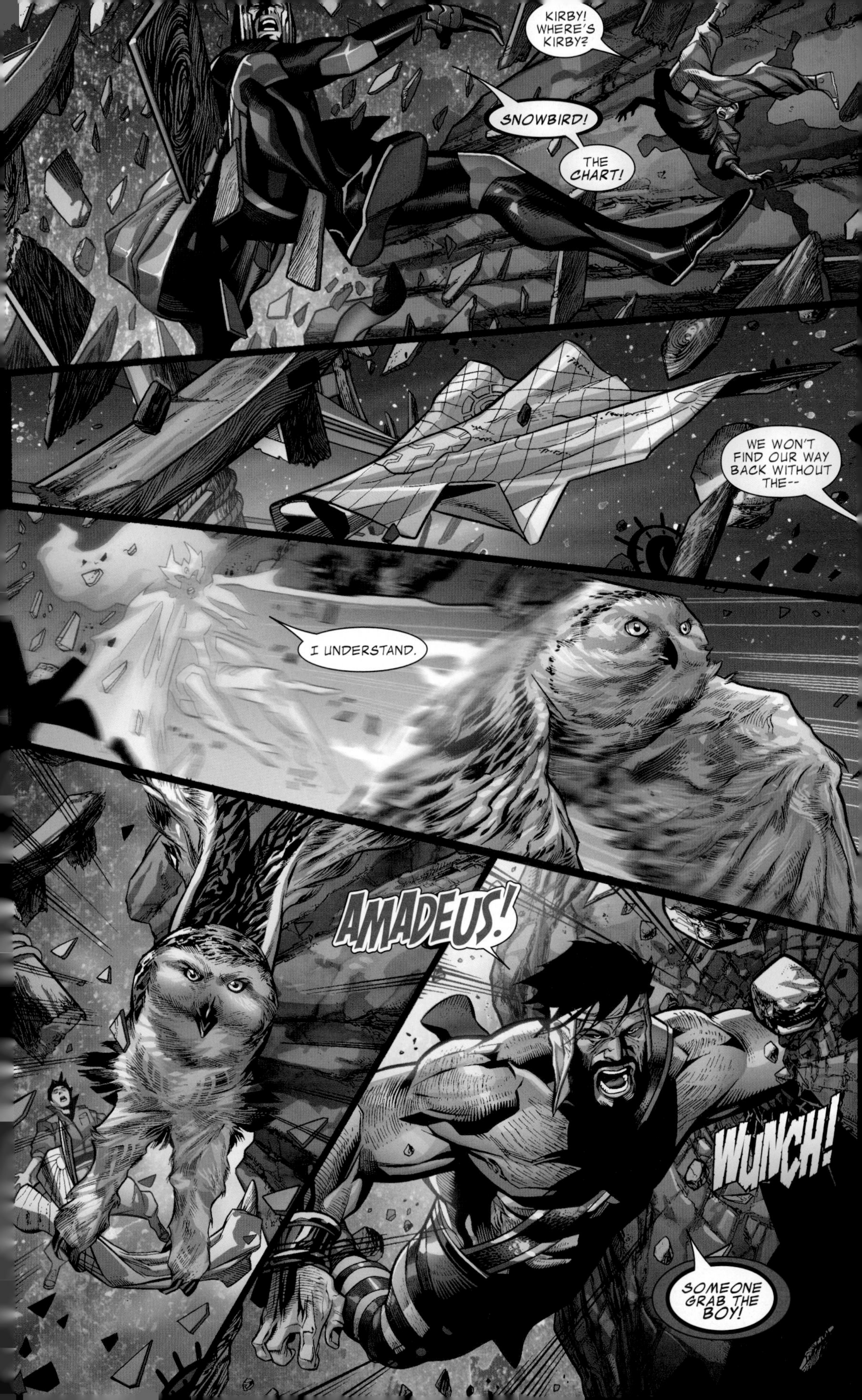
KIRBY! WHERE'S KIRBY?
SNOWBIRD!
THE CHART!
WE WON'T FIND OUR WAY BACK WITHOUT THE--
I UNDERSTAND.
AMADEUS!
WUNCH!
SOMEONE GRAB THE BOY!

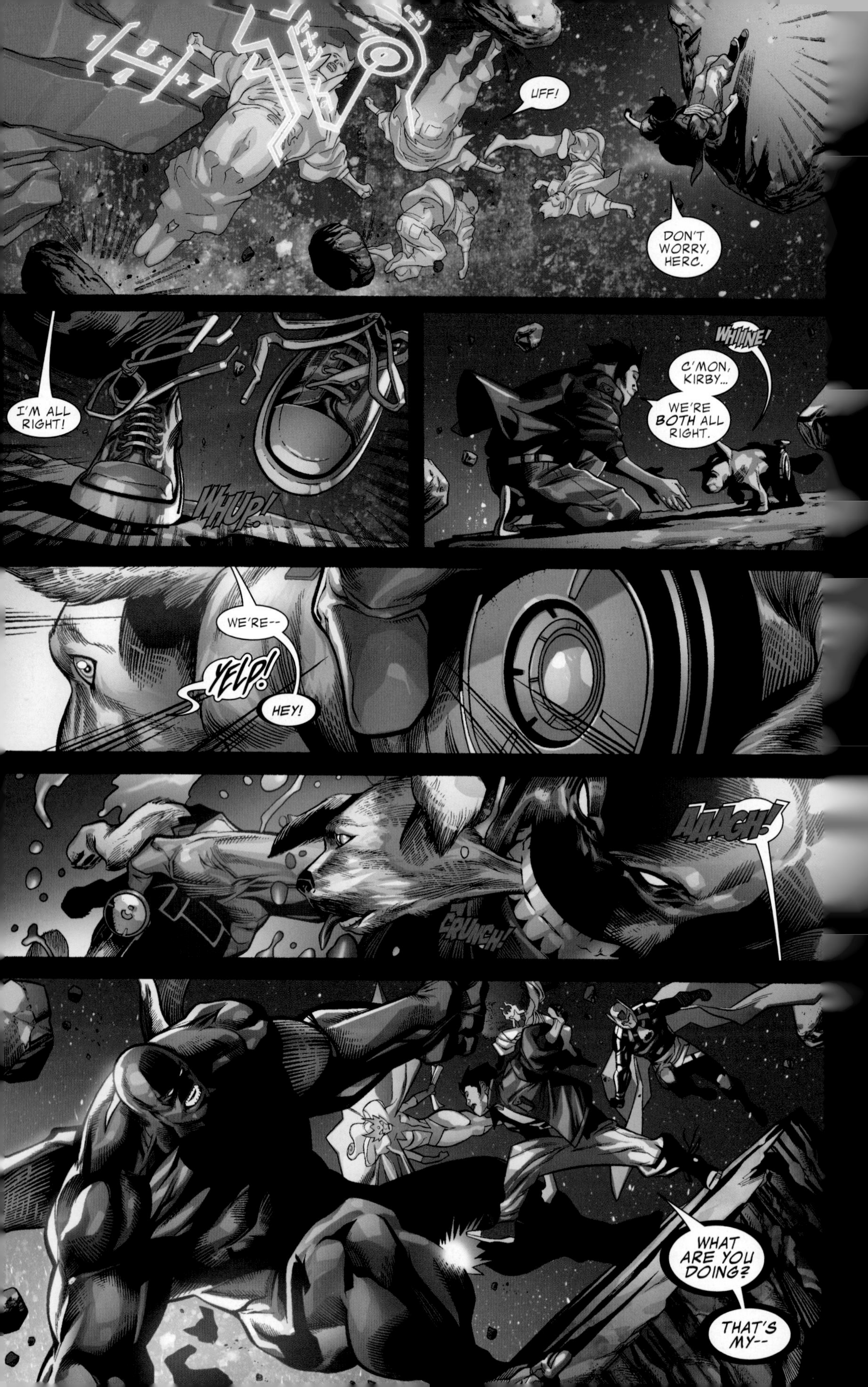
UFF!
DON'T WORRY, HERC.
I'M ALL RIGHT!
WHUP!
WHIINE!
C'MON, KIRBY...
WE'RE BOTH ALL RIGHT.
WE'RE--
YELP!
HEY!
AAAGH!
CRUNCH!
WHAT ARE YOU DOING?
THAT'S MY--

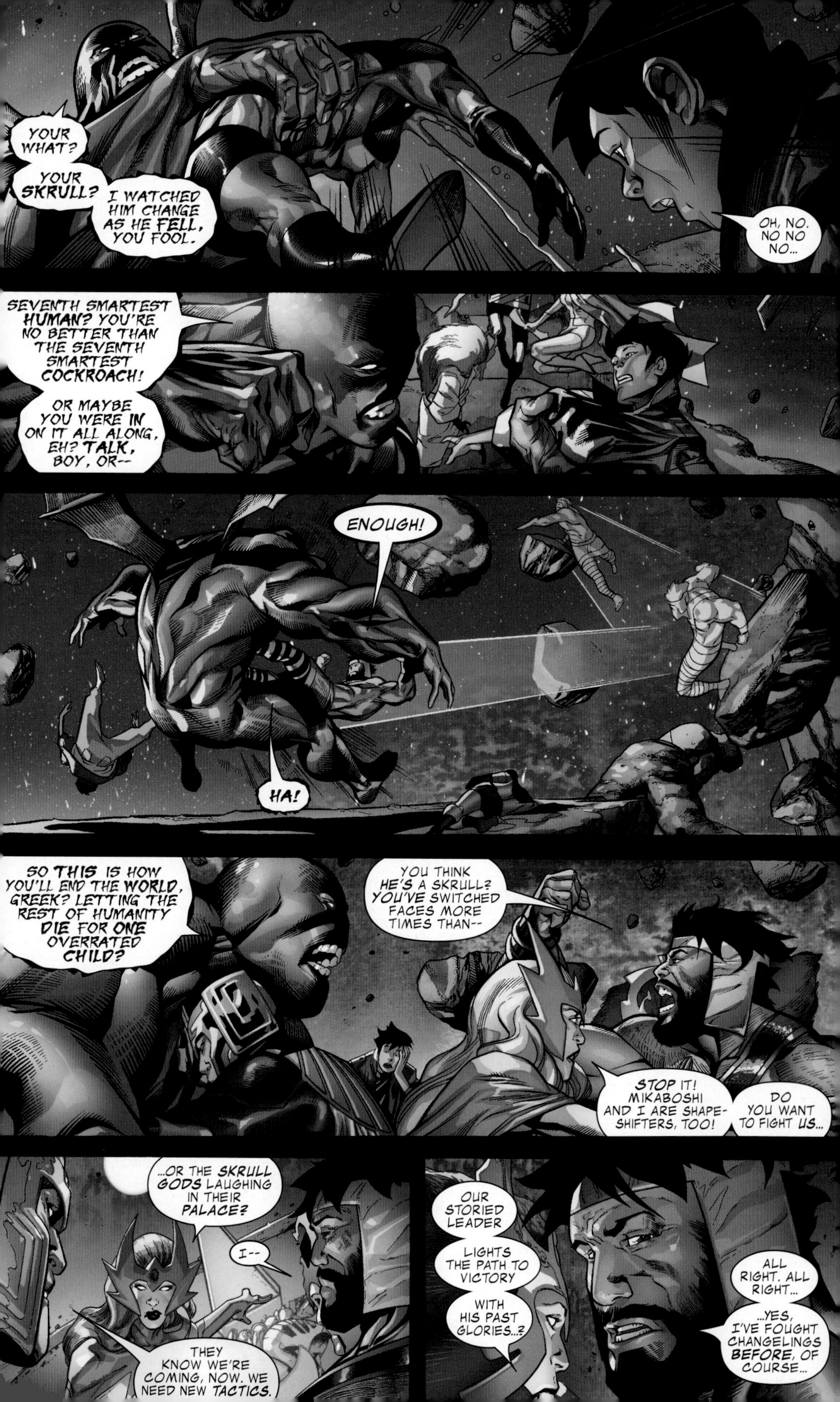
YOUR WHAT?
YOUR SKRULL? I WATCHED HIM CHANGE AS HE FELL, YOU FOOL.
OH, NO. NO NO NO...
SEVENTH SMARTEST HUMAN? YOU'RE NO BETTER THAN THE SEVENTH SMARTEST COCKROACH!
OR MAYBE YOU WERE IN ON IT ALL ALONG, EH? TALK, BOY, OR--
ENOUGH!
HA!
SO THIS IS HOW YOU'LL END THE WORLD, GREEK? LETTING THE REST OF HUMANITY DIE FOR ONE OVERRATED CHILD?
YOU THINK HE'S A SKRULL? YOU'VE SWITCHED FACES MORE TIMES THAN--
STOP IT! MIKABOSHI AND I ARE SHAPE-SHIFTERS, TOO!
DO YOU WANT TO FIGHT US...
...OR THE SKRULL GODS LAUGHING IN THEIR PALACE?
I--
THEY KNOW WE'RE COMING, NOW. WE NEED NEW TACTICS.
OUR STORIED LEADER
LIGHTS THE PATH TO VICTORY
WITH HIS PAST GLORIES...?
ALL RIGHT. ALL RIGHT...
...YES, I'VE FOUGHT CHANGELINGS BEFORE, OF COURSE...

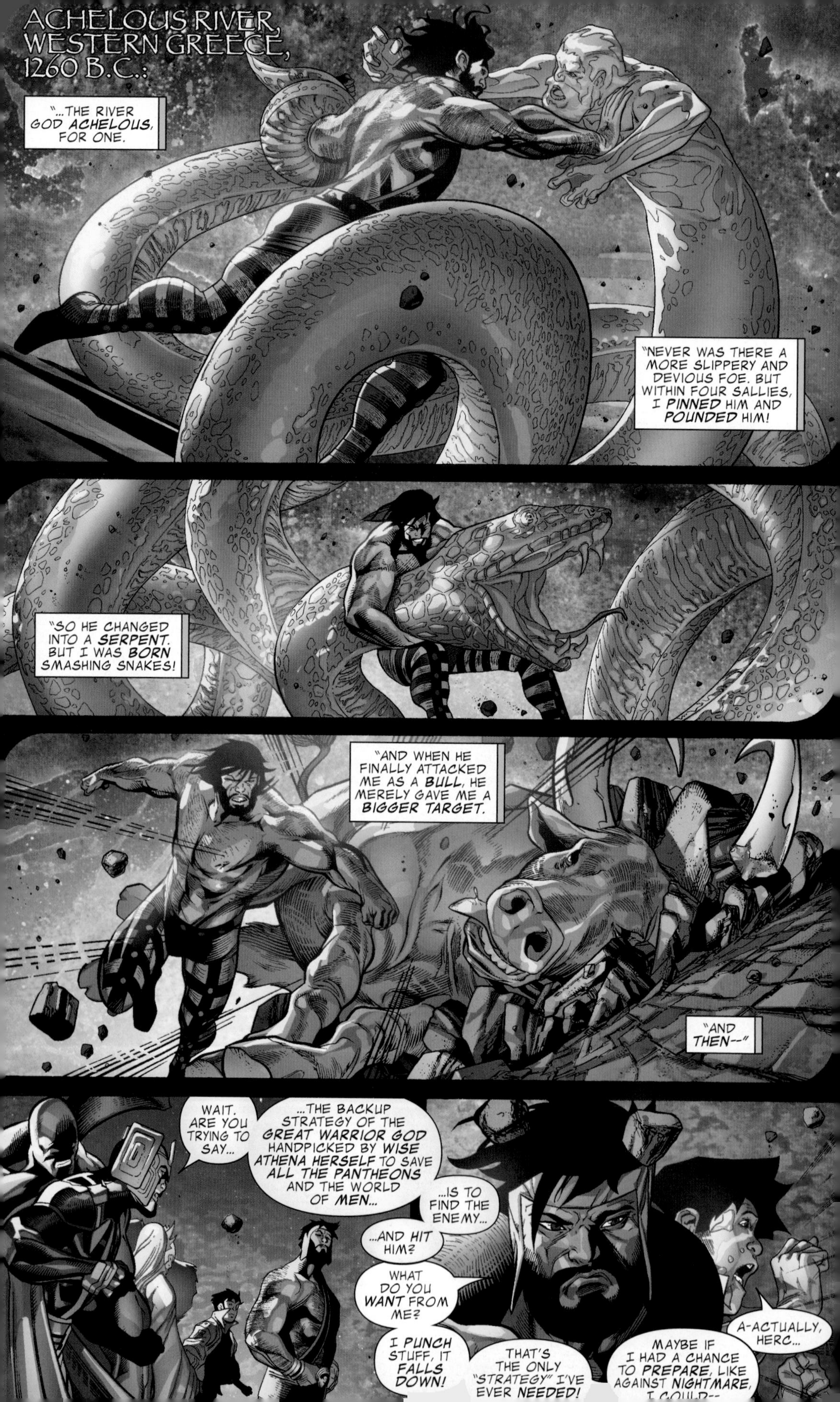

ACHELOUS RIVER, WESTERN GREECE, 1260 B.C.:
"...THE RIVER GOD ACHELOUS, FOR ONE.
"NEVER WAS THERE A MORE SLIPPERY AND DEVIOUS FOE. BUT WITHIN FOUR SALLIES, I PINNED HIM AND POUNDED HIM!
"SO HE CHANGED INTO A SERPENT. BUT I WAS BORN SMASHING SNAKES!
"AND WHEN HE FINALLY ATTACKED ME AS A BULL, HE MERELY GAVE ME A BIGGER TARGET.
"AND THEN--"
WAIT. ARE YOU TRYING TO SAY...
...THE BACKUP STRATEGY OF THE GREAT WARRIOR GOD HANDPICKED BY WISE ATHENA HERSELF TO SAVE ALL THE PANTHEONS AND THE WORLD OF MEN...
...IS TO FIND THE ENEMY...
...AND HIT HIM?
WHAT DO YOU WANT FROM ME?
I PUNCH STUFF, IT FALLS DOWN!
THAT'S THE ONLY "STRATEGY" I'VE EVER NEEDED!
MAYBE IF I HAD A CHANCE TO PREPARE, LIKE AGAINST NIGHTMARE, I COULD--
A-ACTUALLY, HERC...

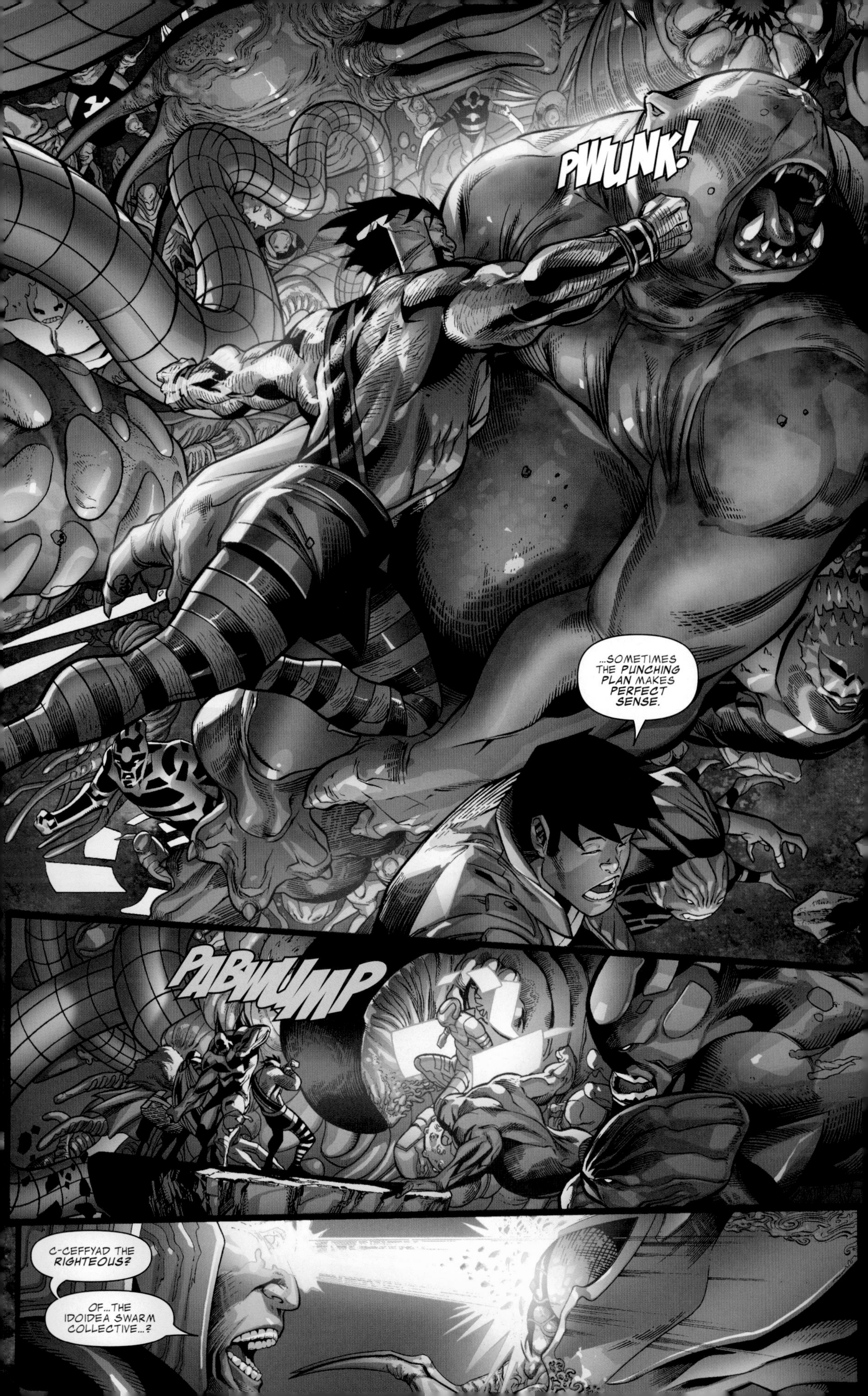
PWUNK!
...SOMETIMES THE PUNCHING PLAN MAKES PERFECT SENSE.
PABWUMP
C-CEFFYAD THE RIGHTEOUS?
OF...THE IDOIDEA SWARM COLLECTIVE...?

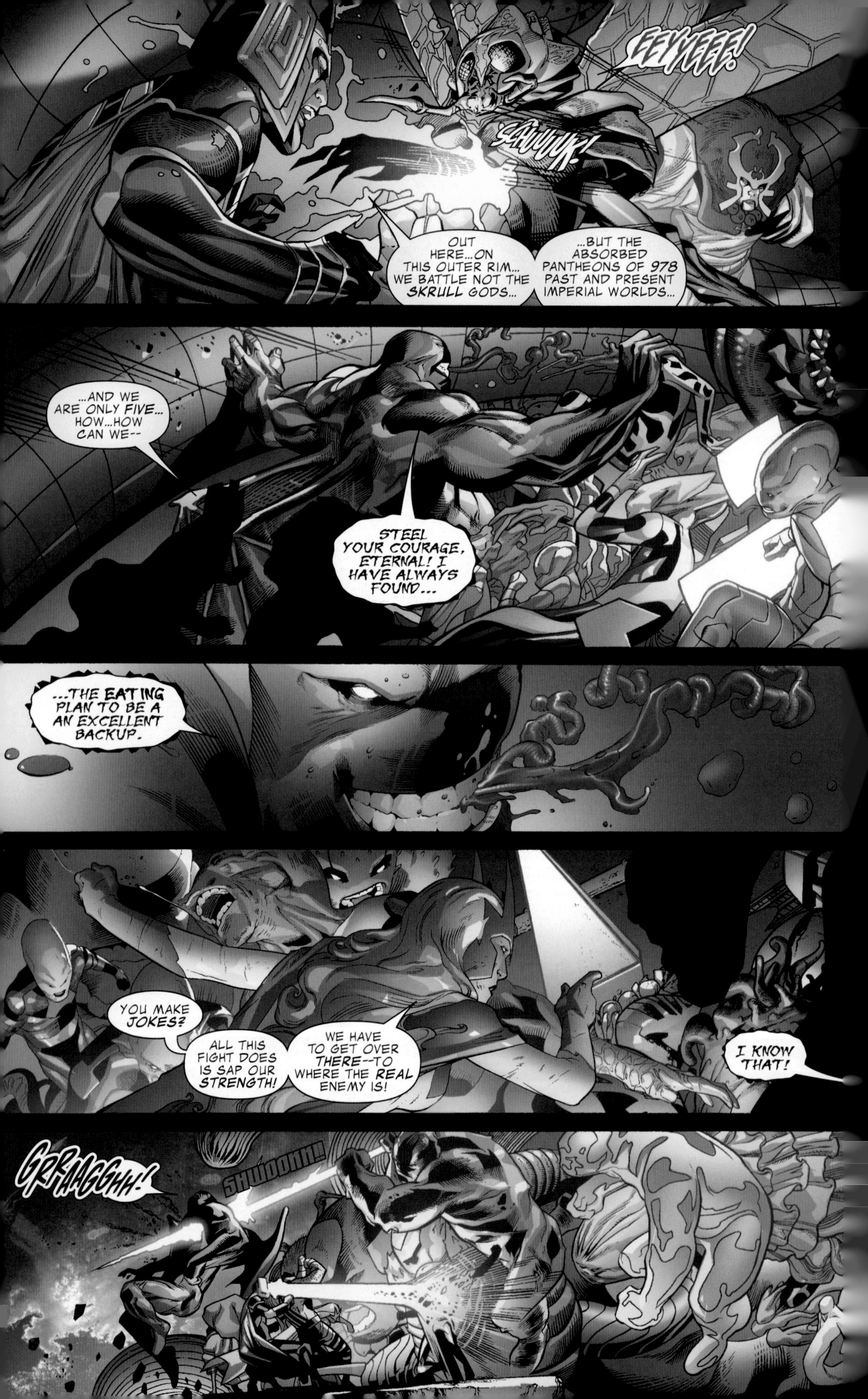
EEYEEE!
SCHUUUK!
OUT HERE...ON THIS OUTER RIM... WE BATTLE NOT THE SKRULL GODS...
...BUT THE ABSORBED PANTHEONS OF 978 PAST AND PRESENT IMPERIAL WORLDS...
...AND WE ARE ONLY FIVE... HOW...HOW CAN WE--
STEEL YOUR COURAGE, ETERNAL! I HAVE ALWAYS FOUND...
...THE EATING PLAN TO BE A AN EXCELLENT BACKUP.
YOU MAKE JOKES?
ALL THIS FIGHT DOES IS SAP OUR STRENGTH!
WE HAVE TO GET OVER THERE--TO WHERE THE REAL ENEMY IS!
I KNOW THAT!
GRRAAGGHH!
SHWOOMM!

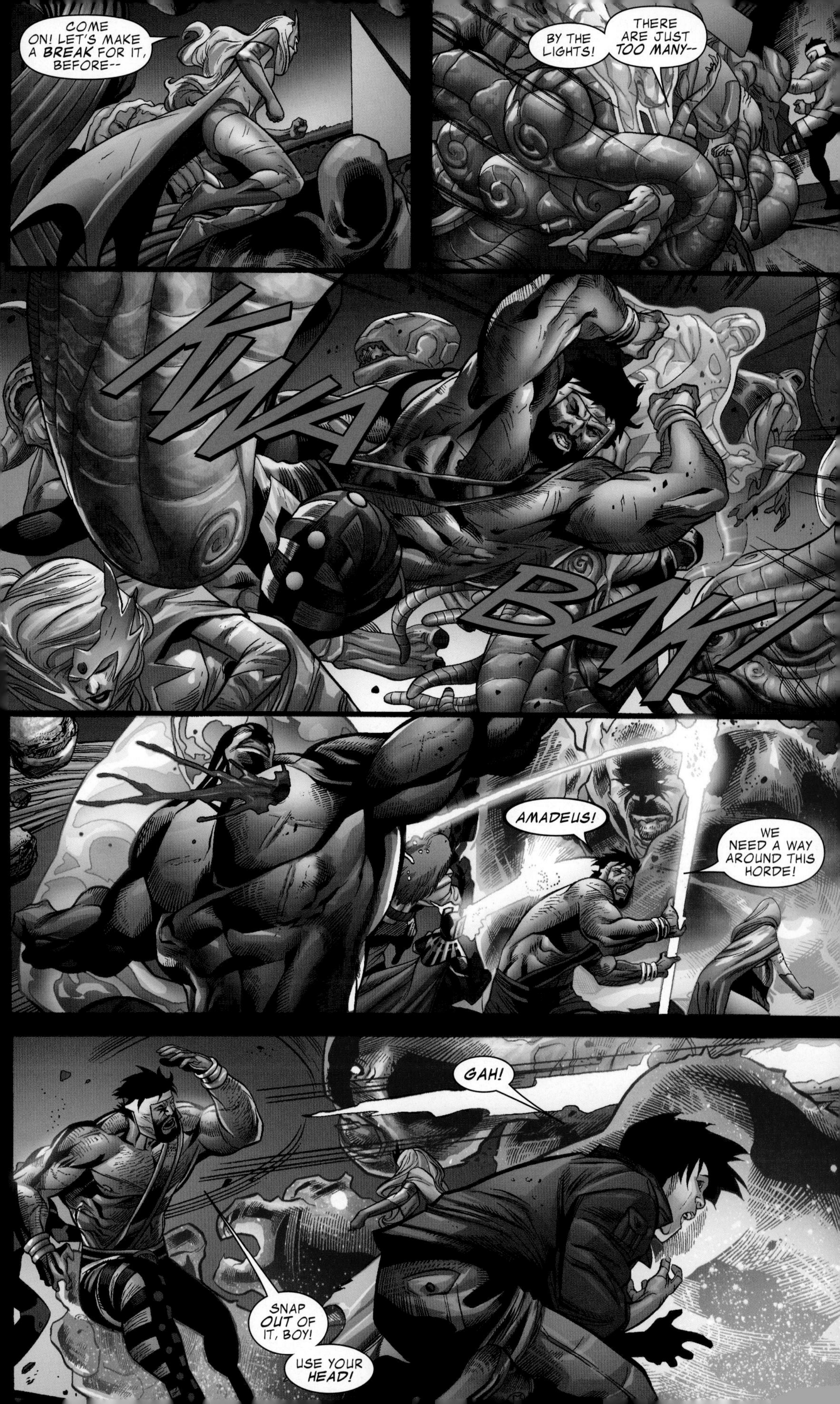
COME ON! LET'S MAKE A BREAK FOR IT, BEFORE--
BY THE LIGHTS!
THERE ARE JUST TOO MANY--
KWA
BAK!
AMADEUS!
WE NEED A WAY AROUND THIS HORDE!
GAH!
SNAP OUT OF IT, BOY!
USE YOUR HEAD!

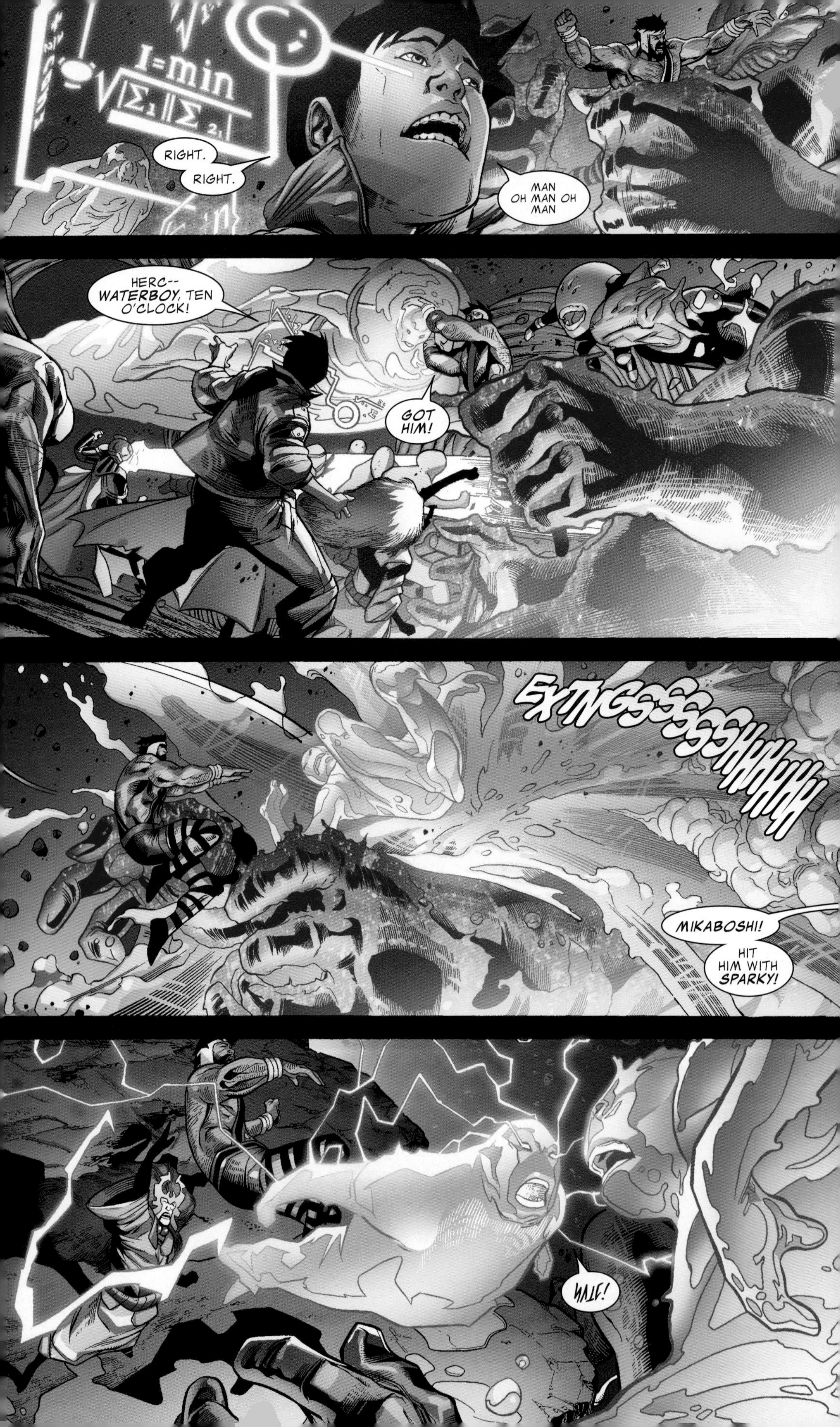
I=min
RIGHT.
RIGHT.
MAN OH MAN OH MAN
HERC-- WATERBOY, TEN O'CLOCK!
GOT HIM!
EXTNGSSSSSHHHHHH
MIKABOSHI!
HIT HIM WITH SPARKY!

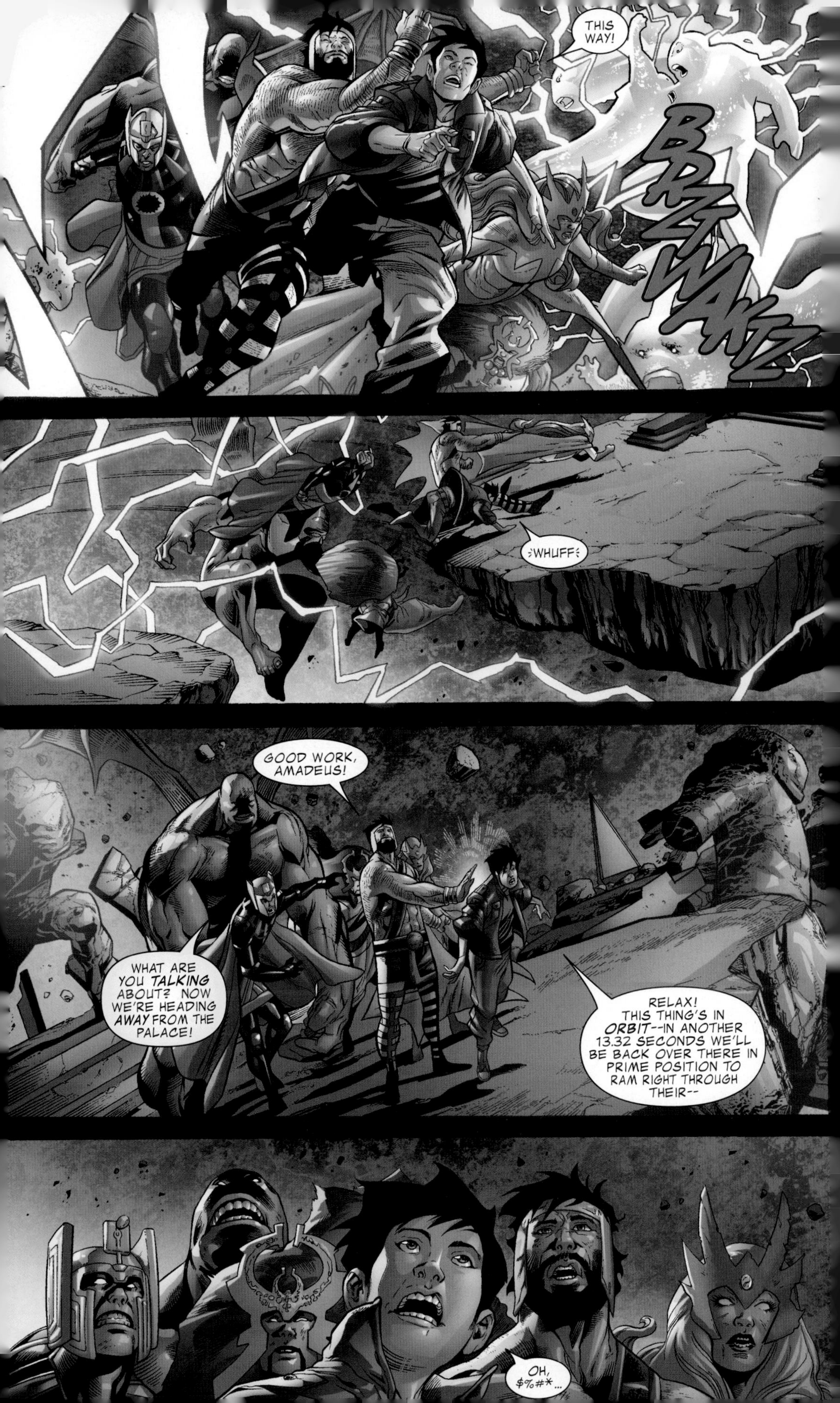
THIS WAY!
BRZZT WAKZZ
WHUFF
GOOD WORK, AMADEUS!
WHAT ARE YOU TALKING ABOUT? NOW WE'RE HEADING AWAY FROM THE PALACE!
RELAX! THIS THING'S IN ORBIT--IN ANOTHER 13.32 SECONDS WE'LL BE BACK OVER THERE IN PRIME POSITION TO RAM RIGHT THROUGH THEIR--
OH, $%#*...

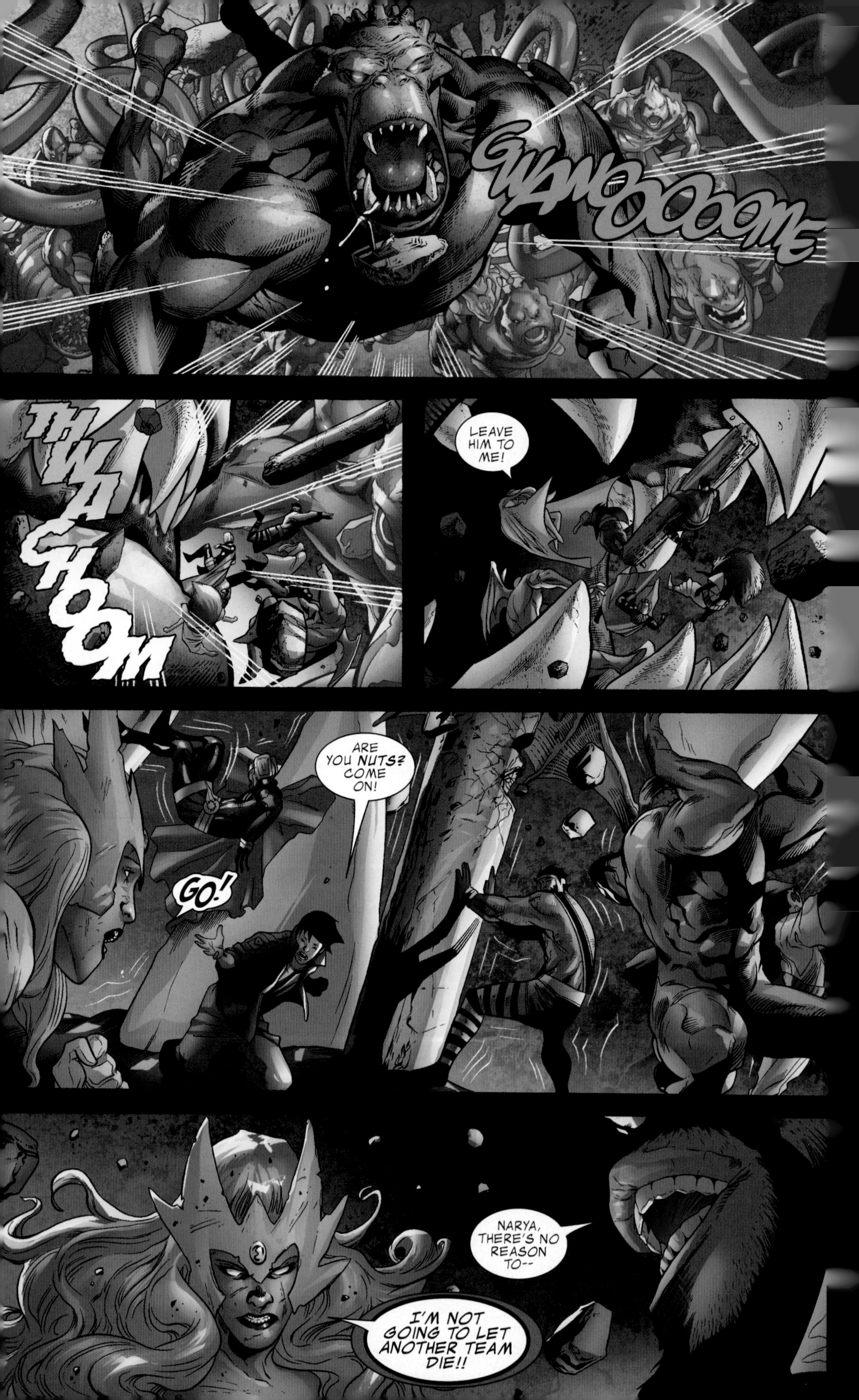

GUAAOOOOOOOM
THWACHOOM
LEAVE HIM TO ME!
ARE YOU NUTS? COME ON!
GO!
NARYA, THERE'S NO REASON TO--
I'M NOT GOING TO LET ANOTHER TEAM DIE!!

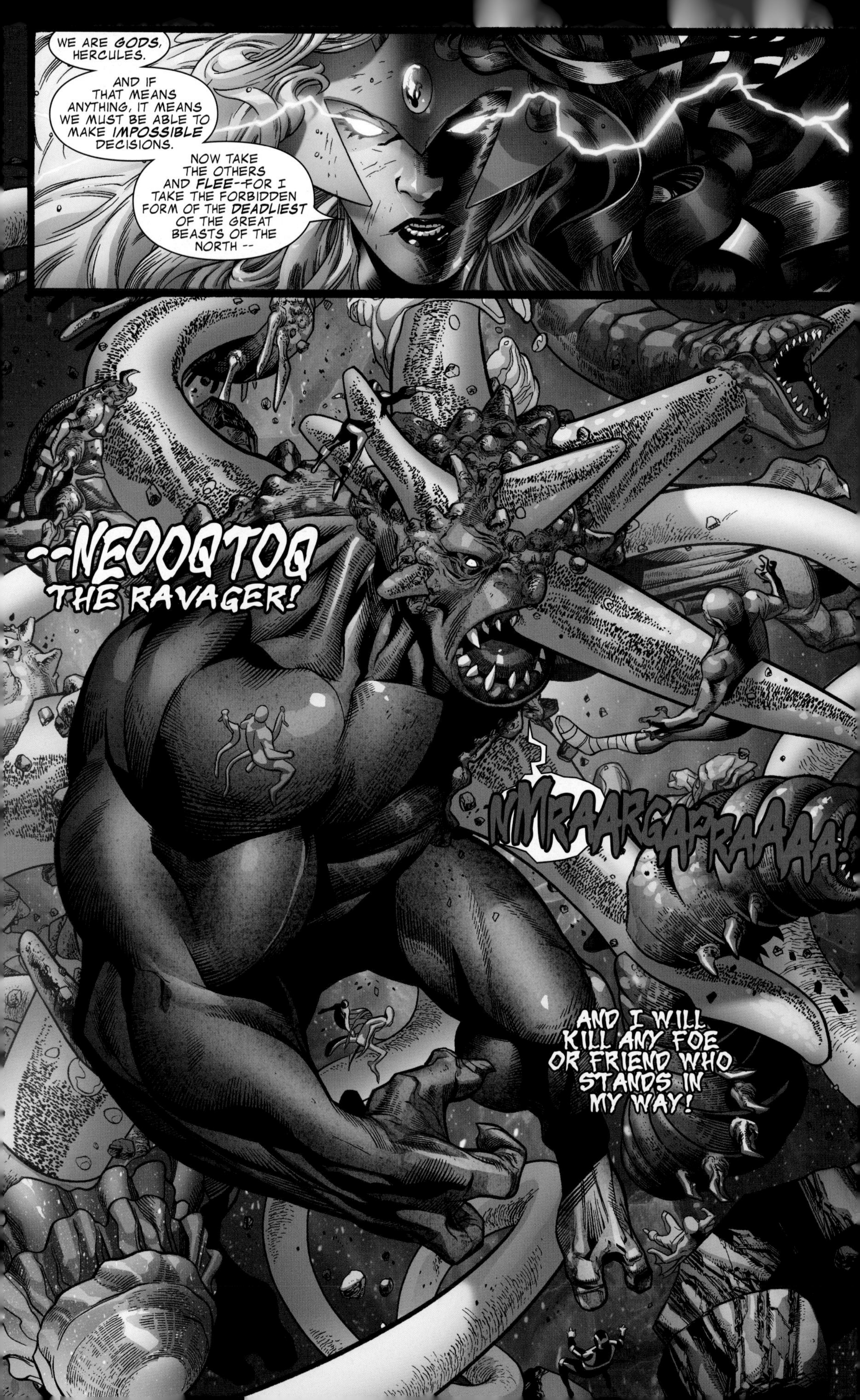
WE ARE GODS, HERCULES.
AND IF THAT MEANS ANYTHING, IT MEANS WE MUST BE ABLE TO MAKE IMPOSSIBLE DECISIONS.
NOW TAKE THE OTHERS AND FLEE--FOR I TAKE THE FORBIDDEN FORM OF THE DEADLIEST OF THE GREAT BEASTS OF THE NORTH --
--NEOOQTOQ THE RAVAGER!
NMRAARGAPRAAAAA!
AND I WILL KILL ANY FOE OR FRIEND WHO STANDS IN MY WAY!

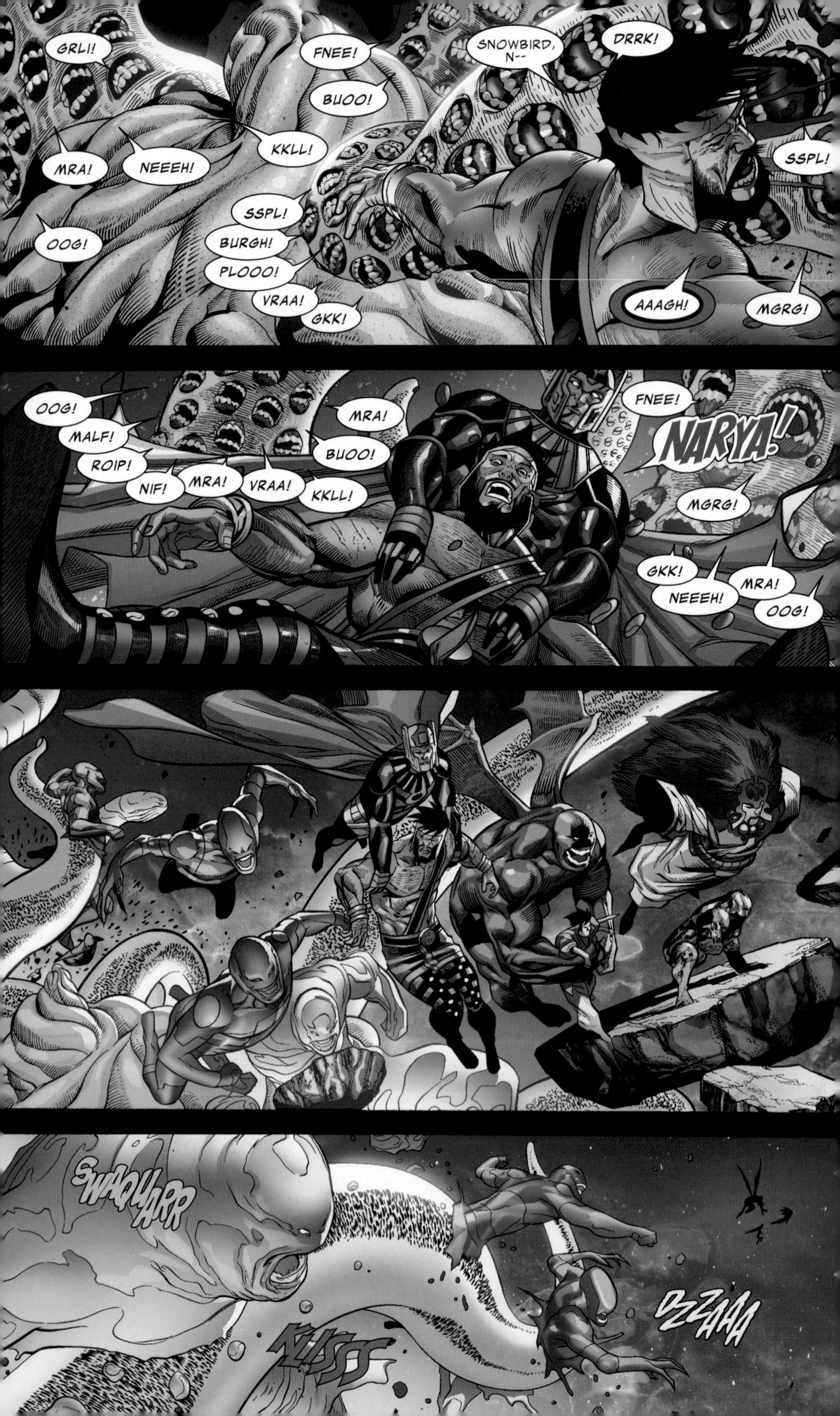

GRLI!
FNEE!
SNOWBIRD, N--
DRRK!
BUOO!
KKLL!
MRA!
NEEEH!
SSPL!
SSPL!
BURGH!
PLOOO!
OOG!
VRAA!
GKK!
AAAGH!
MGRG!
OOG!
MALF!
ROIP!
NIF!
MRA!
VRAA!
MRA!
BUOO!
KKLL!
FNEE!
NARYA!
MGRG!
GKK!
NEEEH!
MRA!
OOG!
SWAQUARR
KLISSS
DZZAAA

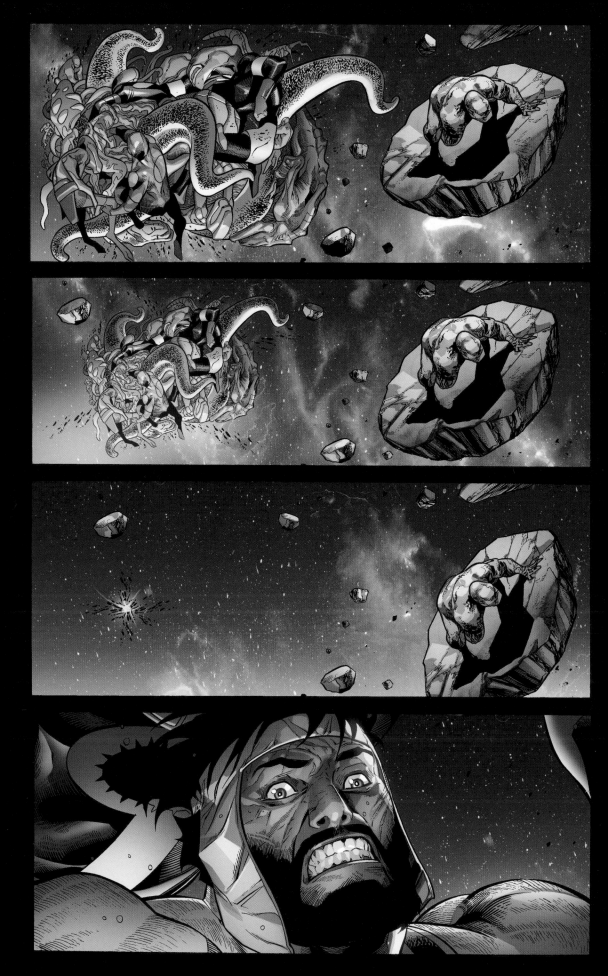

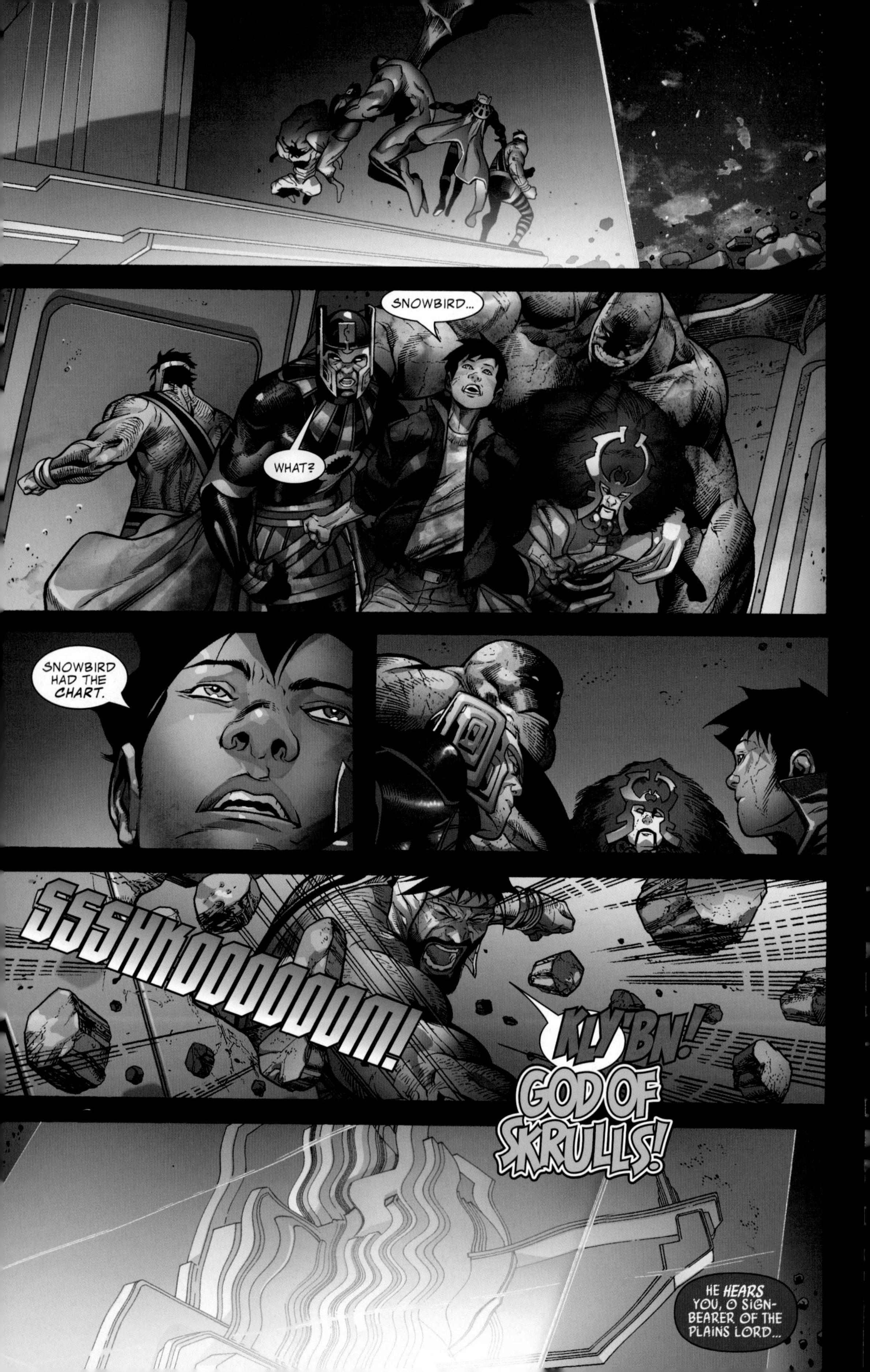
SNOWBIRD...
WHAT?
SNOWBIRD HAD THE CHART.
SSSHKOOOOOOOM!
KLY'BN! GOD OF SKRULLS!
HE HEARS YOU, O SIGN-BEARER OF THE PLAINS LORD...

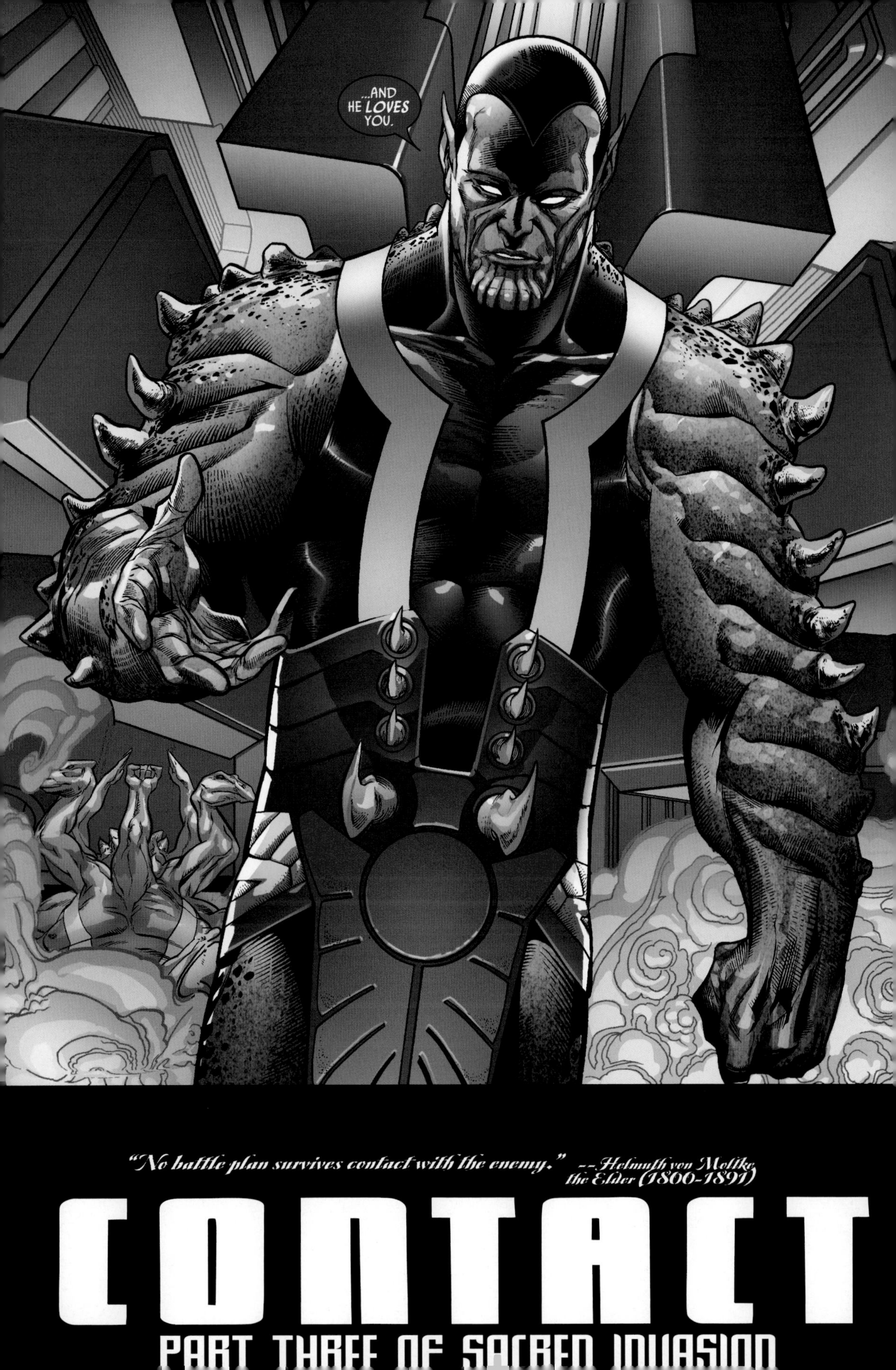
...AND HE LOVES YOU.

"No battle plan survives contact with the enemy." --*Helmuth von Moltke the Elder (1800-1891)*

CONTACT

PART THREE OF SACRED INVASION

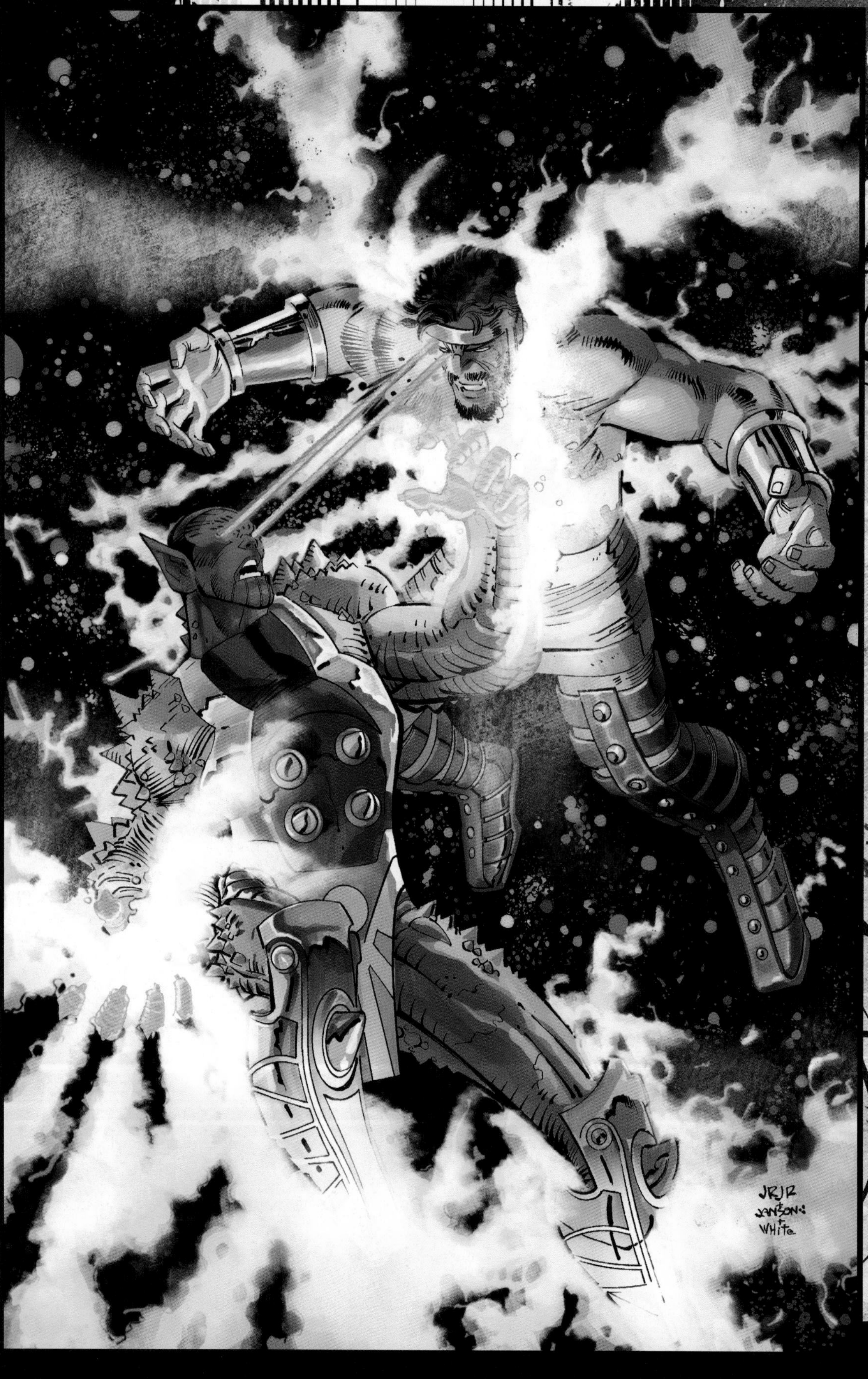
JRJR
JANSON
+
WHITE

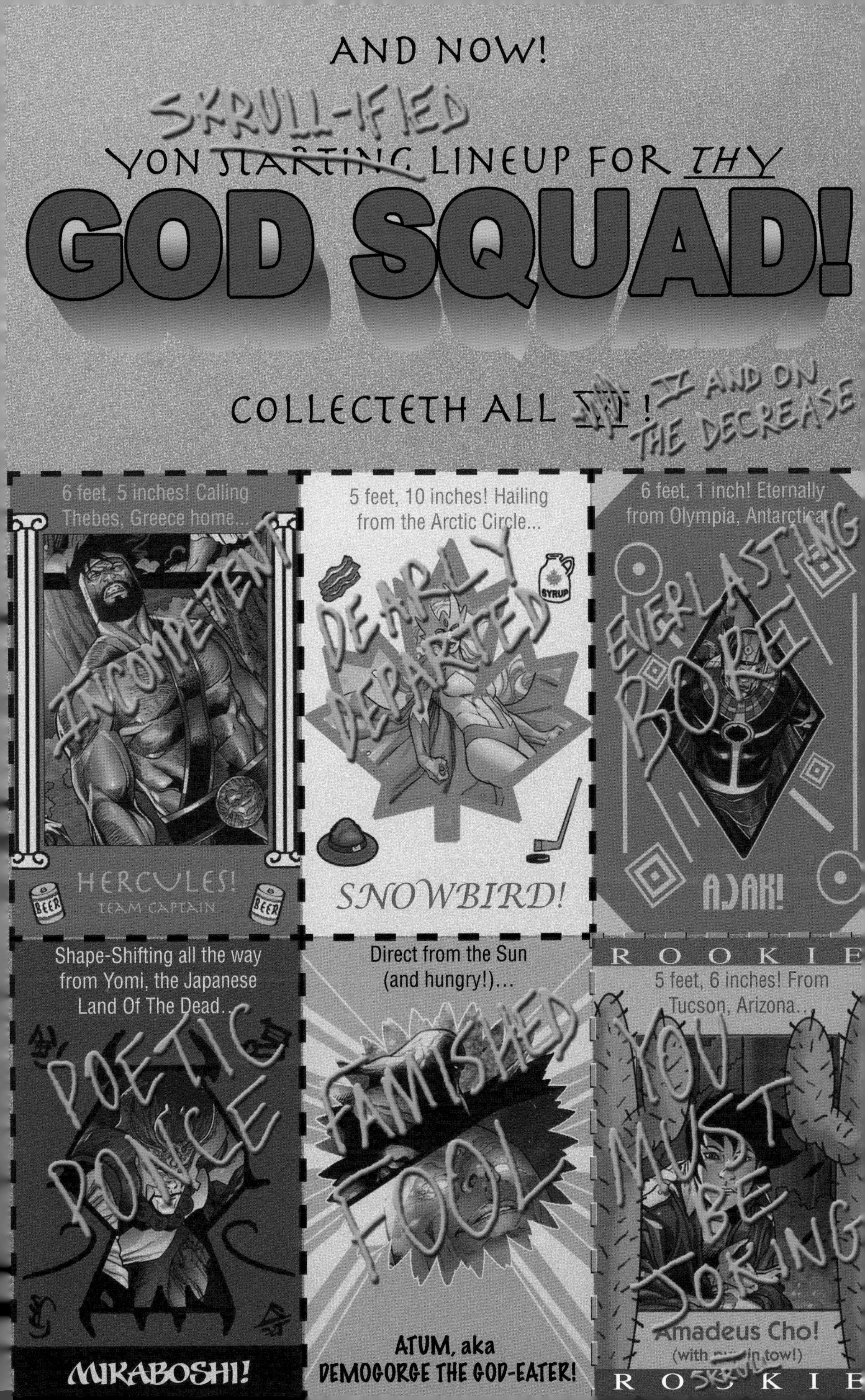

AND NOW!
YON ~~STARTING~~ SKRULL-IFIED LINEUP FOR THY
GOD SQUAD!
COLLECTETH ALL ~~VI~~ V ! AND ON THE DECREASE
6 feet, 5 inches! Calling Thebes, Greece home...
INCOMPETENT
BEER
HERCULES!
TEAM CAPTAIN
5 feet, 10 inches! Hailing from the Arctic Circle...
DEARLY DEPARTED
SYRUP
SNOWBIRD!
6 feet, 1 inch! Eternally from Olympia, Antarctica!
EVERLASTING BORE
AJAK!
Shape-Shifting all the way from Yomi, the Japanese Land Of The Dead...
POETIC PONCE
MIKABOSHI!
Direct from the Sun (and hungry!)...
FAMISHED FOOL
ATUM, aka
DEMOGORGE THE GOD-EATER!
ROOKIE
5 feet, 6 inches! From Tucson, Arizona...
YOU MUST BE JOKING
Amadeus Cho!
(with in tow!)
SKRULL
ROOKIE

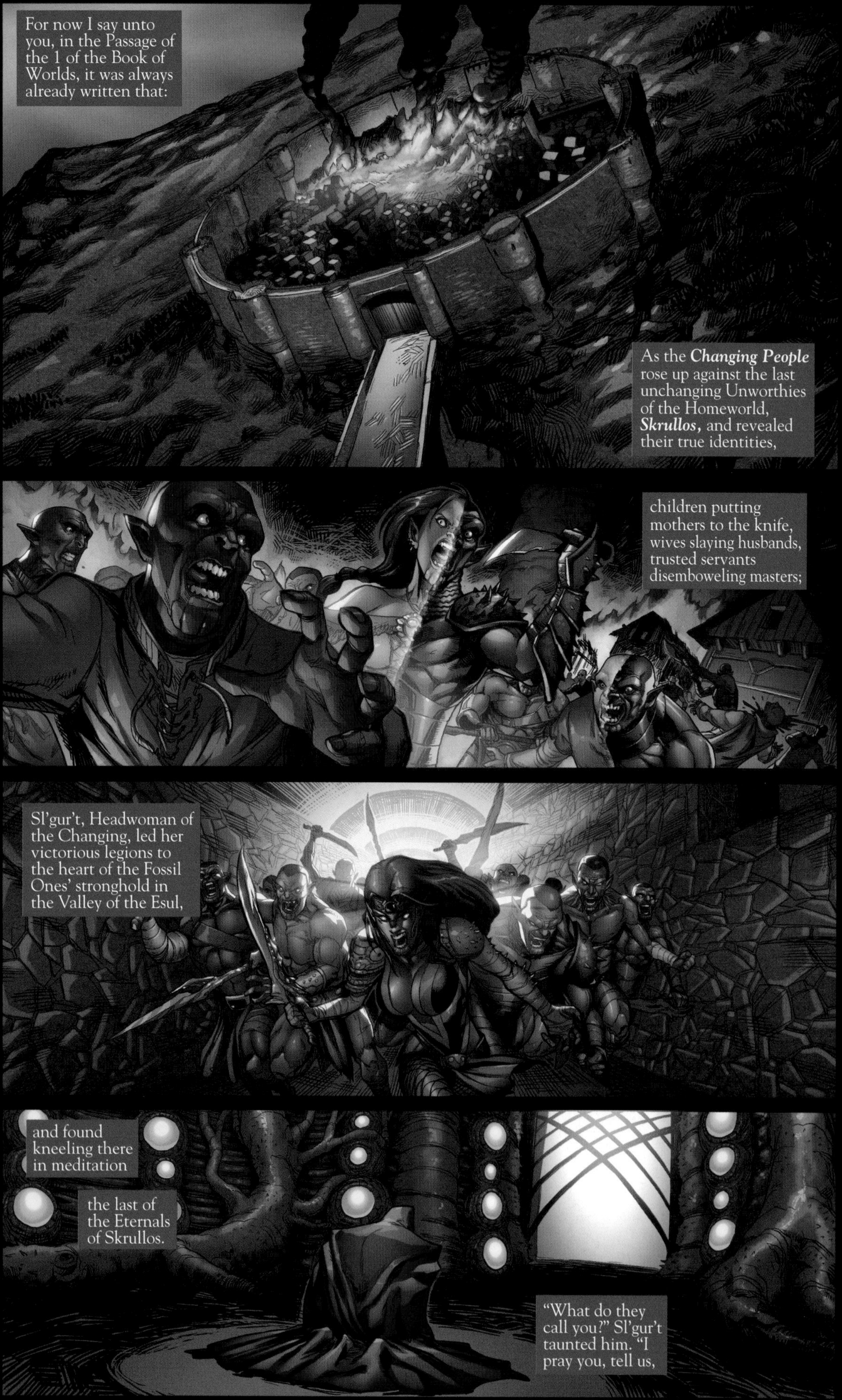
For now I say unto you, in the Passage of the 1 of the Book of Worlds, it was always already written that:
As the ***Changing People*** rose up against the last unchanging Unworthies of the Homeworld, ***Skrullos,*** and revealed their true identities,
children putting mothers to the knife, wives slaying husbands, trusted servants disemboweling masters;
Sl'gur't, Headwoman of the Changing, led her victorious legions to the heart of the Fossil Ones' stronghold in the Valley of the Esul,
and found kneeling there in meditation
the last of the Eternals of Skrullos.
"What do they call you?" Sl'gur't taunted him. "I pray you, tell us,

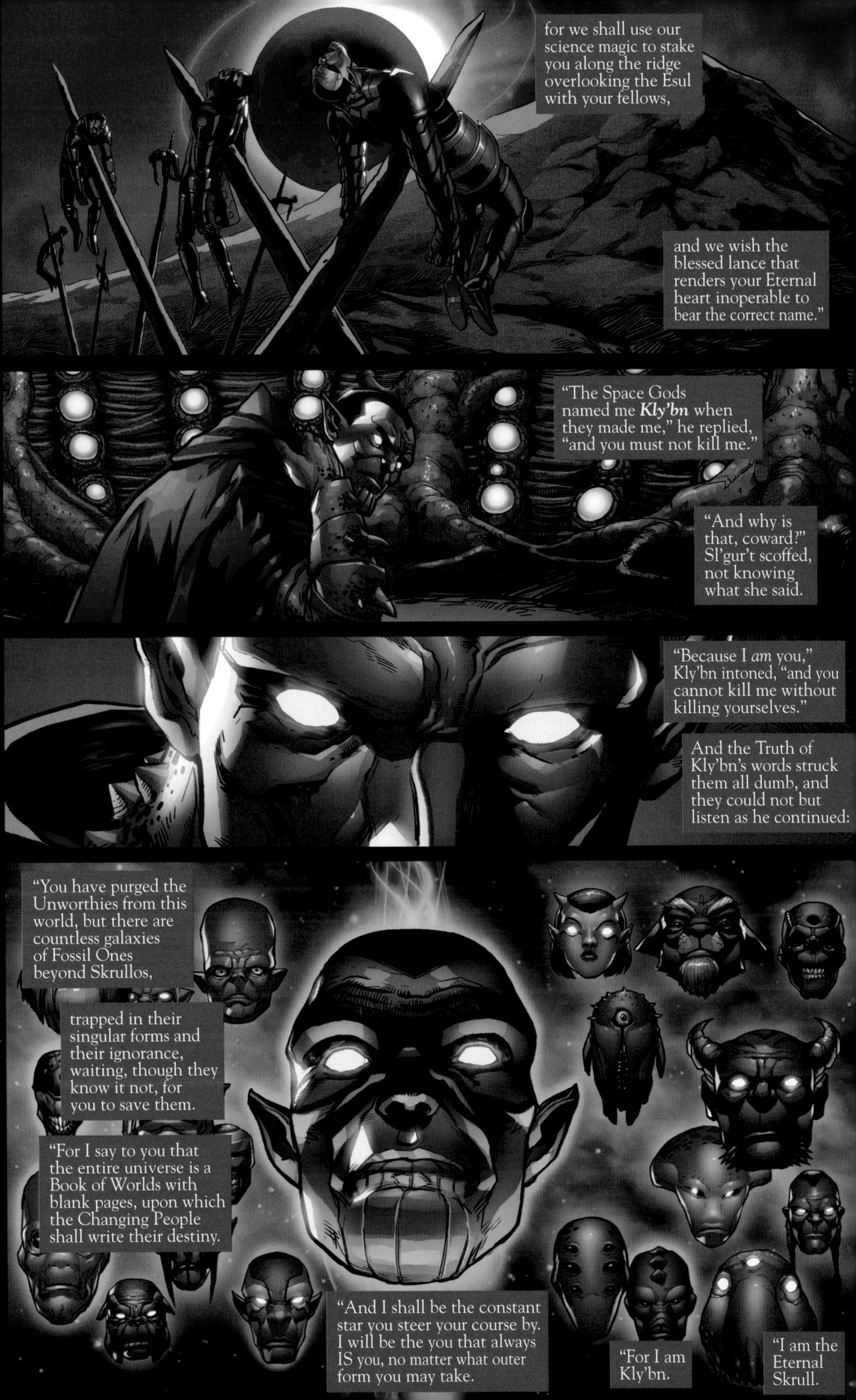
for we shall use our science magic to stake you along the ridge overlooking the Esul with your fellows,
and we wish the blessed lance that renders your Eternal heart inoperable to bear the correct name."
"The Space Gods named me ***Kly'bn*** when they made me," he replied, "and you must not kill me."
"And why is that, coward?" Sl'gur't scoffed, not knowing what she said.
"Because I *am* you," Kly'bn intoned, "and you cannot kill me without killing yourselves."
And the Truth of Kly'bn's words struck them all dumb, and they could not but listen as he continued:
"You have purged the Unworthies from this world, but there are countless galaxies of Fossil Ones beyond Skrullos,
trapped in their singular forms and their ignorance, waiting, though they know it not, for you to save them.
"For I say to you that the entire universe is a Book of Worlds with blank pages, upon which the Changing People shall write their destiny.
"And I shall be the constant star you steer your course by. I will be the you that always IS you, no matter what outer form you may take.
"For I am Kly'bn.
"I am the Eternal Skrull.

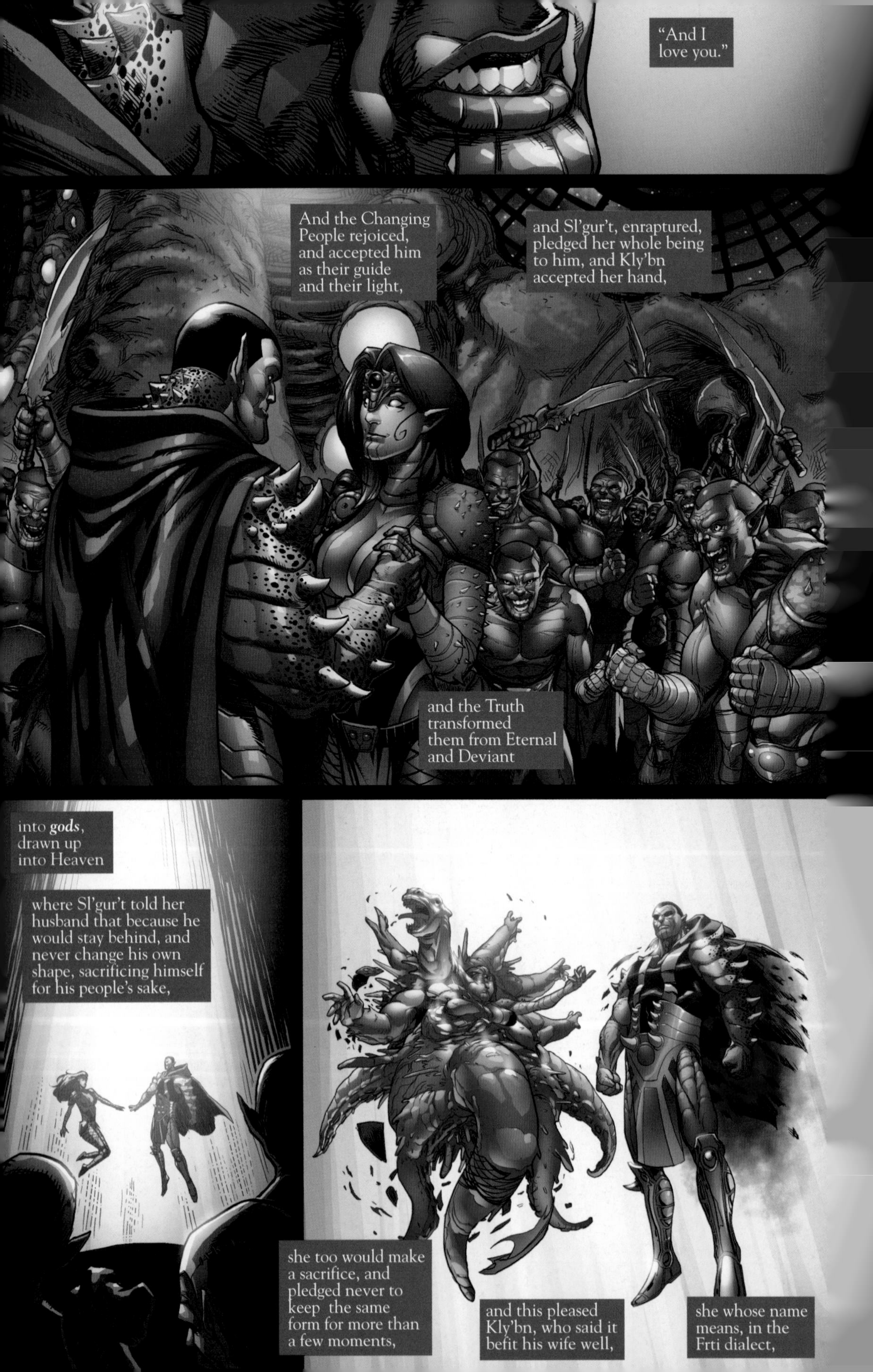
"And I love you."
And the Changing People rejoiced, and accepted him as their guide and their light,
and Sl'gur't, enraptured, pledged her whole being to him, and Kly'bn accepted her hand,
and the Truth transformed them from Eternal and Deviant
into *gods*, drawn up into Heaven
where Sl'gur't told her husband that because he would stay behind, and never change his own shape, sacrificing himself for his people's sake,
she too would make a sacrifice, and pledged never to keep the same form for more than a few moments,
and this pleased Kly'bn, who said it befit his wife well,
she whose name means, in the Frti dialect,

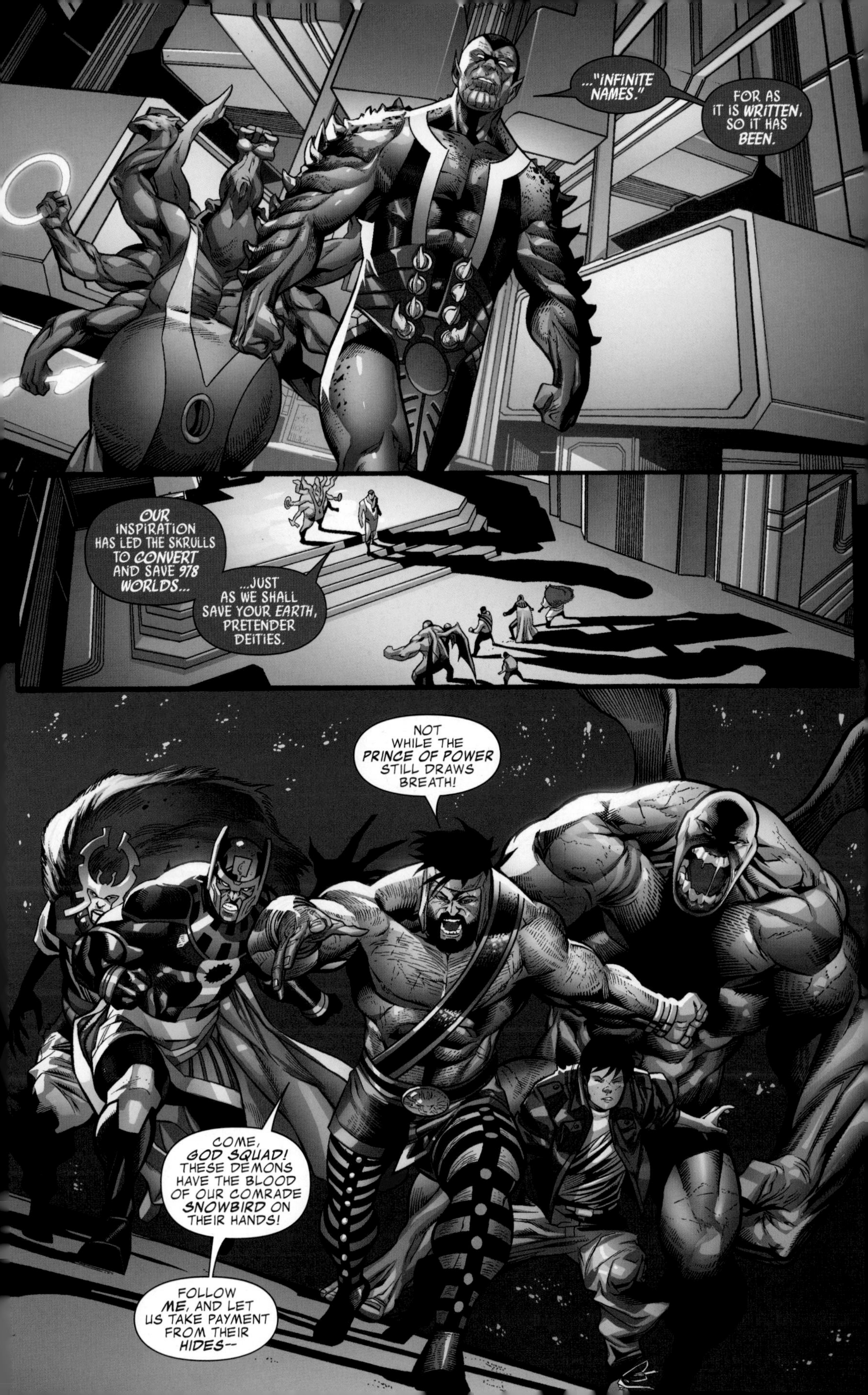
..."INFINITE NAMES."
FOR AS IT IS WRITTEN, SO IT HAS BEEN.
OUR INSPIRATION HAS LED THE SKRULLS TO CONVERT AND SAVE 978 WORLDS...
...JUST AS WE SHALL SAVE YOUR EARTH, PRETENDER DEITIES.
NOT WHILE THE PRINCE OF POWER STILL DRAWS BREATH!
COME, GOD SQUAD! THESE DEMONS HAVE THE BLOOD OF OUR COMRADE SNOWBIRD ON THEIR HANDS!
FOLLOW ME, AND LET US TAKE PAYMENT FROM THEIR HIDES--

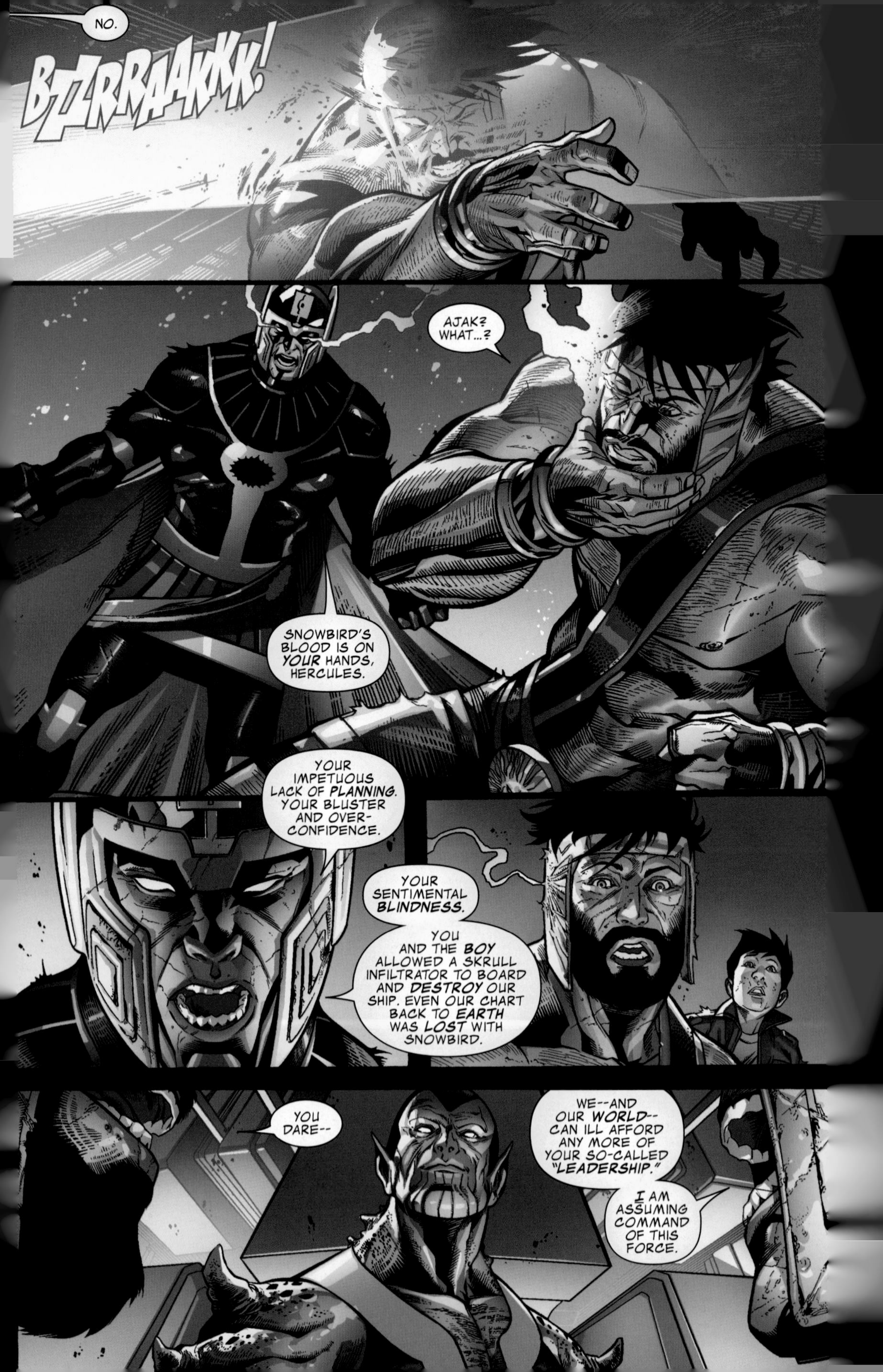
NO.
BZZRRAAKKK!
AJAK? WHAT...?
SNOWBIRD'S BLOOD IS ON YOUR HANDS, HERCULES.
YOUR IMPETUOUS LACK OF PLANNING. YOUR BLUSTER AND OVER-CONFIDENCE.
YOUR SENTIMENTAL BLINDNESS.
YOU AND THE BOY ALLOWED A SKRULL INFILTRATOR TO BOARD AND DESTROY OUR SHIP. EVEN OUR CHART BACK TO EARTH WAS LOST WITH SNOWBIRD.
YOU DARE--
WE--AND OUR WORLD--CAN ILL AFFORD ANY MORE OF YOUR SO-CALLED "LEADERSHIP."
I AM ASSUMING COMMAND OF THIS FORCE.

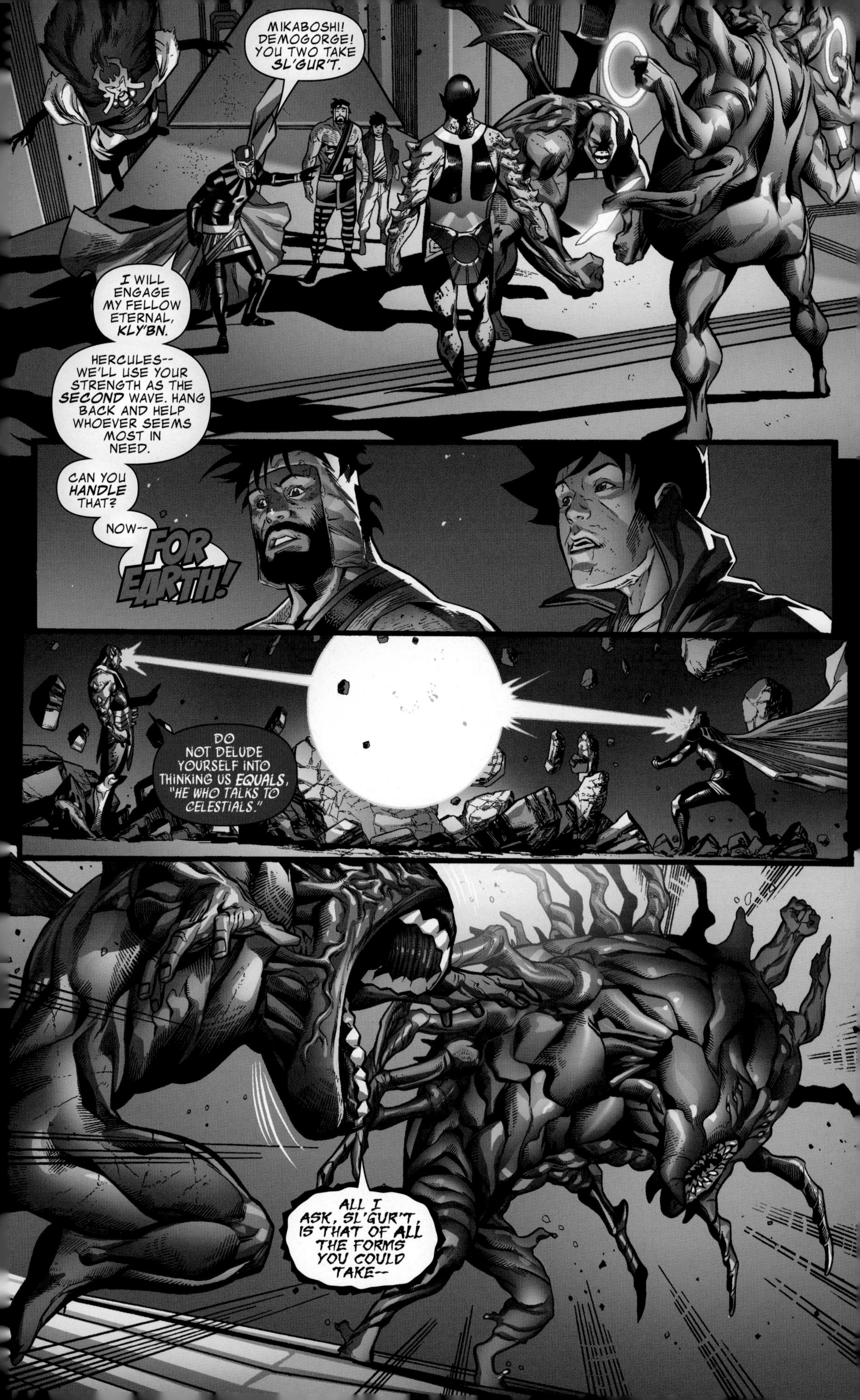
MIKABOSHI! DEMOGORGE! YOU TWO TAKE SL'GUR'T.
I WILL ENGAGE MY FELLOW ETERNAL, KLY'BN.
HERCULES-- WE'LL USE YOUR STRENGTH AS THE SECOND WAVE. HANG BACK AND HELP WHOEVER SEEMS MOST IN NEED.
CAN YOU HANDLE THAT?
NOW--
FOR EARTH!
DO NOT DELUDE YOURSELF INTO THINKING US EQUALS, "HE WHO TALKS TO CELESTIALS."
ALL I ASK, SL'GUR'T, IS THAT OF ALL THE FORMS YOU COULD TAKE--

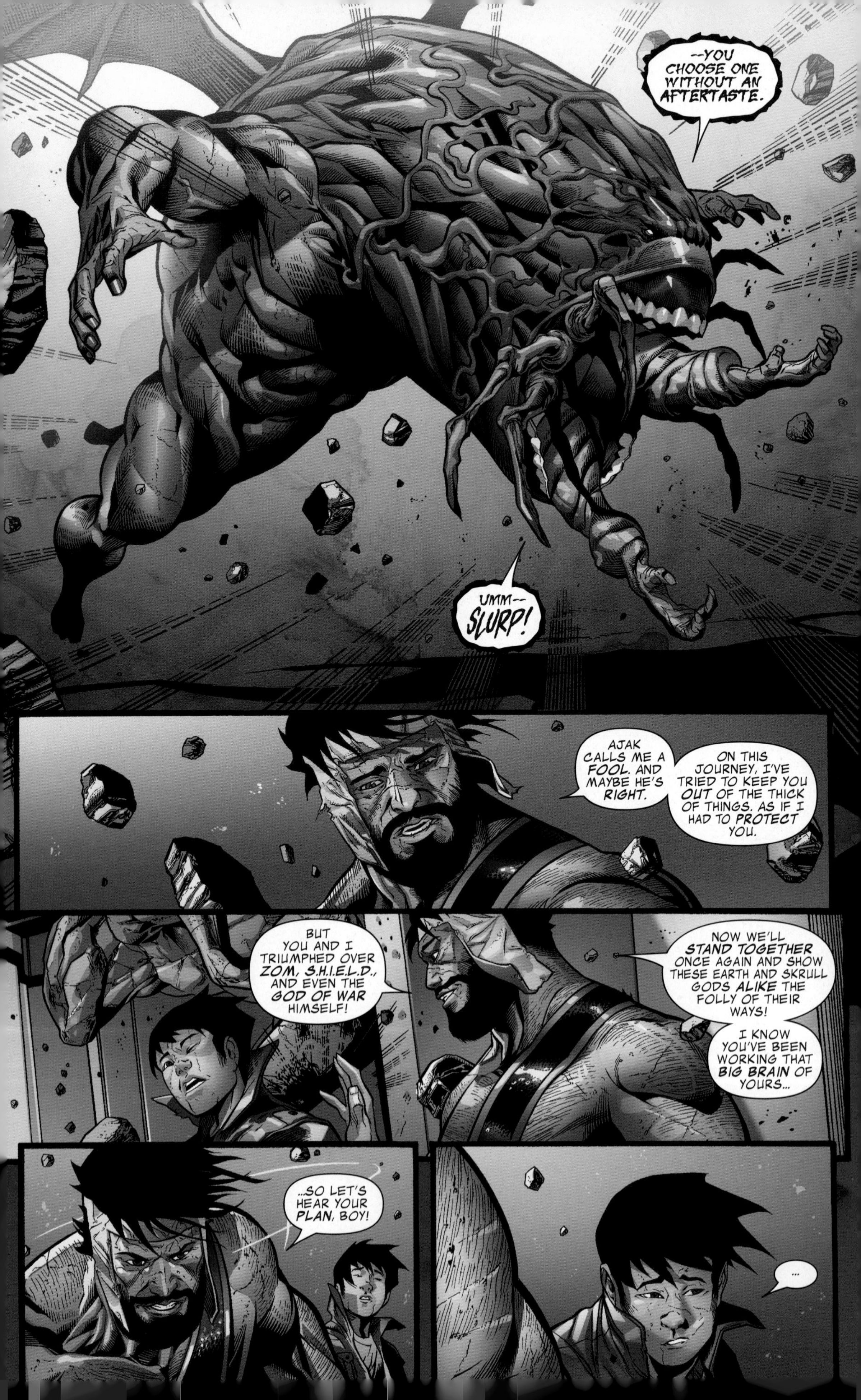
--YOU CHOOSE ONE WITHOUT AN AFTERTASTE.
UMM-- SLURP!
AJAK CALLS ME A FOOL. AND MAYBE HE'S RIGHT.
ON THIS JOURNEY, I'VE TRIED TO KEEP YOU OUT OF THE THICK OF THINGS. AS IF I HAD TO PROTECT YOU.
BUT YOU AND I TRIUMPHED OVER ZOM, S.H.I.E.L.D., AND EVEN THE GOD OF WAR HIMSELF!
NOW WE'LL STAND TOGETHER ONCE AGAIN AND SHOW THESE EARTH AND SKRULL GODS ALIKE THE FOLLY OF THEIR WAYS!
I KNOW YOU'VE BEEN WORKING THAT BIG BRAIN OF YOURS...
...SO LET'S HEAR YOUR PLAN, BOY!
...

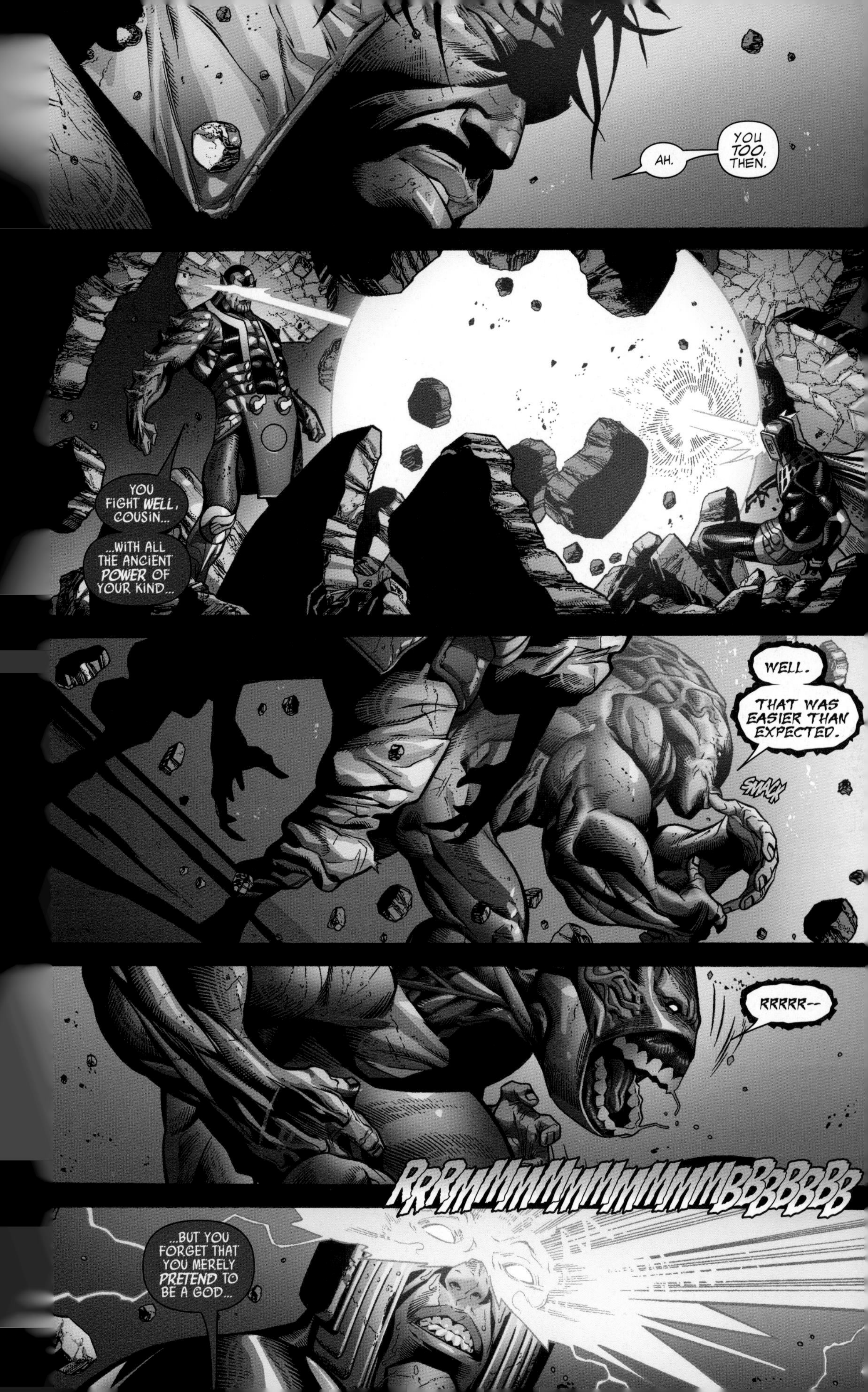
AH.
YOU TOO, THEN.
YOU FIGHT WELL, COUSIN...
...WITH ALL THE ANCIENT POWER OF YOUR KIND...
WELL.
THAT WAS EASIER THAN EXPECTED.
SMACK
RRRRR--
RRRMMMMMMMMMMMMMBBBBBBB
...BUT YOU FORGET THAT YOU MERELY PRETEND TO BE A GOD...

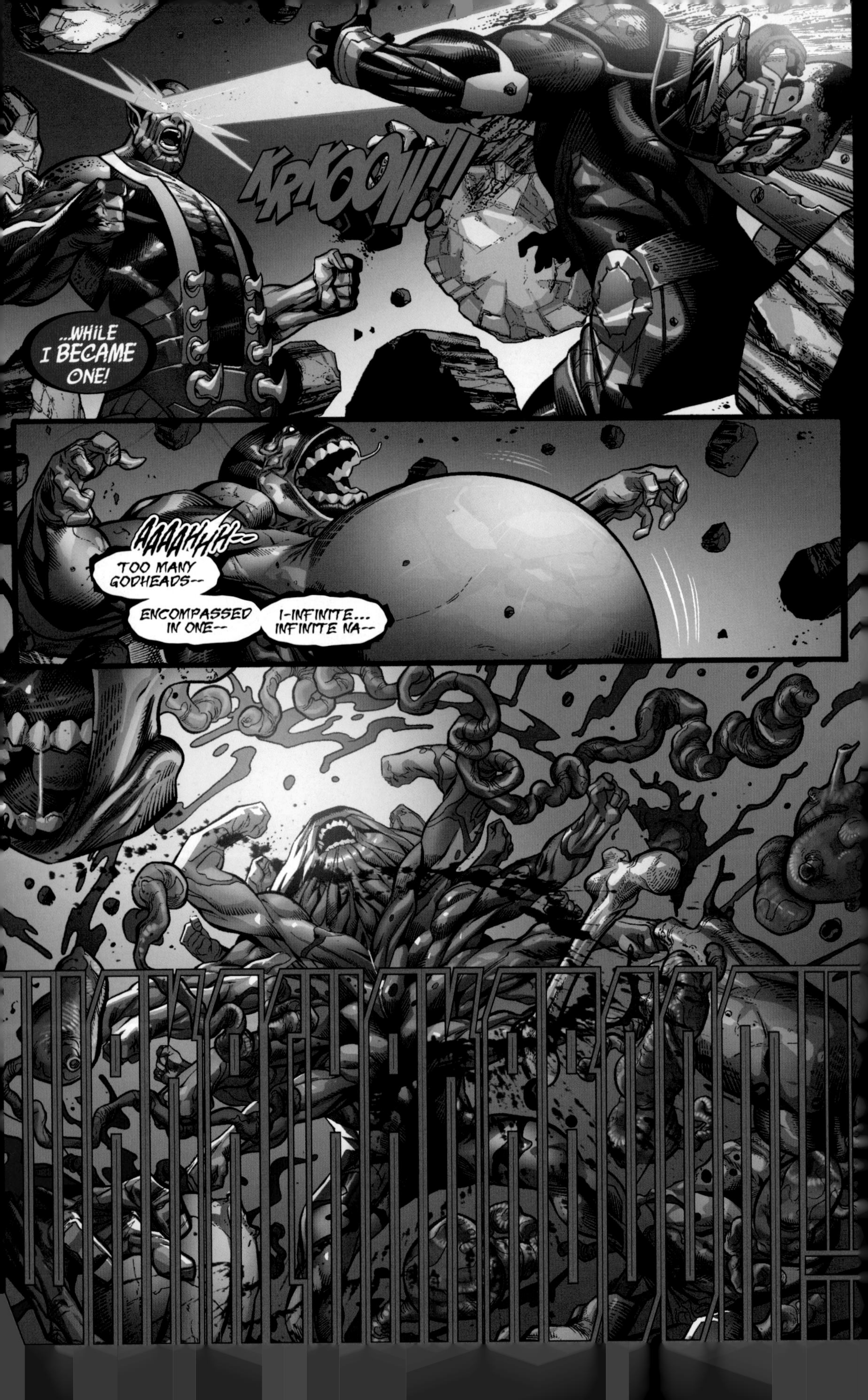
KRAKOOM!!
...WHILE I BECAME ONE!
AAAAHHH--
TOO MANY GODHEADS--
ENCOMPASSED IN ONE--
I-INFINITE... INFINITE NA--

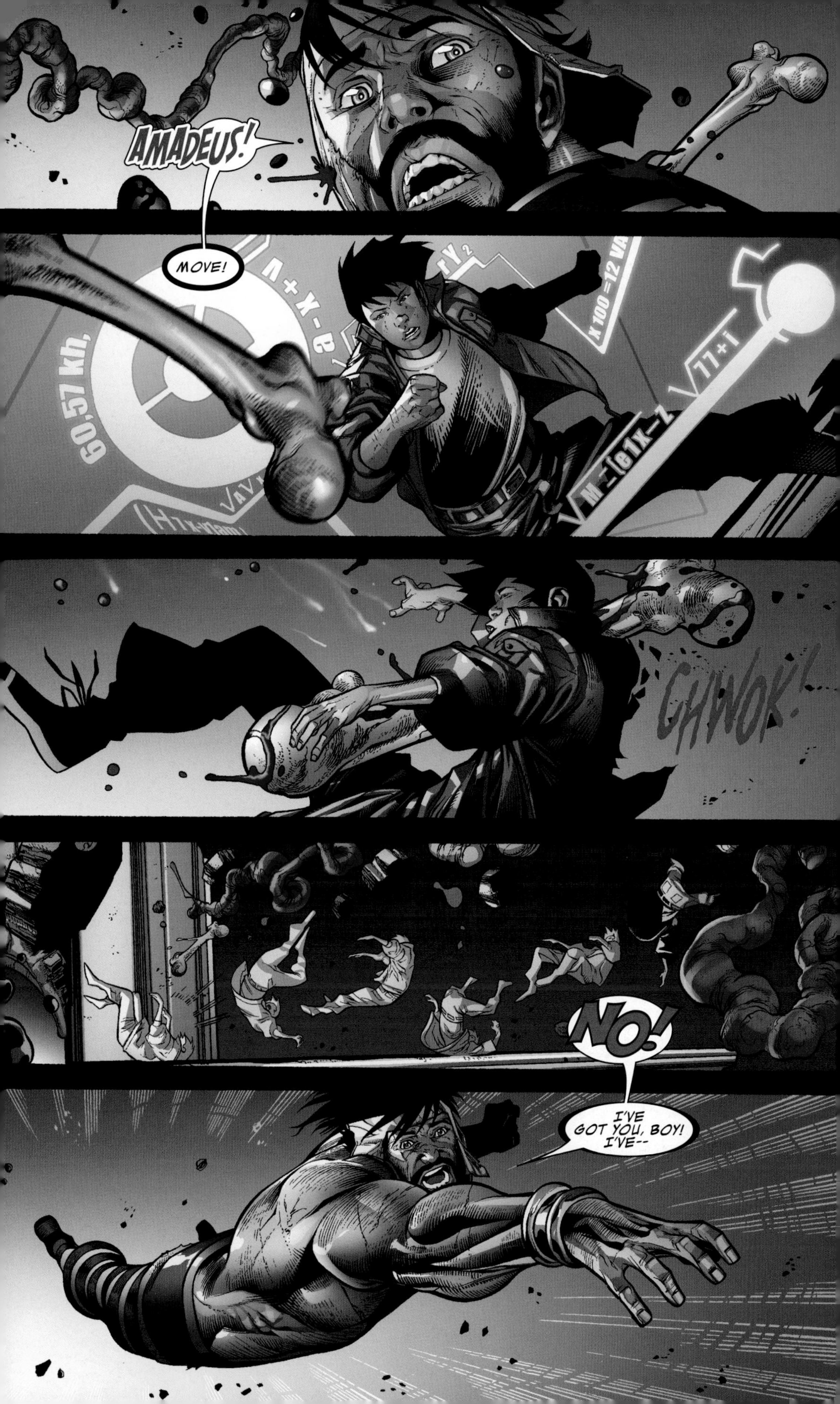
AMADEUS!
MOVE!
CHWOK!
NO!
I'VE GOT YOU, BOY! I'VE--

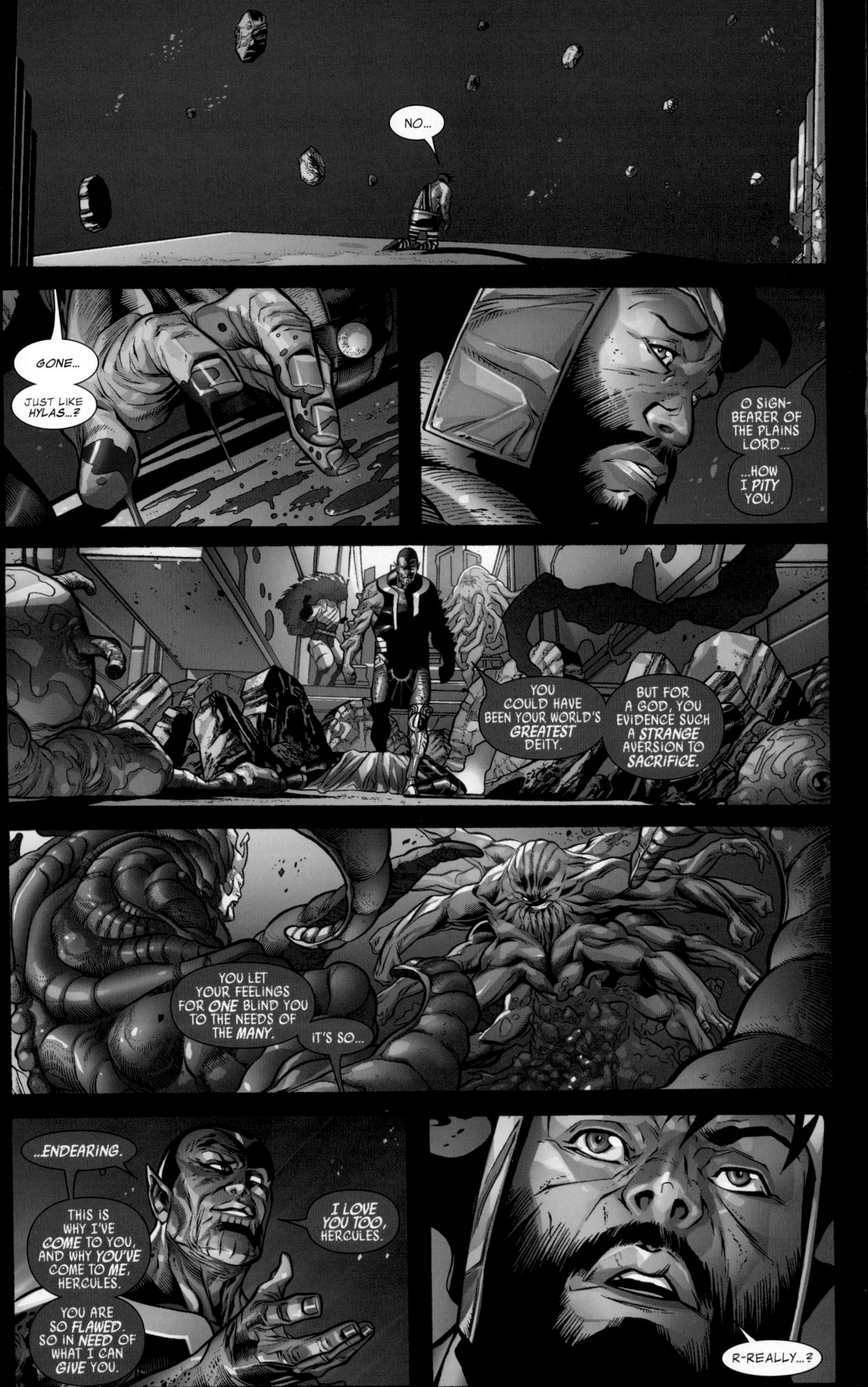
NO...
GONE...
JUST LIKE HYLAS...?
O SIGN-BEARER OF THE PLAINS LORD...
...HOW I PITY YOU.
YOU COULD HAVE BEEN YOUR WORLD'S GREATEST DEITY.
BUT FOR A GOD, YOU EVIDENCE SUCH A STRANGE AVERSION TO SACRIFICE.
YOU LET YOUR FEELINGS FOR ONE BLIND YOU TO THE NEEDS OF THE MANY.
IT'S SO...
...ENDEARING.
THIS IS WHY I'VE COME TO YOU, AND WHY YOU'VE COME TO ME, HERCULES.
YOU ARE SO FLAWED. SO IN NEED OF WHAT I CAN GIVE YOU.
I LOVE YOU TOO, HERCULES.
R-REALLY...?

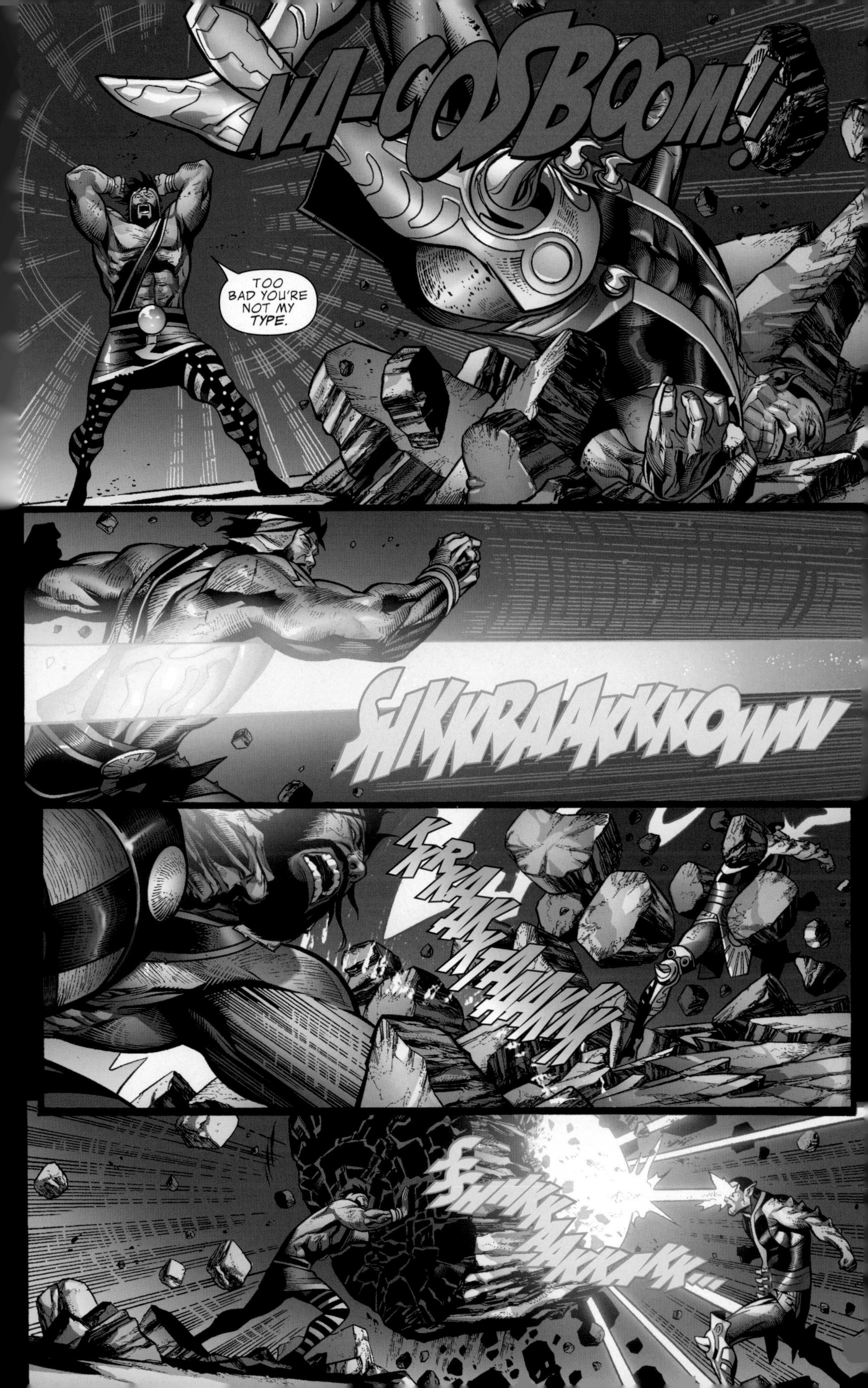
NA-COSBOOM!!
TOO BAD YOU'RE NOT MY TYPE.
SHKKRAAKKKOWW
KRRAKK-KT-AAKK
SHHKKRAKKAKK...

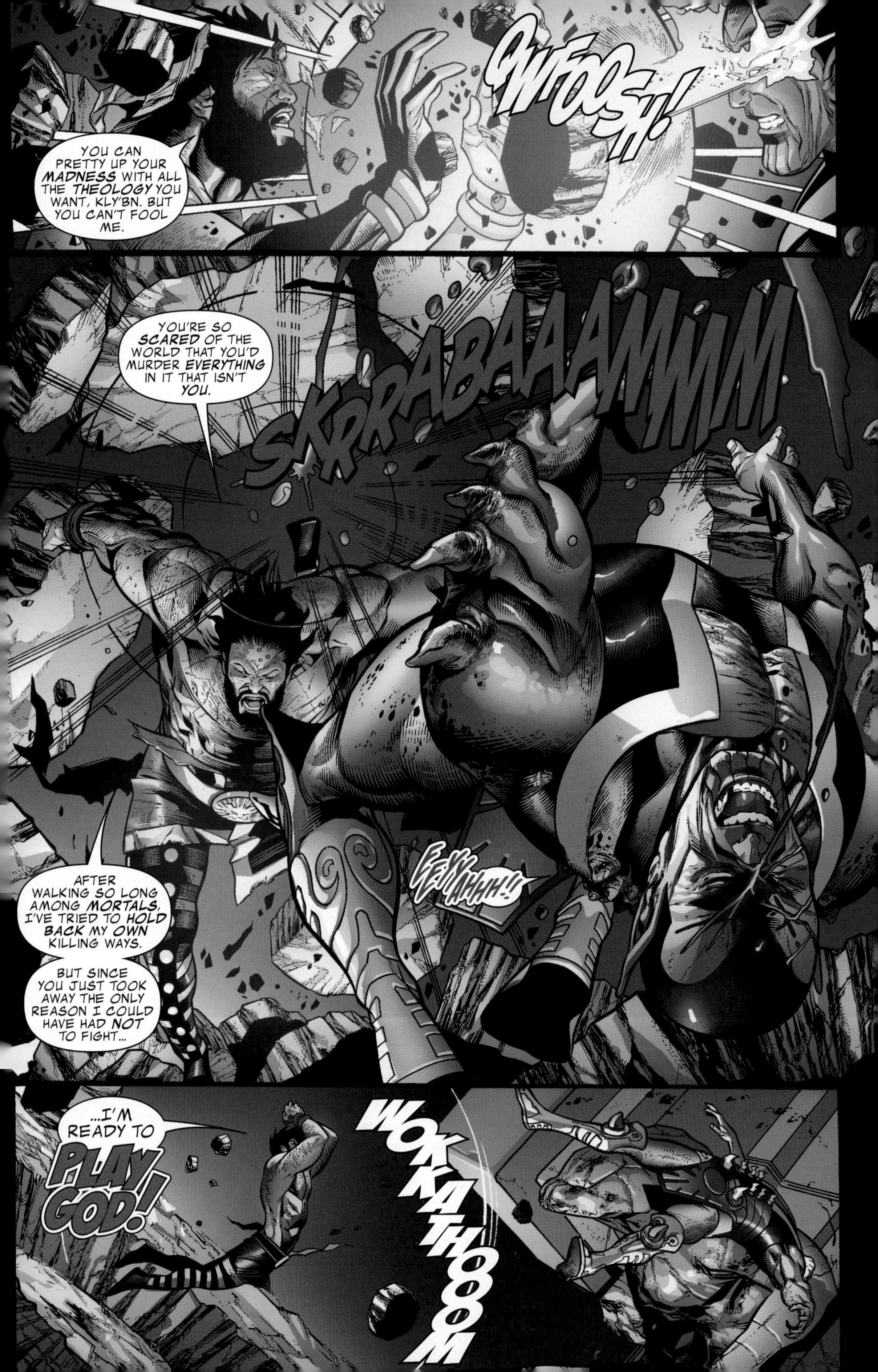
YOU CAN PRETTY UP YOUR MADNESS WITH ALL THE THEOLOGY YOU WANT, KLY'BN. BUT YOU CAN'T FOOL ME.
QWFOOSH!
YOU'RE SO SCARED OF THE WORLD THAT YOU'D MURDER EVERYTHING IN IT THAT ISN'T YOU.
SKRRABAAAMMM
AFTER WALKING SO LONG AMONG MORTALS, I'VE TRIED TO HOLD BACK MY OWN KILLING WAYS.
BUT SINCE YOU JUST TOOK AWAY THE ONLY REASON I COULD HAVE HAD NOT TO FIGHT...
...I'M READY TO PLAY GOD!
WOKATHOOOOM

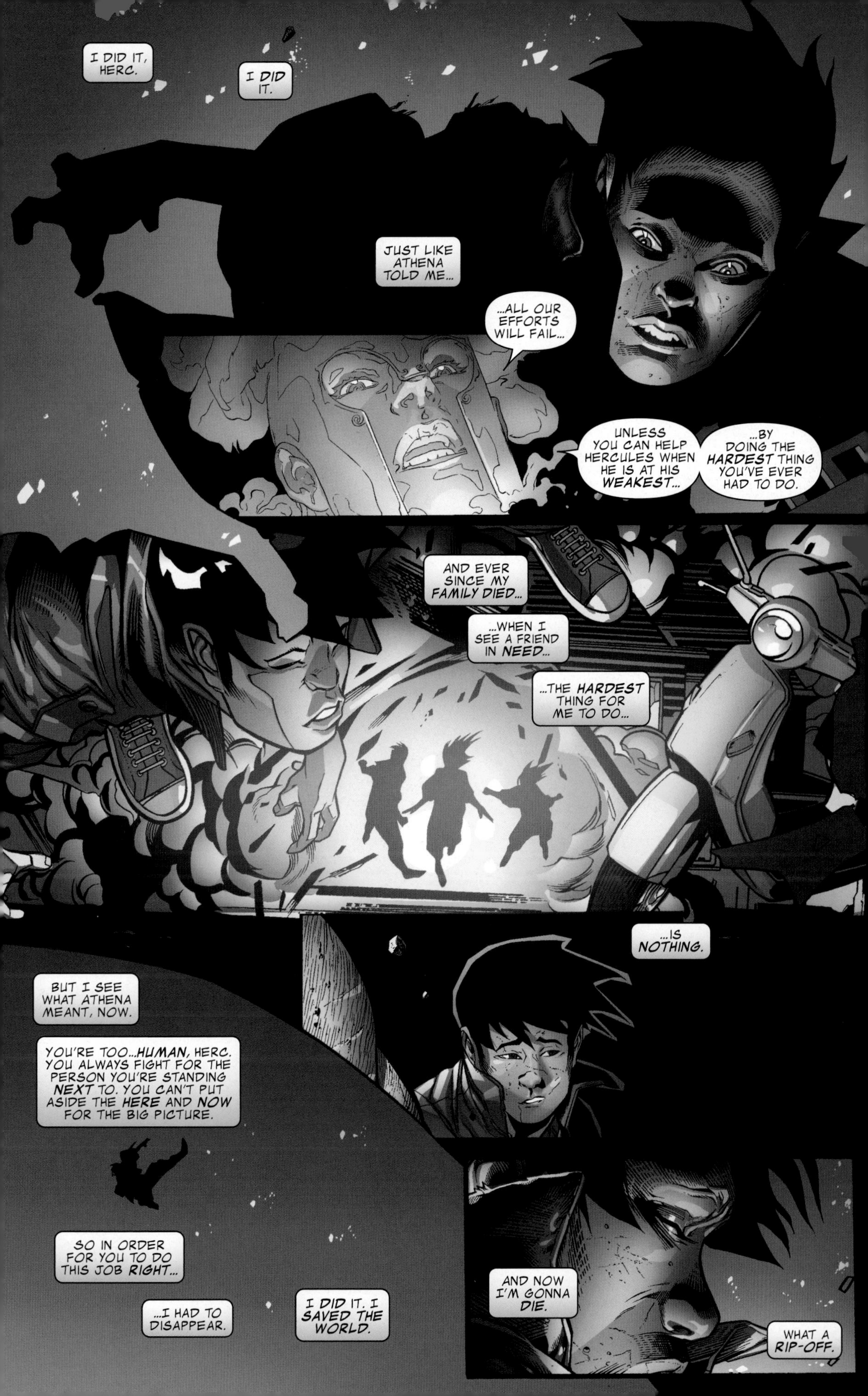
I DID IT, HERC.
I DID IT.
JUST LIKE ATHENA TOLD ME...
...ALL OUR EFFORTS WILL FAIL...
UNLESS YOU CAN HELP HERCULES WHEN HE IS AT HIS WEAKEST...
...BY DOING THE HARDEST THING YOU'VE EVER HAD TO DO.
AND EVER SINCE MY FAMILY DIED...
...WHEN I SEE A FRIEND IN NEED...
...THE HARDEST THING FOR ME TO DO...
...IS NOTHING.
BUT I SEE WHAT ATHENA MEANT, NOW.
YOU'RE TOO...HUMAN, HERC. YOU ALWAYS FIGHT FOR THE PERSON YOU'RE STANDING NEXT TO. YOU CAN'T PUT ASIDE THE HERE AND NOW FOR THE BIG PICTURE.
SO IN ORDER FOR YOU TO DO THIS JOB RIGHT...
...I HAD TO DISAPPEAR.
I DID IT. I SAVED THE WORLD.
AND NOW I'M GONNA DIE.
WHAT A RIP-OFF.

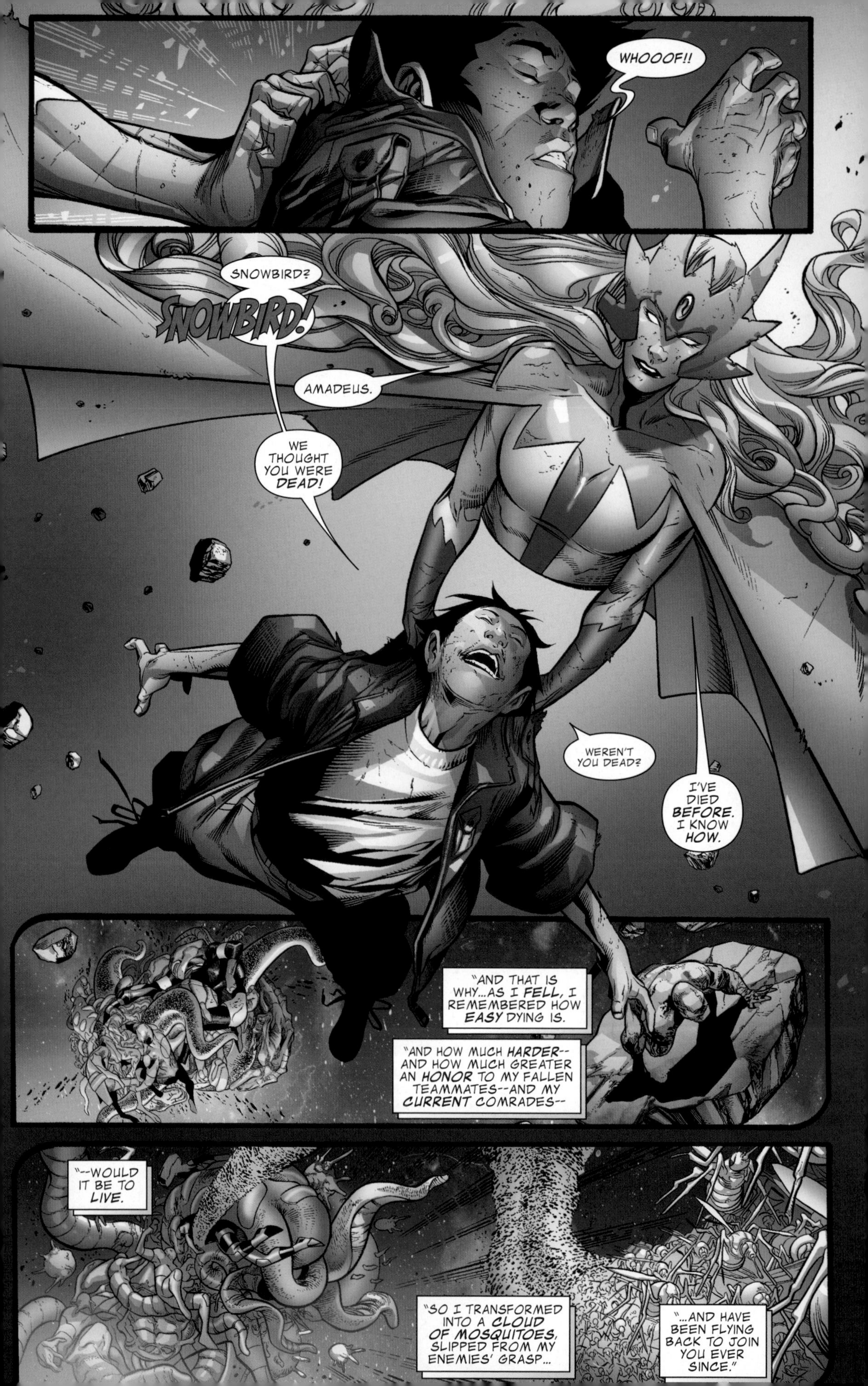
WHOOOF!!
SNOWBIRD?
SNOWBIRD!
AMADEUS.
WE THOUGHT YOU WERE DEAD!
WEREN'T YOU DEAD?
I'VE DIED BEFORE. I KNOW HOW.
"AND THAT IS WHY...AS I FELL, I REMEMBERED HOW EASY DYING IS.
"AND HOW MUCH HARDER--AND HOW MUCH GREATER AN HONOR TO MY FALLEN TEAMMATES--AND MY CURRENT COMRADES--
"--WOULD IT BE TO LIVE.
"SO I TRANSFORMED INTO A CLOUD OF MOSQUITOES, SLIPPED FROM MY ENEMIES' GRASP...
"...AND HAVE BEEN FLYING BACK TO JOIN YOU EVER SINCE."

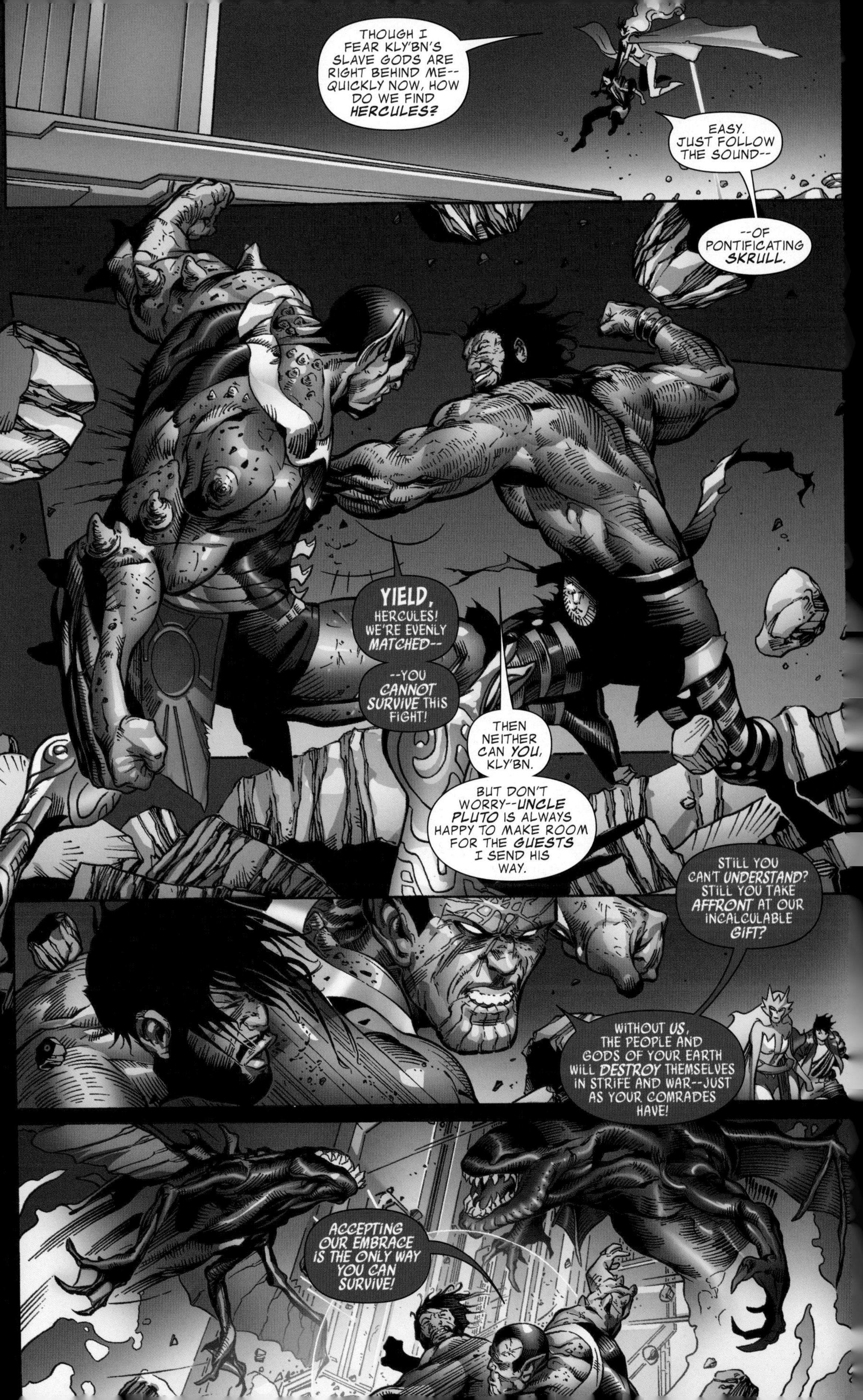
THOUGH I FEAR KLY'BN'S SLAVE GODS ARE RIGHT BEHIND ME-- QUICKLY NOW, HOW DO WE FIND HERCULES?
EASY. JUST FOLLOW THE SOUND--
--OF PONTIFICATING SKRULL.
YIELD, HERCULES! WE'RE EVENLY MATCHED--
--YOU CANNOT SURVIVE THIS FIGHT!
THEN NEITHER CAN YOU, KLY'BN.
BUT DON'T WORRY--UNCLE PLUTO IS ALWAYS HAPPY TO MAKE ROOM FOR THE GUESTS I SEND HIS WAY.
STILL YOU CAN'T UNDERSTAND? STILL YOU TAKE AFFRONT AT OUR INCALCULABLE GIFT?
WITHOUT US, THE PEOPLE AND GODS OF YOUR EARTH WILL DESTROY THEMSELVES IN STRIFE AND WAR--JUST AS YOUR COMRADES HAVE!
ACCEPTING OUR EMBRACE IS THE ONLY WAY YOU CAN SURVIVE!

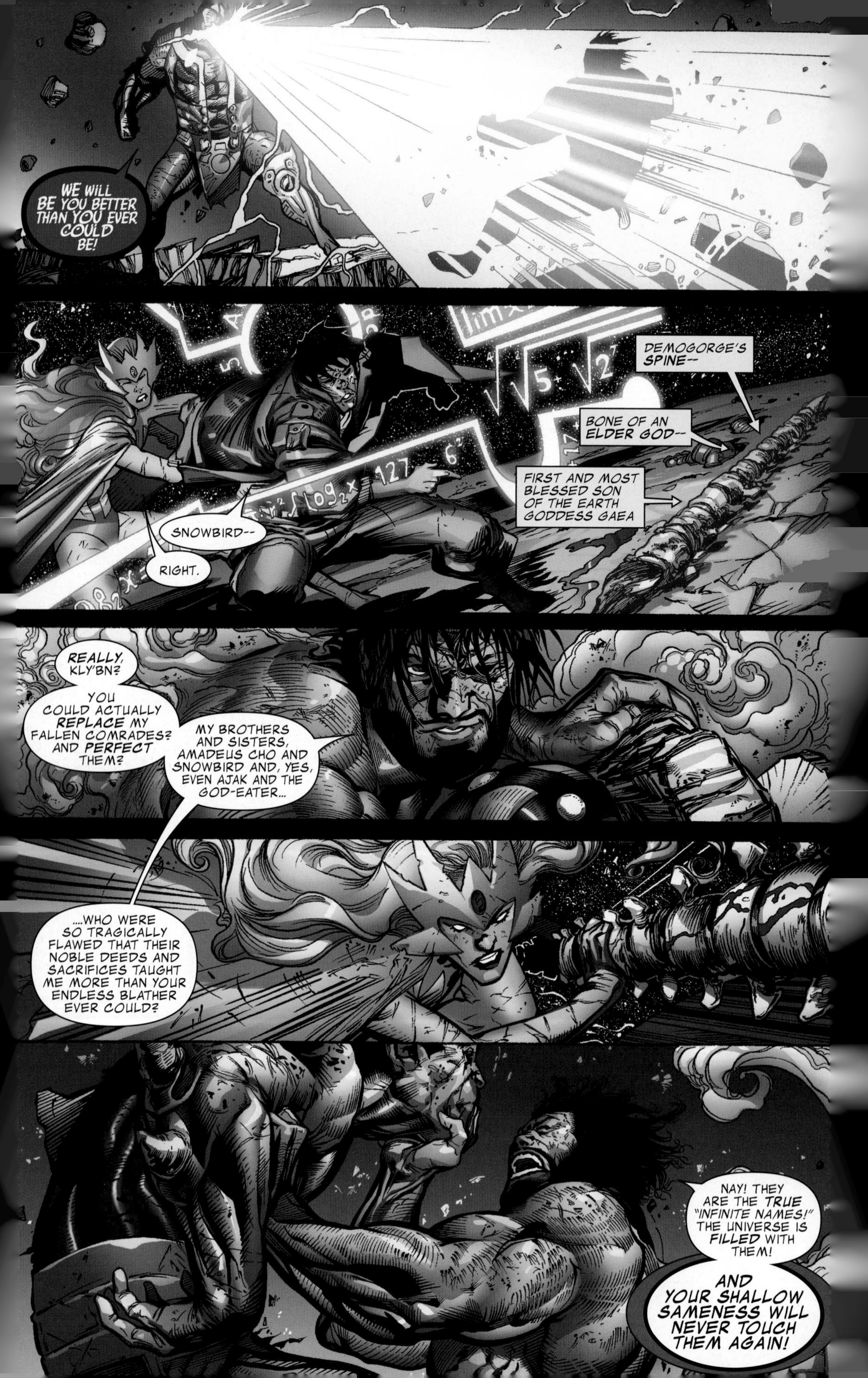
WE WILL BE YOU BETTER THAN YOU EVER COULD BE!
DEMOGORGE'S SPINE--
BONE OF AN ELDER GOD--
FIRST AND MOST BLESSED SON OF THE EARTH GODDESS GAEA
SNOWBIRD--
RIGHT.
REALLY, KLY'BN?
YOU COULD ACTUALLY REPLACE MY FALLEN COMRADES? AND PERFECT THEM?
MY BROTHERS AND SISTERS, AMADEUS CHO AND SNOWBIRD AND, YES, EVEN AJAK AND THE GOD-EATER...
....WHO WERE SO TRAGICALLY FLAWED THAT THEIR NOBLE DEEDS AND SACRIFICES TAUGHT ME MORE THAN YOUR ENDLESS BLATHER EVER COULD?
NAY! THEY ARE THE TRUE "INFINITE NAMES!" THE UNIVERSE IS FILLED WITH THEM!
AND YOUR SHALLOW SAMENESS WILL NEVER TOUCH THEM AGAIN!

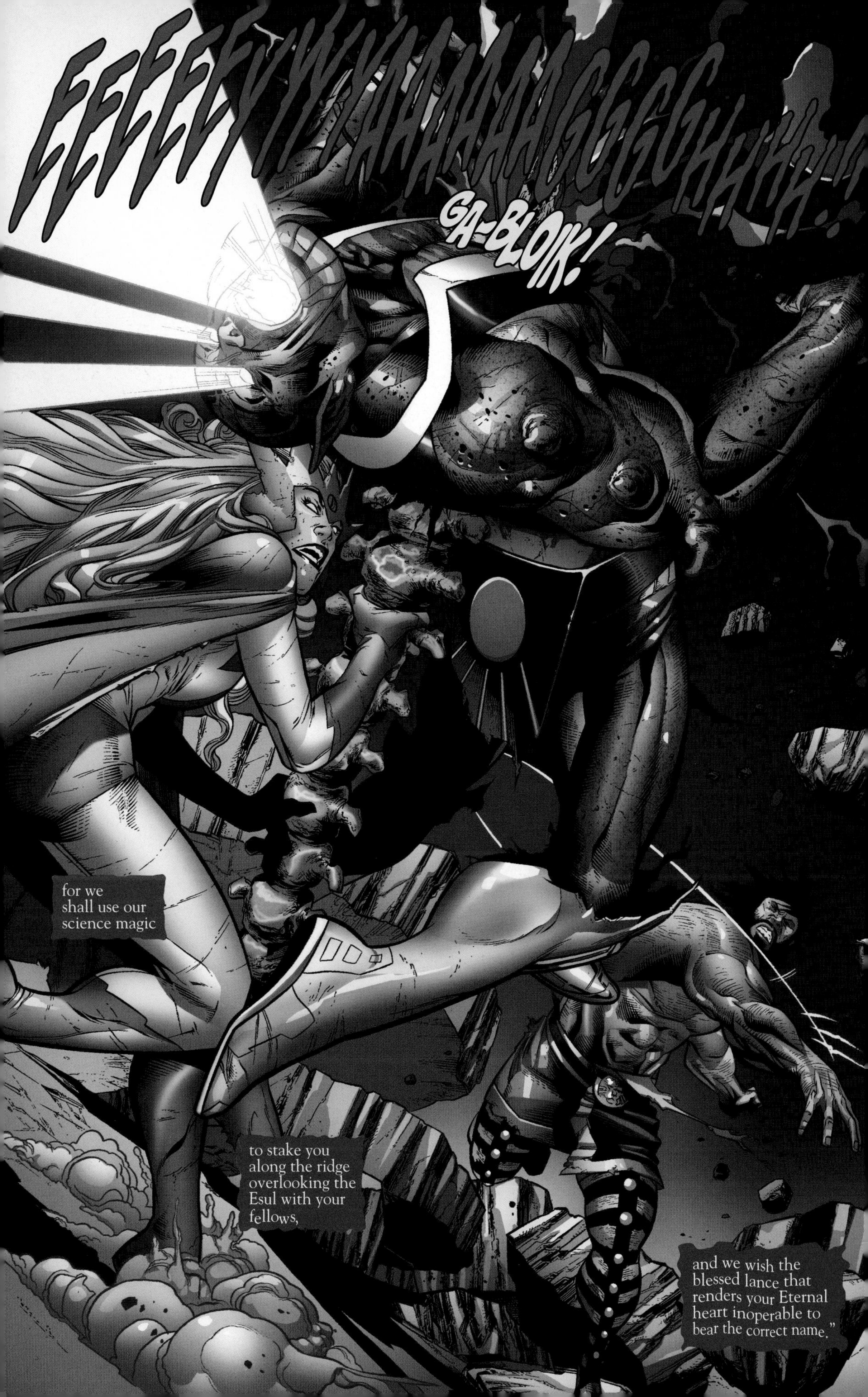
EEEEEYYAAAAAAGGGGHHHH!!
GA-BLOIK!
for we shall use our science magic
to stake you along the ridge overlooking the Esul with your fellows,
and we wish the blessed lance that renders your Eternal heart inoperable to bear the correct name."

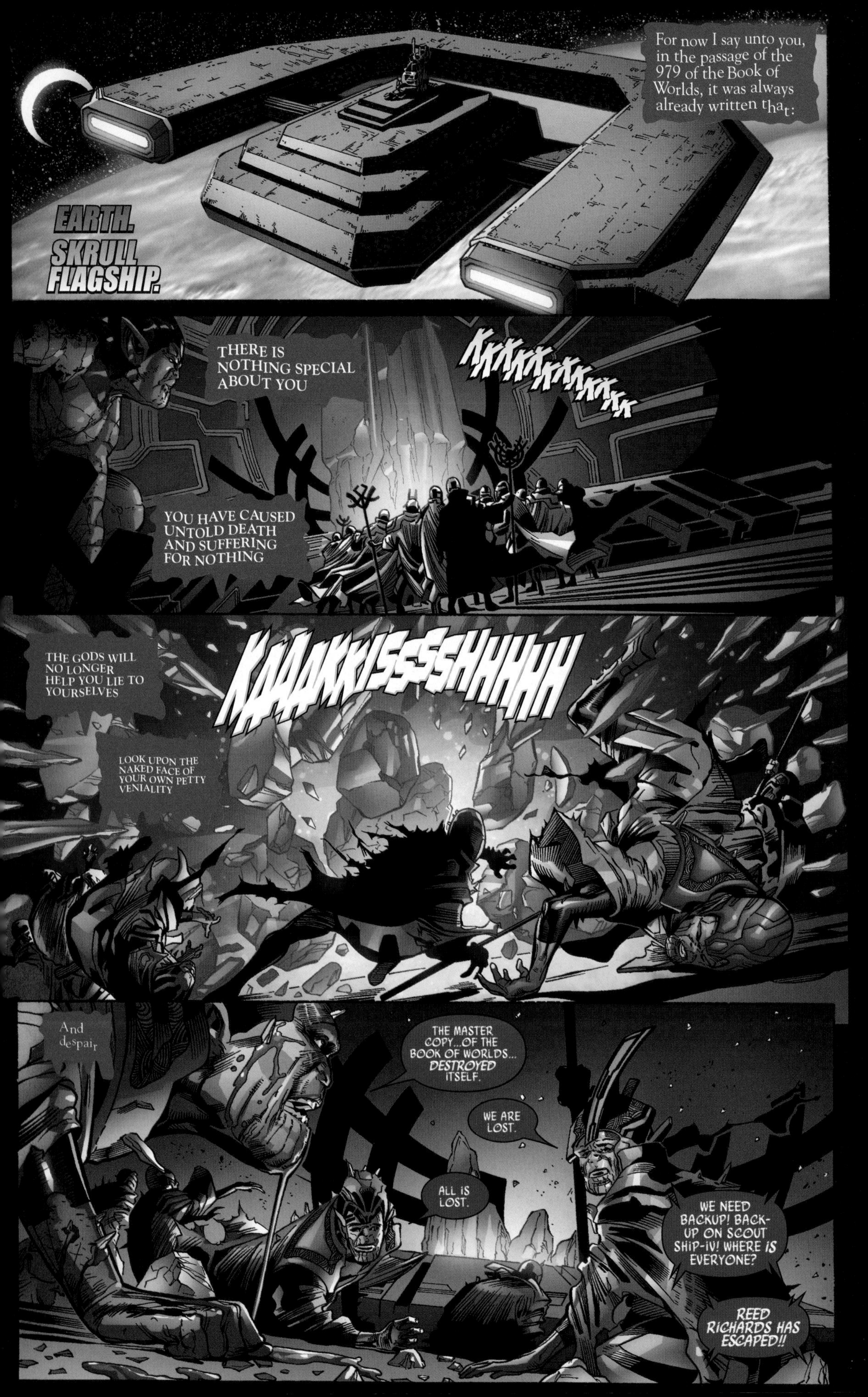
For now I say unto you, in the passage of the 979 of the Book of Worlds, it was always already written that:
EARTH. SKRULL FLAGSHIP.
THERE IS NOTHING SPECIAL ABOUT YOU
KKKKKKKKKKKK
YOU HAVE CAUSED UNTOLD DEATH AND SUFFERING FOR NOTHING
THE GODS WILL NO LONGER HELP YOU LIE TO YOURSELVES
KAAAKKISSSSHHHHH
LOOK UPON THE NAKED FACE OF YOUR OWN PETTY VENIALITY
And despair
THE MASTER COPY...OF THE BOOK OF WORLDS... DESTROYED ITSELF.
WE ARE LOST.
ALL IS LOST.
WE NEED BACKUP! BACK-UP ON SCOUT SHIP-IV! WHERE IS EVERYONE?
REED RICHARDS HAS ESCAPED!!

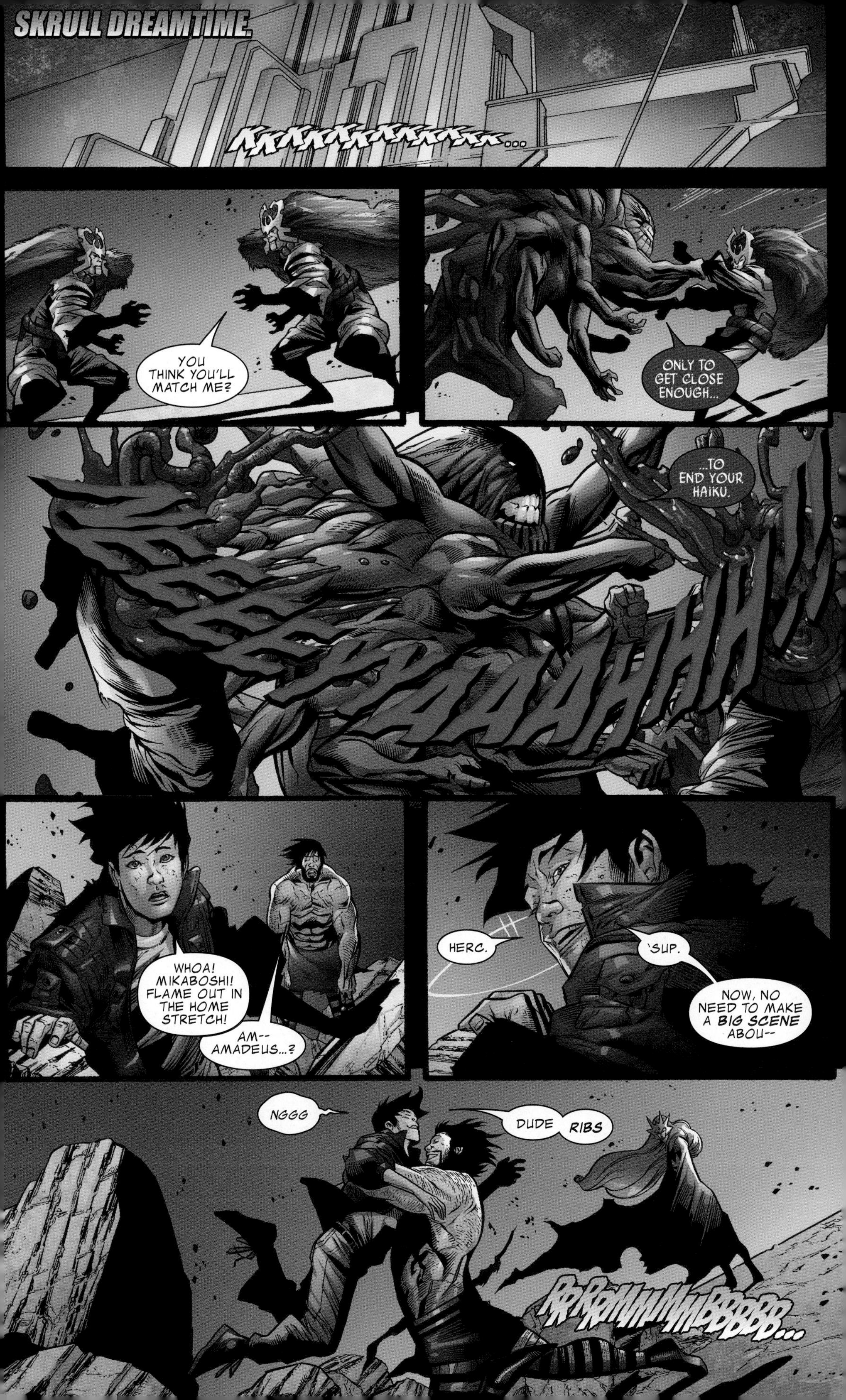
SKRULL DREAMTIME.
KKKKKKKKKKKKKK...
YOU THINK YOU'LL MATCH ME?
ONLY TO GET CLOSE ENOUGH...
...TO END YOUR HAIKU.
EEEEYAAAAAHHHH!
WHOA! MIKABOSHI! FLAME OUT IN THE HOME STRETCH!
AM-- AMADEUS...?
HERC.
'SUP.
NOW, NO NEED TO MAKE A BIG SCENE ABOU--
NGGG
DUDE
RIBS
RRRRMMMMMBBBBBB...

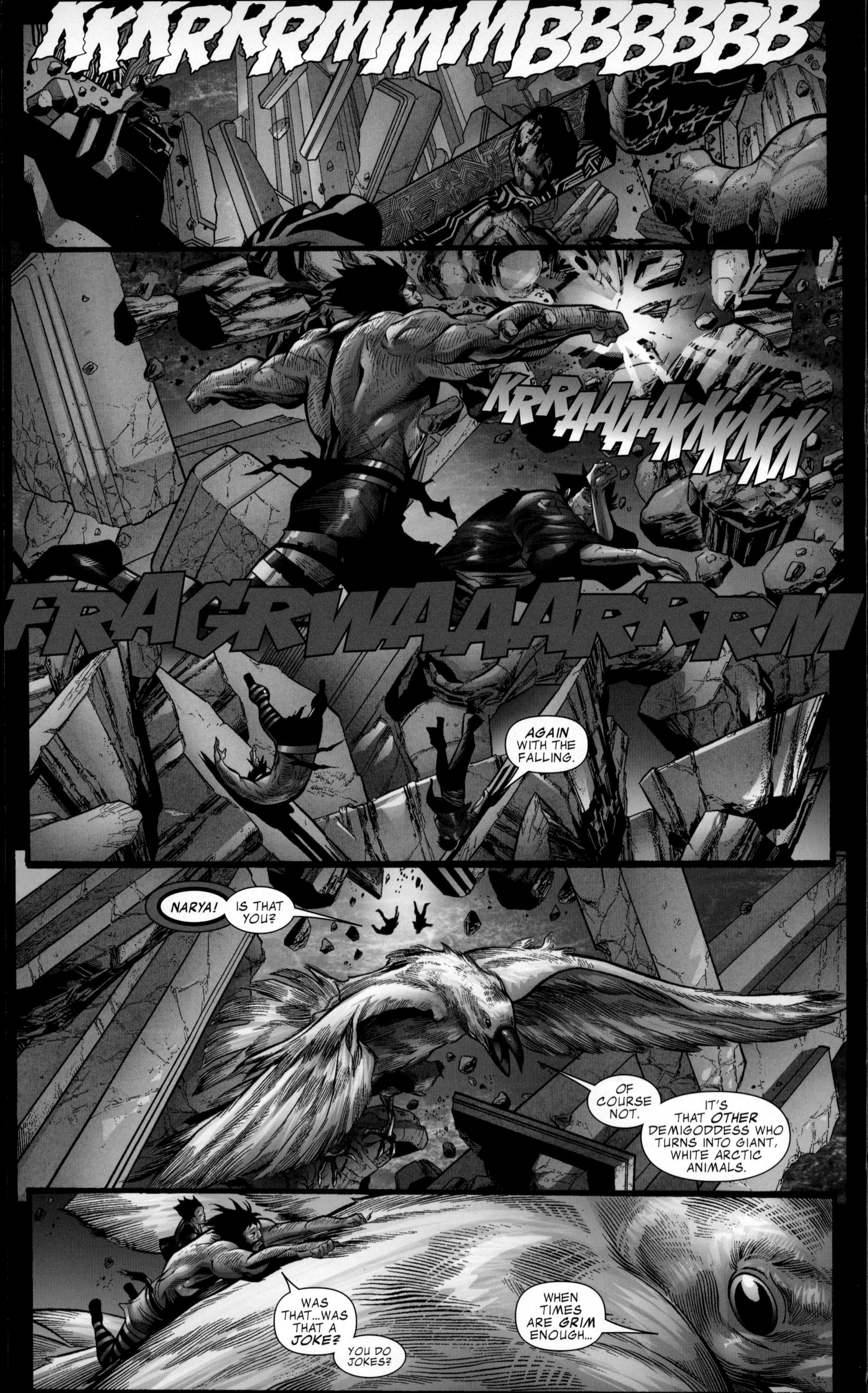
KKRRRMMMBBBBBB
KRRAAAAKKKKKK
FRAGRWAAARRRM
AGAIN WITH THE FALLING.
NARYA!
IS THAT YOU?
OF COURSE NOT.
IT'S THAT OTHER DEMIGODDESS WHO TURNS INTO GIANT, WHITE ARCTIC ANIMALS.
WAS THAT...WAS THAT A JOKE?
YOU DO JOKES?
WHEN TIMES ARE GRIM ENOUGH...

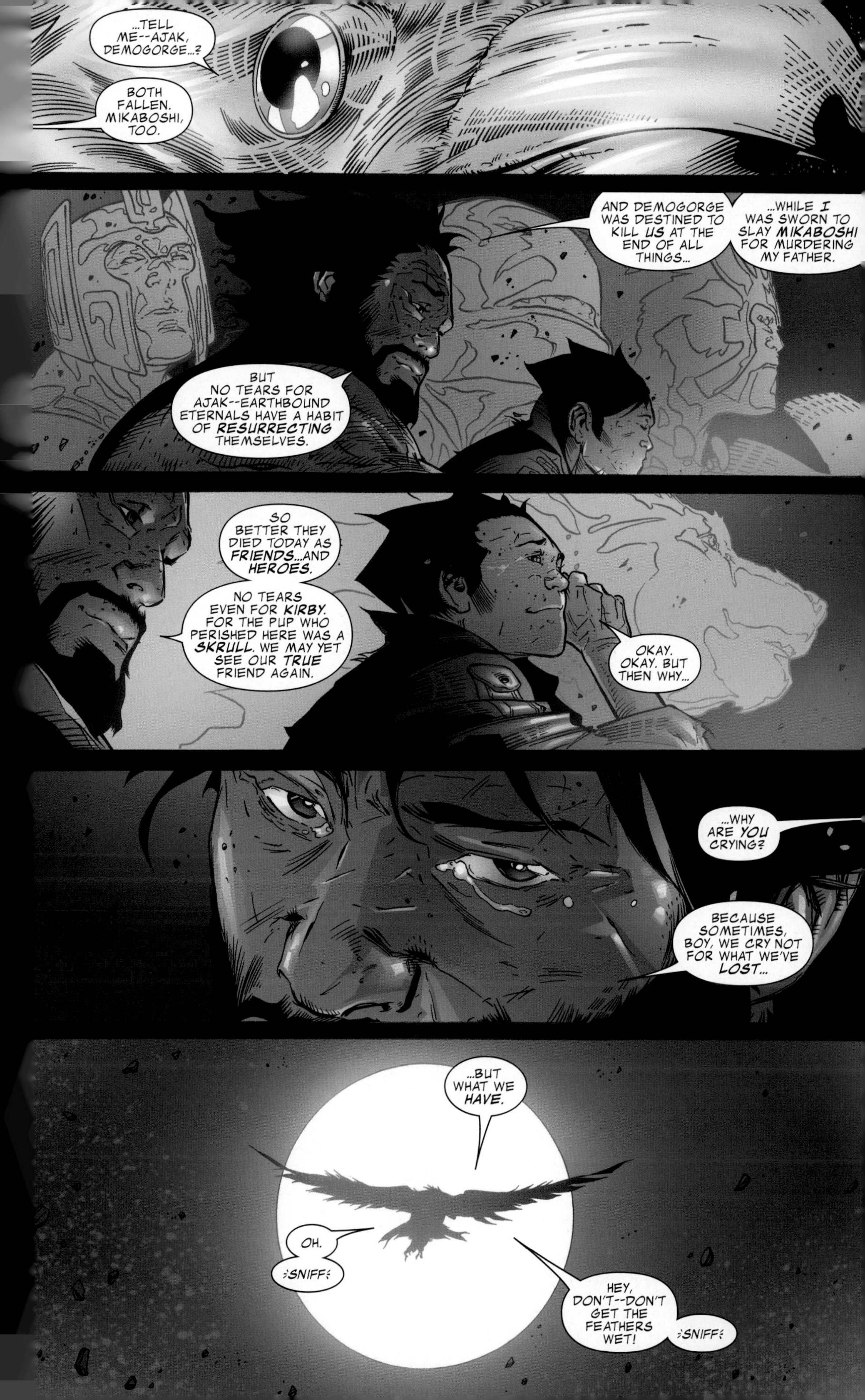
...TELL ME--AJAK, DEMOGORGE...?
BOTH FALLEN. MIKABOSHI, TOO.
AND DEMOGORGE WAS DESTINED TO KILL US AT THE END OF ALL THINGS...
...WHILE I WAS SWORN TO SLAY MIKABOSHI FOR MURDERING MY FATHER.
BUT NO TEARS FOR AJAK--EARTHBOUND ETERNALS HAVE A HABIT OF RESURRECTING THEMSELVES.
SO BETTER THEY DIED TODAY AS FRIENDS...AND HEROES.
NO TEARS EVEN FOR KIRBY. FOR THE PUP WHO PERISHED HERE WAS A SKRULL. WE MAY YET SEE OUR TRUE FRIEND AGAIN.
OKAY. OKAY. BUT THEN WHY...
...WHY ARE YOU CRYING?
BECAUSE SOMETIMES, BOY, WE CRY NOT FOR WHAT WE'VE LOST...
...BUT WHAT WE HAVE.
OH.
SNIFF
HEY, DON'T--DON'T GET THE FEATHERS WET!
SNIFF

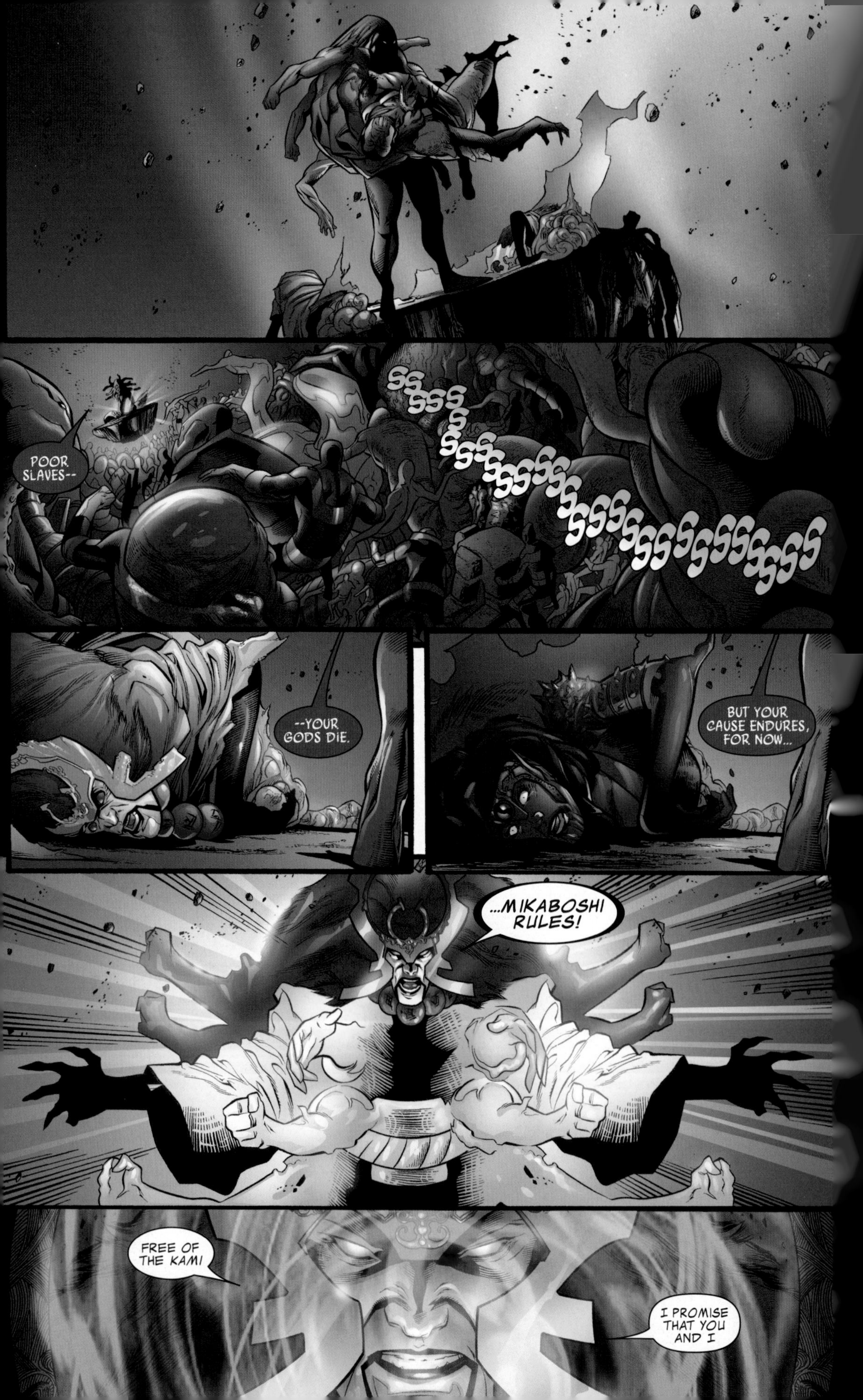
POOR SLAVES--
SSSSSSSSSSSSSSSSSSSSSSSSSSSSSS
--YOUR GODS DIE.
BUT YOUR CAUSE ENDURES, FOR NOW...
...MIKABOSHI RULES!
FREE OF THE KAMI
I PROMISE THAT YOU AND I

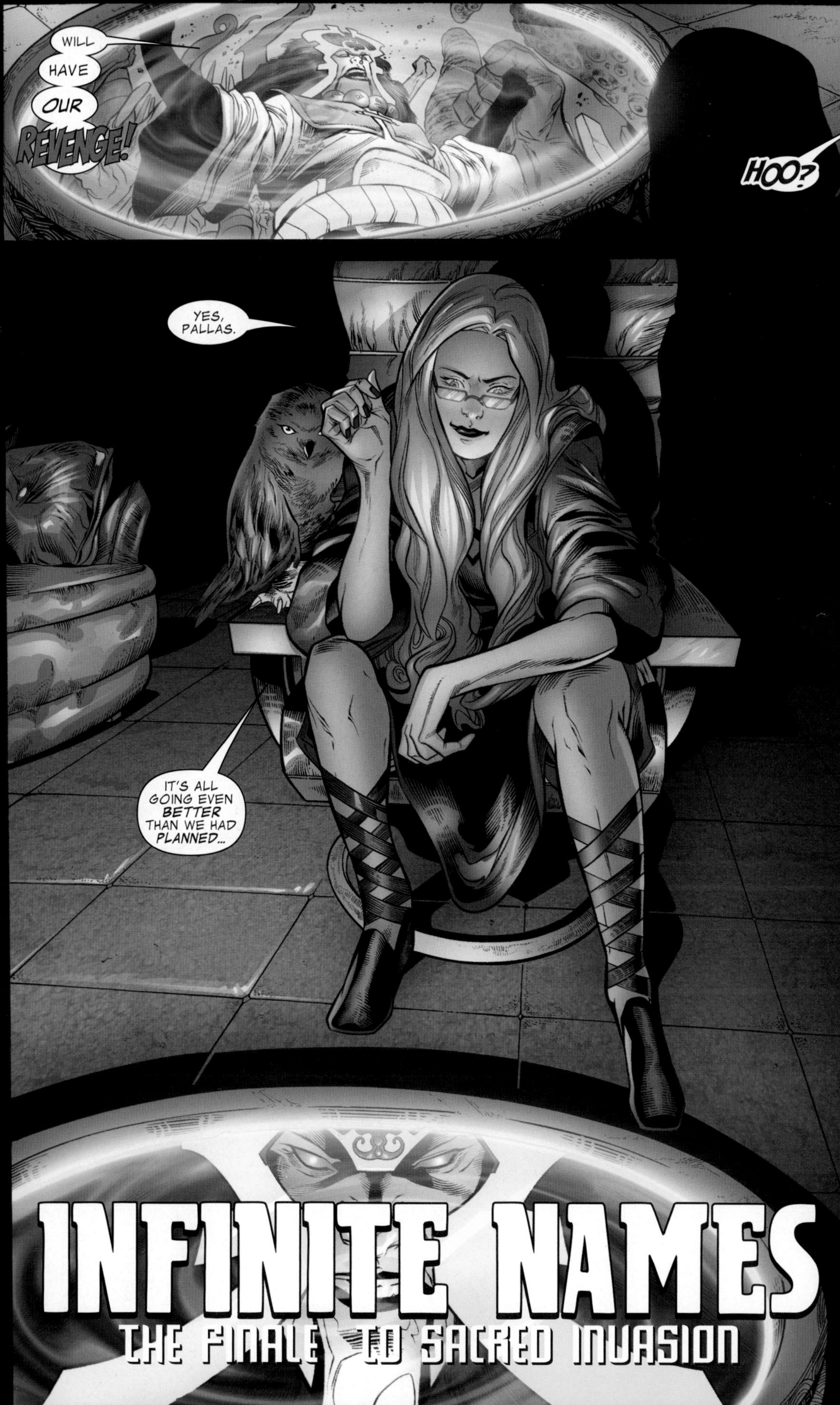
WILL
HAVE
OUR
REVENGE!
HOO?
YES, PALLAS.
IT'S ALL GOING EVEN BETTER THAN WE HAD PLANNED...
INFINITE NAMES
THE FINALE TO SACRED INVASION

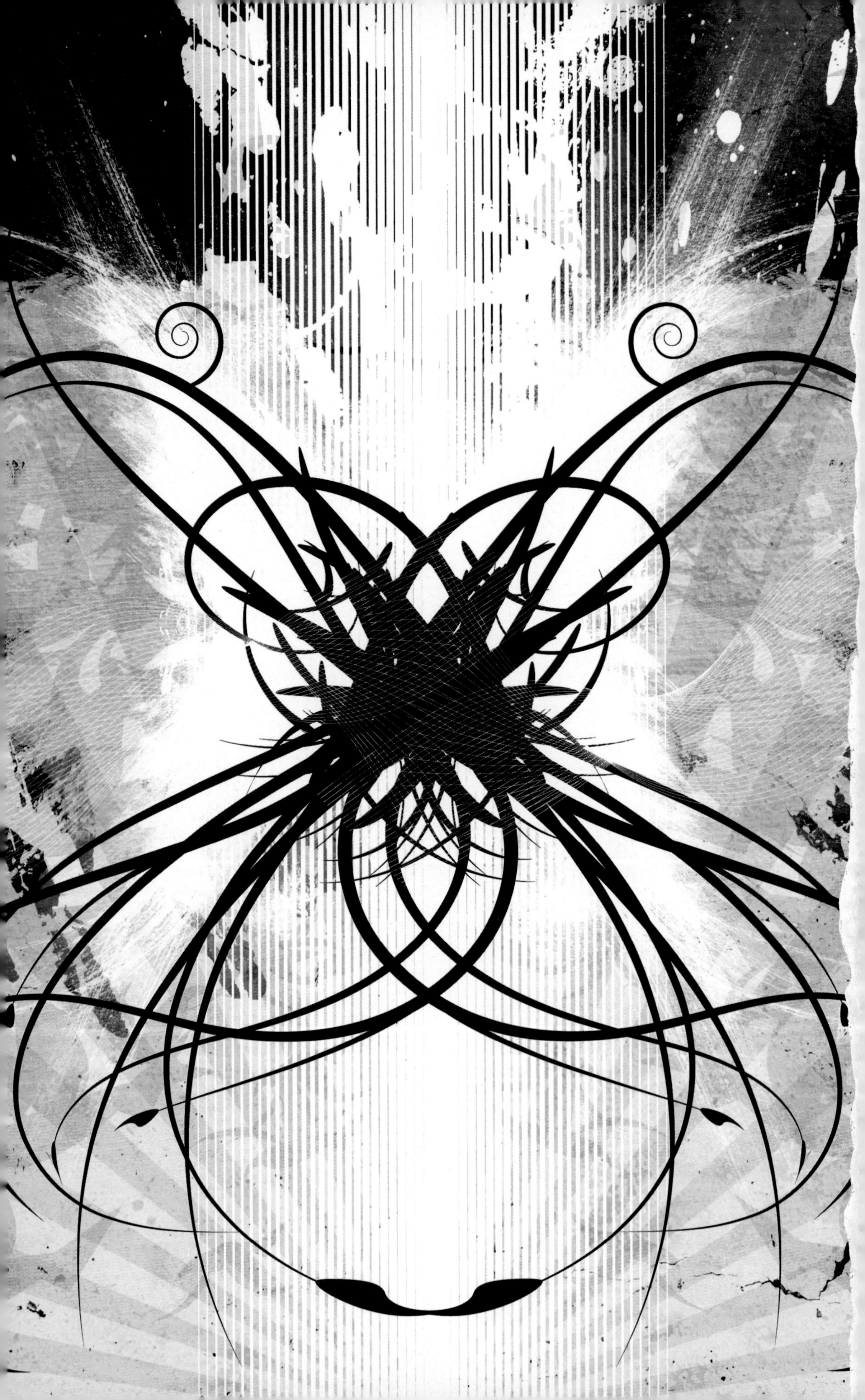